The Practice of Prolog

Logic Programming

Ehud Shapiro, editor

Koichi Furukawa, Jean-Louis Lassez, Fernando Pereira, and David H. D. Warren, associate editors

The Art of Prolog: Advanced Programming Techniques, Leon Sterling and Ehud Shapiro, 1986

Logic Programming: Proceedings of the Fourth International Conference (volumes 1 and 2), edited by Jean-Louis Lassez, 1987

Concurrent Prolog: Collected Papers (volumes 1 and 2), edited by Ehud Shapiro, 1987

Logic Programming: Proceedings of the Fifth International Conference and Symposium (volumes 1 and 2), edited by Robert A. Kowalski and Kenneth A. Bowen, 1988

Constraint Satisfaction in Logic Programming, Pascal Van Hentenryck, 1989

Logic-Based Knowledge Representation, edited by Peter Jackson, Han Reichgelt, and Frank van Harmelen, 1989

Logic Programming: Proceedings of the Sixth International Conference, edited by Giorgio Levi and Maurizio Martelli, 1989

Meta-Programming in Logic Programming, edited by Harvey Abramson and M. H. Rogers, 1989

Logic Programming: Proceedings of the North American Conference 1989 (volumes 1 and 2), edited by Ewing L. Lusk and Ross A. Overbeek, 1989

PROLOG and Its Applications, edited by Alan Bond and Basuki Soetarman, 1990

Logic Programming: Proceedings of the 1990 North American Conference, edited by Saumya Debray and Manuel Hermenegildo, 1990

Concurrent Constraint Programming Languages, Vijay A. Saraswat, 1990

Logic Programming: Proceedings of the Seventh International Conference, edited by David H. D. Warren and Peter Szeredi, 1990

Prolog VLSI Implementations, Pierluigi Civera, Gianluca Piccinini, and Maurizio Zamboni, 1990

The Craft of Prolog, Richard A. O'Keefe, 1990

The Practice of Prolog, Leon S. Sterling, 1990

The Practice of Prolog

Edited by Leon S. Sterling

The MIT Press
Cambridge, Massachusetts
London, England

Library of Congress Cataloging-in-Publication Data

The Practice of Prolog / [edited by] Leon S. Sterling.
     p.   cm. -- (Logic programming)
   Includes bibliographical references.
   ISBN 0-262-19301-9
   1. Prolog (Computer program language) I. Sterling, Leon.
 II. Series.
QA76.73.P76P73   1990   90-42397
005.13'3--dc20   CIP

To my father, Joseph Sterling, a truth seeker.

Contents

Contents

List of Figures

List of Tables

The Authors

Paul Drongowski is an Associate Professor of Computer Engineering and Science at Case Western Reserve University in Cleveland, Ohio. Dr. Drongowski earned his doctorate at the University of Utah in 1982, his M.S. in Computer Engineering from Case in 1977, and his B.S. in Mathematics from Carnegie–Mellon University in 1974. Previously he was a computer engineer with Ford Aerospace and Communications Corporation involved in the design of distributed and secure systems. He was an original contributor to the N.mPc system for register transfer level modelling and analysis of hardware systems. His current interests include the specification, manipulation and analysis of combined hardware and software architectures – a field which is certainly ready for a practical expert systems approach!

Eran Gabber is currently a PhD research student at the Computer Science Department of Tel–Aviv University, Israel. His thesis investigates methods for developing portable and efficient software for multiprocessors. He received his B.Sc. in mathematics and computer science and M.Sc. in computer science in 1981 and 1985, respectively, from Tel-Aviv University. He is currently the chief programmer of the parallel computing laboratory at the Computer Science Department of Tel-Aviv University. He previously worked for seven years as a systems programmer on IBM mainframes and on UNIX systems. His interests include parallel computation, programming languages and tools, software engineering and computer architecture.

Toni Kazic is an Instructor in the Department of Genetics, Washington University School of Medicine, and a Visiting Scientist in the Mathematics and Computer Science Division at Argonne National Laboratory. She received her Ph.D. in genetics from the University of Pennsylvania in 1984, and worked in DNA repair and chromosome structure of *Escherichia coli* for several years. Her present research interests include interactions of multiple biochemical pathways, biological databases, and computational biology.

Arun Lakhotia is an Assistant Professor in the Center for Advanced Computer Studies at the University of Southwestern Louisiana. He received his M. Sc. (Tech.) in Computer Science from the Birla Institute of Technology and Science (BITS) in 1982 and his Ph.D. in Computer Science from Case Western Reserve University in 1990. During the course of his Ph.D. he spent three summers with the Computer Science Center of Texas Instruments. Before joining CWRU he worked for three years in Indian companies, Madras Computer Laboratories and Zenith Computers Limited, as a software engineer and project leader. His interests include logic programming, software development methodologies, and software engineering.

Ewing Lusk is a senior computer scientist in the Mathematics and Computer Science Division at Argonne National Laboratory and Scientific Director of Argonne's Advanced Computing Research Facility. After receiving his Ph. D. in mathematics at the University of Maryland in 1970, he served first in the Mathematics Department and later in the Computer Science Department at Northern Illinois University before joining the Automated Reasoning group at Argonne in 1982. His current research is in automated theorem proving, logic programming, and parallel computing.

Chris Mellish is a lecturer and SERC Advanced Fellow in the Department of Artificial Intelligence at the University of Edinburgh. He graduated as a mathematician from Oxford University in 1976 and was awarded a PhD by the University of Edinburgh in 1981. After further postdoctoral work, he moved to the University of Sussex to take up a lectureship in Computing and AI in the Cognitive Studies Programme. In 1987, he returned to Edinburgh as a lecturer in the AI Department. Since October 1985 he has been supported by an SERC Advanced IT Fellowship. His main interests are logic programming and natural language processing. He is co-author of a textbook on Prolog and of three versions of a textbook on natural language processing.

Richard O'Keefe received his undergraduate training at the University of Auckland, before moving to the Department of Artificial Intelligence at the University of Edinburgh where he received a Ph.D. At Edinburgh, Richard become an outspoken but highly regarded member of the Prolog community. He worked several years for Quintus Prolog in Silicon Valley before returning down under, where he is now a lecturer in Computer Science at the Royal Melbourne Institute of Technology. He is author of a book on the craft of Prolog programming.

Robert Olson received his B.S. in Computer Science from the University of Illinois at Urbana in 1989 and is a currently holds a research assistantship in the Computer Science department. He is also pursuing a doctorate in Computer Science within the graduate college at Urbana. Robert was a scientific assistant in the Mathematics and Computer Science Division at Argonne National Laboratory for the year previous to his graduation. In addition, he participated in student research programs under the supervision of Ross Overbeek at Argonne for the five years prior to his appointment as a scientific assistant. He is presently working with multiprocessor performance instrumentation and visualization, and has an ongoing interest in developing tools for portable parallel computing.

Ross Overbeek is a senior computer scientist at Argonne National Laboratory. He received his B.Ph. from Grand Valley State College and his M.S. from Penn. State University in 1970. He got his Ph.D. in computer science from Penn. State in 1971. He then taught at Northern Illinois University for 11 years, before taking a brief retirement in Maui for a year. Since 1983, he has been a member of the Mathematics and Computer Science Division at Argonne doing research in automated deduction, logic programming, and parallel computation. For the last two years, he has focused on applications of logic programming in molecular biology. He is now on the Joint Informatics Task Force, a working group advising the NIH and DOE on computational requirements of the Human Genome Initiative.

D. Stott Parker is an Associate Professor in the Computer Science Department at UCLA in Los Angeles. He received his B.A. in Mathematics in 1974 from Princeton University cum laude, and his Ph.D. in Computer Science in 1978 from the University of Illinois. Before arriving at UCLA he spent a period of postdoctoral research at the University of Grenoble in France. During the years 1984–1985 he served as director of research on Knowledge-Based Systems at Silogic, Inc., a Los Angeles startup company. His interests include logic programming, data- and knowledge-base systems, and constraint-based modeling.

Peter Reintjes has been a Member of Technical Staff of the Microelectronics Center of North Carolina (MCNC) since 1982. He received a BS in Physics from the University of North Carolina at Chapel Hill where he also worked in the Computer Graphics Laboratory. After two years writing microcode and doing UNIX development work for Data General Corporation, he joined MCNC, where he has been working on VLSI/CAD software and the design of special purpose hardware for computational molecular biology. He spent the year 1989 on loan from MCNC to IBM Corporation, doing technology-transfer in Prolog-based CAD tools.

Leon Sterling is an Associate Professor in the Department of Computer Engineering and Science at Case Western Reserve University (CWRU), and co–Director of the Center for Automation and Intelligent Systems Research there. He received his B.Sc.(hons.) in Mathematics and Computer Science from the University of Melbourne in 1976 and his Ph.D. in Pure Mathematics from Australian National University in 1981. He spent three years in the Artificial Intelligence Department at the University of Edinburgh, and one year at the Weizmann Institute before joining CWRU in 1985. His interests include logic programming, expert systems and new foundations for artificial intelligence.

Steve Tuecke is a scientific assistant in the Mathematics and Computer Science Division at Argonne National Laboratory. He received his B.A., with a major in Mathematics, from St. Olaf College in 1989. As an undergraduate, he began working at Argonne in a student program under the supervision of Ross Overbeek. During this time he studied and worked on parallel computing and logic programming. After graduating from St. Olaf and one brief semester of graduate studies, he began his current position at Argonne. His current interests include concurrent logic programming, parallel computing, and the application of graphical user interfaces to parallel programming.

Introduction

The raison d'être of this book is to encourage programmers to use Prolog in their day-to-day work. Personally, I find the language exciting to use, and wish to share the excitement with others. More pragmatically, I have seen how certain moderately–sized pieces of software are far easier to write in Prolog than in any other language with which I am familiar. Further, the code, if written clearly, can be easily maintained by persons other than the original author.

Why is the encouragement necessary? Why is Prolog not being widely taught and used in software engineering projects? In fact, reception to Prolog has been mixed, ranging from excitement in Europe, adoption by consensus in Japan and prejudiced ambivalence by the mainstream computer science community in the United States. A major reason for the mixed reception of Prolog has been, in my opinion, the relative inaccessibility of good educational material showing how the language should be used. Indeed, five years ago there was only one widely available book on Prolog, the well-known primer "Programming in Prolog" [?]. Many popular misconceptions abounded about the significance of Prolog's constructs and programming techniques, for example the role of cut, which suggested that Prolog was not a good general language. Popular misconceptions take a long time to subside, and need new material to challenge the old.

The lack of introductory textbooks for Prolog has been addressed. There has been an explosion of texts in recent years, including "The Art of Prolog" [?] in this Logic Programming Series. By and large, however, the current crop of textbooks address programming in the small. It is still necessary to show how to extend the small examples in the texts to programming projects.

This book, in contrast, is intended to help Prolog programming in the moderate to large. It is a collection of programming projects and applications. Each chapter explains a particular application, and presents a Prolog program written to solve the application. It stands apart in the level of detail and the sophistication and quality of the code.

The chapters are not homogeneous, neither in writing style nor in the level of background knowledge expected by the reader, nor in the experience the authors have in programming in Prolog. However, therein lies a strength. There is no single correct way to develop code in any programming language, and Prolog is no exception. This book, due to the variety of authors, shows a variety of styles for effectively developing programs in Prolog. Furthermore, readers at different levels of programming expertise should see that Prolog may be useful for them.

The common thread between the chapters is the effective use of Prolog. For each application, the author was convinced of the appropriateness of Prolog, and borrowed and developed the necessary programming techniques. Prolog is not always an easy language to use. There are a lot of subtle effects brought on by the power of unification and backtracking. Seemingly very similar programs can perform very differently. However with a clear logical understanding of a problem, a programmer can write a very clear program, as is illustrated in each chapter.

This book is intentionally unusual in its level of detail of presenting code. Unlike collections of research papers where code is essentially shunned, enough of the code is given so that the reader knowledgeable in the given application area should be able to reconstruct the application. The significant advantage gained in this book is giving an appreciation of the pragmatic issues that arise when developing a sizable application in Prolog. Pragmatic considerations cannot be easily explained in an introductory textbook or with small programs. Expressed as generalities, such considerations can sound very hollow. In contrast, in the context of a real example, the point comes through forcefully.

The first chapter of this book concerns the prototyping of databases in Prolog. It starts with a simple example of modelling a video rental store that would come easily to a student of relational database technology. Indeed a relational database is an example of a simple logic program. Just this level of Prolog programming is useful to rapidly construct a database. Lusk and Overbeek, two of the co-authors of this chapter, used Prolog databases to coordinate the reviewing of conference papers when they were program conference chairs. At Case Western Reserve University, the graduate student coffee club has been maintained as a Prolog database. This paper is concerned primarily, however, with a more exciting example, namely how a Prolog database can serve as a research tool for molecular biology, specifically in the context of the Human Genome project. The practicality of Prolog for the small example carries over to the large, and the authors sketch their database design and some of the important issues that arise when one is using Prolog for large databases.

The second chapter also advocates the use of Prolog as a tool, this time for the computer–aided design of digital circuits. Specifically, Preditor is described which is a practical VLSI CAD system. There are two key advantages claimed by the author, Peter Reintjes. The first is the clarity of the code which leads to its easier maintenance. The Prolog version is an order of magnitude smaller than the C counterpart. The second advantage is the extensibility of the tool due to the availability of Prolog for inferencing.

The third chapter indeed shows how high level inferencing can be incorporated into a research tool for VLSI CAD. Paul Drongowski describes a component of the AGENT system which works with a graphical design language to assist with hardware design at the register transfer level. As argued in the paper, Prolog was good for this application due to the ease of editing new examples. One Prolog feature exploited was the grammar rule formalism of DCGs which makes parsing straightforward.

The fourth chapter also uses Prolog parsing technology, but this time illustrates the strength of Prolog in one aspect of software engineering - namely compiler writing. The essential techniques used in this paper arise from David H.D. Warren's landmark Ph.D. thesis about a Prolog compiler, naturally written largely in Prolog. The relevant sections for software engineering in Prolog can be found in [?], and is also reproduced in Chapter 23 of [?]. Eran Gabber demonstrates in this chapter how Warren's research can be applied to a parallelizing compiler for a version of Pascal.

The fifth chapter is another example of using Prolog for software engineering. The application area this time is Prolog itself. Arun Lakhotia and Leon Sterling present ProMiX, a partial evaluator for Prolog. A partial evaluator for pure Prolog is a very simple task. However, taking into account the extra-logical system predicates of Prolog such as I/O and cut complicates the programming task tremendously. The paper explains the complications in the partial evaluator due to Prolog side-effects, and how they can be accommodated. It demonstrates how to handle low-level procedural concerns cleanly.

The sixth chapter by Chris Mellish discusses a program for generating natural language explanations of plans. The code is presented very clearly and systematically, and exemplifies the standard of coding that can be achieved when developing Prolog applications. Again advantage is taken of DCG grammar rules.

The seventh chapter also concerns natural language, but is presented in a different style. We look over the shoulder of Richard O'Keefe, arguably the world's best Prolog programmer, as he develops a Prolog program. The application domain is learning English pronouns, but the significance of the paper lies in the process rather than the final application.

The final chapter by Stott Parker shows an important aspect of Prolog programming, namely developing embedded languages to add expressive power. The application described here is manipulating streams. Stream-to-stream translators (transducers) cannot be implemented directly in Prolog easily, but can be in the language Log(F), which in turn can be compiled into Prolog. Designing languages on top of Prolog which can be easily translated into Prolog is a good development method, especially for expert systems.

Finally, in this introduction, I would like to acknowledge and thank the people that made this book possible. First and foremost are the authors of the chapters for their cooperation and interest in assembling the book. Without them there would be no book. This book was prepared as camera-ready copy using LaTeX in the Department of Computer Engineering and Science at Case Western Reserve University. For logistic help with LaTeX, thanks are due to Arun Lakhotia, Michael Howley, Umit Yalcinalp, and especially Jwahar Bammi for his painstaking grappling needed to wrestle with the mysterious interactions of LaTeX, PicTeX and the MIT Press macros. More generally, thanks to Terry Ehling at MIT Press for her patience, and series editor Ehud Shapiro for supporting this book. Thanks also to Frederica Flanagan, Lynn Austin and especially Marcy Sanford for their general secretarial support.

In conclusion, I hope the applications encourage the reader to use Prolog when it would be helpful. The widespread use of Prolog is still developing and the best programming techniques need to become available. I trust this book is a contribution in that direction.

Leon Sterling

The Practice of Prolog

Chapter 1

Prototyping Databases in Prolog

Toni Kazic

Department of Genetics
Washington University School of Medicine
St.Louis, MO 63110, USA

Ewing Lusk, Robert Olson, Ross Overbeek, Steve Tuecke

Mathematics and Computer Science Division
Argonne National Laboratory
Argonne, IL 60439, USA

Abstract

We discuss here some of the issues that arise in designing databases and implementing them in Prolog. The first two examples, of databases for a small video store and for a library, are presented as tutorial examples to illustrate some of the issues in a simple context. We then introduce a very real database problem, that of maintaining the growing body of genetic sequence data that is being made available by new laboratory techniques in molecular biology.

1.1 Introduction

One of the most significant aspects of the computer revolution has been the concept of a database: the storage of information in a way that enhances our ability to use it. Databases themselves are as old as stone tablets. The first computerized databases were flat files, little different from the stone tablets except for the computer's ability to store them compactly and read them rapidly.

Database technology evolved swiftly, driven by the rapid computerization of existing "manual" databases during the 1970's. First came the large software systems called Database Management Systems (DBMS's). These systems often required weeks of programming in a low-level language such as COBOL, together with considerable expertise in the language of some particular DBMS just to install a single new transaction type. They are still in use.

(Bad) experience with these systems led to the study of databases from a more theoretical standpoint. Most theory was developed in the context of *relational* databases, which were more abstract than their vendor-dependent predecessors. Eventually implementations of the relational model appeared, dramatically reducing the cost for creating and accessing databases.

A greater level of abstraction was needed, however, to guide the development of flexible databases that could evolve beyond their original purposes without major and expensive reorganization. The *Entity–Relationship(ER) Approach* is one of the more successful methods of formulating useful abstract models. By focusing on the entities and their relationships, it structured the way designers approached the problem of creating extensible databases. Gradually, the database community became aware that the ER approach was a powerful conceptual tool, and it became the key design aid for databases implemented under a wide variety of commercially available systems. Many designers realized that the worst mistakes were made by failing to develop an adequate overview of the data to be accessed, and that making the implementation step substantially less difficult could not directly address this problem. The essential need was to systematically describe the aspects of the world that were to be modeled by the database, and to do so without including any details of the implementation.

Relational databases have grown rapidly in popularity. However, the current implementations represent only one way to implement a database of relations. Prolog is a programming language that contains within it the language of relations. The complete language allows even complex queries to be expressed concisely. It can thus be used in a very direct way to implement relational databases. However, it is still necessary to begin with an abstract model of that part of the world about which one is trying to manage data.

In this paper we describe a methodology for designing databases. It begins with an entity-relationship model, progresses in a straightforward way to a relational model, and continues on with a translation of the relational model into Prolog. We will begin with a relatively simple example in order to illustrate the technique.

If our motives in this article were only to present a methodology for database design and implementation, we would then progress to a more complex application that would be familiar to most readers. However, another motive has influenced our presentation: we believe that logic programming has a fundamental role to play in the computational support of molecular biologists, and we wish to encourage members of the logic programming community to investigate this particular application area. Our reasons for believing that molecular biology will be an application area of particular significance are as follows:

- Breakthroughs in the technology of DNA sequencing have produced an immediate need to create and support a rapidly growing database.

- The results of effectively storing, maintaining, and using a biological database might well prove critical to understanding exactly how fundamental mechanisms in the cell operate. The potential benefits, both in terms of medical applications and in terms of basic research, are immense.

- Computer users within the community of biologists have not yet committed to specific computing environments and packages. We believe that "fifth generation" technology can play a useful role in this particular area of science, and the construction of an integrated database represents one obvious contribution that can be made.

- The projects arising internationally to map the human genome represent one of the most exciting efforts in science of the 20th century.

Logic programming offers an integration of database technology, high-level programming, and logic. Molecular biology is an application area that will be driven by a growing, rapidly changing database, and already commands wide interest. If fifth-generation technology has a role to play in the support of science, this application is the place to demonstrate it.

Hence, we illustrate our methodology for database design using an important application for molecular biologists: the accumulation and management of data for mapping the genomes of various organisms. This problem is presently being approached with conventional technology. Current biological databases exist in the form of flat files or simple relational databases. Attempts to formulate an integrated view are just emerging; each of the existing databases offers a very circumscribed view, with extremely limited abilities to search or integrate new forms of data. What is needed is an integration of the existing data into a single conceptual framework, along with a means of easily extracting information from it. We believe that a properly designed database should be rapidly prototyped in Prolog, and that Prolog offers the query capabilities required to support unpredictable requests. Finally, because the original biological databases, while quite complex, will contain a fairly limited amount of data, we believe that the "prototype" might well prove to be a useful production database.

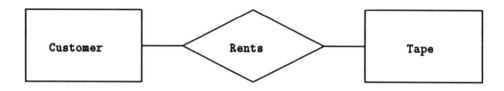

Figure 1.1: A Simple Model

1.2   Designing a Prolog Database

Prolog is a useful database implementation language, but such an implementation should only be undertaken after the database is properly designed. In this section we will describe an effective design process and illustrate it with a solution to a simple database problem. In the next section, we will apply this design and implementation technique to a more complex example, a database for a library. Finally, we will consider a quite complex application, a database for maintaining genetic information.

1.2.1   Creating the Entity-Relationship Model

For our first example, we will choose the database that might be required to operate a small videotape rental store. The store needs to maintain data on what tapes it owns, its customers, and the rentals of tapes to customers. The first step in designing the database is to concentrate on the entities that the database is to keep track of and how they relate to one another. This level of the design is called the "Entity-Relationship Model". In our example, the entities and relationships are given in the informal description of the database found in the second sentence of this paragraph. This database will be about customers and tapes, and these entities are related because customers rent tapes. The database will maintain data about these two entities (*customers* and *tapes*) and one relationship (*rents*). It is often useful to represent this level of a database design by a diagram, in which entities are represented by rectangles and relationships by diamonds connected to the entities they relate. So our model looks like Figure 1.1. Note that one might later expand this database to keep track of more data; for example, about the suppliers from whom the store buys tapes. The business may expand, selling tapes to customers as well as renting them. A future diagram might be as shown in Figure 1.2.

If the original entity-relationship model is done with careful attention to "real-world" entities and their relationships, then one can expect it to be stable and

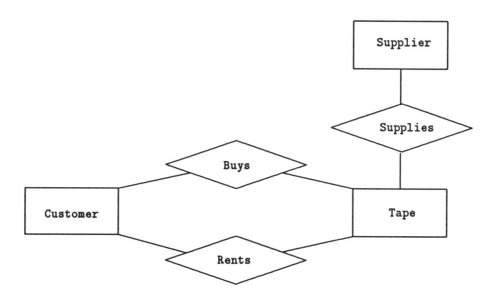

Figure 1.2: An Expanded Model

easily extended. The video store may expand its business or the amount of data it wants to maintain, but (one hopes) customers will always rent tapes. Only a major change in the business or in the goals of its database would require a substantial change to the entity-relationship model.

1.2.2 Specifying the Relational Representation

Once the overall abstract structure of a database has been specified in an entity-relationship diagram, the next step is to fill in more detail by specifying exactly which data items are to be included in the representation of each entity and each relationship. These data items are called the *attributes* of the entities and relationships.

In our example, let us suppose that all the data we need to know for each tape is its *key* (the unique identifying number for the tape), *title*, and *format* (VHS or Beta). Note that the title cannot serve as a key because the store carries multiple copies of some tapes. It is convenient to represent this level of detail in our database design by tables. For the videotape entity, the table has the following structure:

tape-id	title	format
3264	Raiders of the Lost Ark	VHS
7912	E.T.	VHS
3663	E.T.	Beta

Each row in the table represents a single *instance* of the entity; in this case, a physical tape. The table for the *customer* entity might look like this:

cust-id	name	phone	address
1234	George Bates	(312) 789-3423	721 First Avenue Naperville, IL 60532
5678	Fred Jones	(815) 758-6757	2341 Pleasant Road DeKalb, IL 60115

By convention, the first attribute of the table is the key.

The relationship table includes the keys of the entities being related, together with attributes of the relationship itself. In our case, suppose that all we want to record about rentals is the date and whether or not the tape has been returned:

cust-id	tape-id	date	returned
1234	3264	12/1/88	not_returned
1234	3663	12/2/88	returned

With these tables, we have specified a relational representation of the database. This intermediate representation of the database has more detail than the entity-relationship model, and forces several decisions about exactly what data will be maintained in the database. Yet many implementation decisions have been postponed, allowing flexibility in implementation.

1.2.3   Implementation in Prolog

The previous two steps have laid the groundwork for the implementation. Even if one were intending a non-Prolog implementation, the previous steps would still be the appropriate ones. However, it is particularly easy to translate the relational representation into Prolog, since Prolog is a language of relations. As a starting point, one can assign a predicate to each entity and relationship, with an argument for each attribute. Thus, our Prolog database would contain:

```
videotape(3264,'Raiders of the Lost Ark',vhs).
```

Prolog also offers a particularly convenient means for representing a structured attribute. For example, the implementation of the *customer* entity might look like

```
customer(1234,'George Bates',telephone(312,789,3423),
        address(['721 First Av.','Suite 7b'],
              'Naperville', 'IL', 60532)).
```

Here, the telephone number and address are represented as attributes with structure, allowing significant subitems to be directly referenced. The use of a list to represent a varying number of unstructured lines in the address is particularly convenient. Most Prolog systems provide built-in indexing on the first argument of each predicate, so that sequential searches are avoided as much as possible when the first argument is supplied. For this reason the key field occurs first in our Prolog predicates.

Once a Prolog representation of the data exists, there are a number of ways to support queries.

1. The simplest is to just have the user formulate queries in Prolog. For those with a background in logic programming, this is both natural and convenient.

2. In situations in which one can easily define the classes of queries to be supported, defining the Prolog routines to implement such customized access is normally straightforward.

3. Occasionally, it makes sense to offer "natural language" interfaces to databases.

4. Finally, it is possible to support a number of structured query languages (most notably SQL) in the Prolog environment.

The best approach depends on who uses the database, how often they use it, and how many resources can be expended to support query capability.

The invention of relational databases represented a major step forwards. It allowed a particularly natural representation of data (as tables), and permitted a number of query languages to be invented. There also arose a body of research relating to "normal forms" for relational databases. This work centered on deriving the correct relational representation of a set of attributes, given the attributes and functional dependencies among attributes. In retrospect, it appears as if the goal was to automatically determine what entities and relationships were being represented. Such a task is quite difficult, and it has produced an enormous number of highly technical research papers. In our opinion, these papers are largely irrelevant to the actual goal of implementing well-designed databases, although the use of normal forms does provide one means of verifying a database design.

A good entity-relationship model offers the best first step to a properly normalized relational implementation, and the best way to acquire such an ER-model is through discussions with people familiar with the application area. The advantages of databases in normal form, namely the absence of the dreaded "update anomalies", accrue naturally to databases in which entities and relationships have been accurately identified.

1.3   A More Advanced Example

Our previous example was a bit too simple to be realistic, even for a small video store. As a next step toward a realistic application, we describe in this section a library database. It shares several concepts with the video store example, but here we will attempt to flesh out the model a bit more, while following precisely the same methodology as before.

1.3.1   An Entity-Relationship Model for a Library

We will still make several simplifying assumptions. We attempt here to model only the part of a library's activities having to do with loaning books to users of the library. We also assume that the items that the library deals with are books, though in practice a library might also loan out magazines, audio and video tapes, films, records, and various kinds of equipment. It should be easy to generalize from the discussion given here.

It is immediately obvious that two primary entities will be *users* of the library and *books*. A little reflection reminds us that libraries carry multiple copies of books, and that the individual copies, which are the entities checked out to users, are not the same things as the books as represented in the card catalog. For example, a user may request that a book be reserved for him, but he does not care which copy he gets. This leads us to consider two separate entities: *book*, with attributes shared by all copies of the same book, and *copy*, with attributes of the individual copy. These entities will be related by the *book/copy* relationship. It will be necessary to access the *book* entities in a variety of ways besides their unique identifying reference numbers: by author, title, subject, and perhaps a list of keywords. The rest of the E-R diagram is shown in Figure 1.3. If a user reserves a book, a *request* relationship is created, linking the user to the book (not to an individual copy). When he checks out a copy, a *loan* relationship node is created, containing the date the copy is due. If the user fails to return it on time, a *fine* node is created, related to the user by an *owes* relationship and to the copy by the *for* relationship.

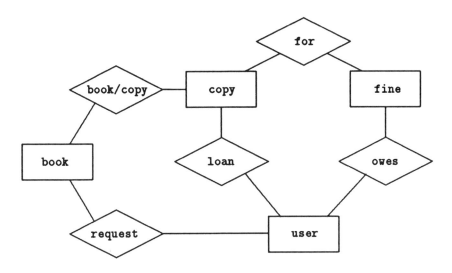

Figure 1.3: Library ER Diagram

1.3.2 The Relational Representation for the Library Database

The next step is to fill out the relational representation by specifying the attributes of each entity and relationship. One set of choices is represented in Table 1.1. (The fields representing the keys are italicized.) Structured data might be used for the user address and phone, as in the video store example. A reasonable choice for the *copynum* is a pair consisting of the *refnum* of the book (identifying the book) and a sequence number identifying the copy. For example, the *copynum* for the third copy of *Semigroups* might be

```
copynum('QA 774.1R4',3)
```

so that the representation of the copy itself would be

```
copy(copynum('QA 774.1R4',3),'Science Reading Room').
```

Another type of structured data might be used for the list of authors and list of keywords associated with a book. We will discuss later the option of treating the authors and keywords as separate entities.

Entity	Attributes
book	*refnum*, title, authorlist, publisher, keywords
user	*usernum*, name, phone, address
copy	*copynum*, location
fine	*finenum*, amount, status (paid or unpaid)

Relationship	Attributes
request	*refnum, usernum*, date
loan	*usernum, copynum*, date of loan, date due
owes	*usernum, finenum*
for	*finenum, copynum*
book/copy	*refnum, copynum*

Table 1.1: Attributes for Library Database

1.3.3   Implementing the Library Database in Prolog

The Prolog implementation of most of the library database design is for the most part as straightforward as the video store example. However, the library database provides a setting in which several new issues can be discussed.

Implementation of Entities and Relationships   The most straightforward approach to translating an ER model into a Prolog database implementation is the one we followed in the video store example. Each node of the ER model becomes a table in the relational representation, and then each table becomes a Prolog predicate in the Prolog representation. This one–to–one–to–one relationship is appealingly simple, but the performance of the database can be improved by the addition of some new Prolog predicates and the elimination of others.

For example, the simple-minded translation of the library database ER model into Prolog would produce a *copyofbook* predicate to implement the *book/copy* relationship. Since our relational model includes no data associated with an instance of this relationship, the only arguments of the *copyofbook* predicate would be the key of the *book* entity (refnum) and the key of the *copy* entity (copynum). If we choose as the *copynum* a structure containing the book's *refnum*, then the predicate is redundant: one can readily access the copies of a book given its *refnum* and access the book given its *copynum*.

Auxiliary Access Structures A common addition is the inclusion of extra predicates to support efficient access to the contents of the database. As an example, consider looking up a book by one of its authors. It is possible to do this by writing the query in Prolog like this:

```
lookup_author(Author,Refnum) :-
    book(Refnum, Title, Authorlist, Keywordlist, Publisher),
    member(Author,Authorlist).
```

If this predicate is called with the `Author` variable instantiated to a given name, but with `Refnum` uninstantiated, it returns the first book written by the given author, and on backtracking returns all the other books by that author. It thus does what we require, but does so very inefficiently since it examines each book in the entire database. On the other hand, if we include an "inversion" predicate

```
lookup_author(Author,Refnum)
```

in our database, then standard Prolog indexing on the first argument provides us with rapid access to books by a given author. Note that higher-level queries which may call the `lookup_author` predicate need not be aware of the implementation. A similar inversion predicate would be appropriate for keywords.

It is worth noting that the index on authors might have arisen via the straightforward approach if we had treated authors as entities. Then the `lookup_author` predicate would be the translation of the relationship between authors and their books. We choose not to look at the author index in this way because we are not storing any attributes of authors, and the approach seems far less natural in the case of, say, keywords. Therefore we prefer, in this example, to treat both authors and keywords as attributes of the *book* entity.

We can now define the predicates that will make up our library database:

```
book(Refnum,Title,Authorlist,Publisher,Keywordlist).
user(Usernum,Name,Address,Phone).
copy(Copynum,Location).
fine(Finenum,Amount,Status).

request(Refnum,Usernum,Date).
loan(Usernum,Copynum,Loandate,Datedue).
owes(Usernum,Finenum).
for(Finenum,Copynum).
```

To illustrate the usefulness of this approach, we consider some sample queries that would be easy to express directly in Prolog:

- "What books are checked out to user 1234?"

- "What books on biology has Lusk been fined for?"

- "What users have checked out books on African archeology in the last two years?"

1.4   A Database to Support Molecular Biology

Now we consider a more substantial application of the ideas that we have been discussing. In this section, we wish to explore the problem of creating a database to support research in molecular biology. Our intent here is not to offer a complete presentation of the issues involved in the design of biological databases; indeed, this is an area in which substantial resources are now being focused, and the issues are far from straightforward. However, the techniques that we have been discussing do form the foundation for examining the relevant issues, and we believe the area can be used effectively for purposes of illustration.

1.4.1   New Problems in Computational Biology

We will begin this section by covering some relevant aspects of molecular biology. Our treatment will be necessarily brief. We will not attempt to offer a true biology tutorial; rather, we will summarize a minimal number of concepts to allow the reader to follow our discussion.

Suppose that you were given a disk drive that contained the operating system and data from a fabulous computer. Further suppose that, if you understood how the machine and the operating system actually worked, you might well have the keys to knowledge of incredible value. To properly motivate your effort, suppose that it appears that you would get keys to understanding life itself (minimally, you will be able to cure cancer, AIDS, and the common cold). However, all you have is a disk drive and the ability (with a lot of effort) to extract character sequences from the drive. You do not know the instruction set of the machine or how any of the algorithms implemented on the machine work. However, you do know that versions of the machine actually do work, and occasionally you have glimpses of an operating machine.

Suppose that you have already spent a few years looking at the problem. You've extracted a few sequences from a number of spots on the disk, and they seem to come in several different types. In fact, you might be fairly sure that some sequences correspond to programs. You have even located the directory where all of the operating system resides. Other friends seem to be able to recognize the start of subroutines. In a few cases, they even know what the function of some of the routines must be, although they usually don't understand how the actual code of the machine relates to implementing the function.

Further suppose that a breakthrough occurs in how to read sequences from the disk, so that all of a sudden you can start looking at a much larger sampling of sequences. One of your more inspired friends, grasping the significance of progress to date, proposes that teams cooperate to extract all of the sequences from the disk. The task will be expensive (hundreds of millions of dollars will be required) and time consuming (it will probably take 10-15 years). It is not even clear that you could accurately interpret the data, but it would certainly initiate a large-scale effort to really solve the problem.

The piece of detective work required to unravel the meaning of the encoded programs would certainly take a substantial effort. The first part of the effort would be to start producing a complete set of characters from the disk. The second part would be to gather and coordinate insights as researchers from around the world study different aspects of the problem. This situation is, in many ways, analogous to that facing molecular biologists.

Rather than sequences from a computer disk, biologists have acquired the ability to read the genetic sequences that specify the activity of living cells. DNA is a chemical encoding of genetic information. It is based on the 4-character alphabet a, c, g, t. The genetic information about a person is encoded in long strings of characters from this very limited alphabet. These strings convey instructions for building all of the variety of mechanisms required to make the organism function properly. Some simple organisms contain only a single large molecule of DNA. However, in more complex organisms, each cell contains a number of molecules; each of these is called a *chromosome*. A human cell has 46 chromosomes. "The entire complement of genetic material in the set of chromosomes of a particular organism is defined as its *genome*" [Ass88]. A total of about $3 \cdot 10^9$ characters make up the genome for a human being.

Over the last five years substantial technical advances have reduced the cost of determining the sequences of characters in sections of DNA. Essentially, biologists have developed a technology for cutting up the chromosomes and then determining the exact sequence of characters in these pieces. If enough overlapping pieces of DNA are "sequenced", the complete sequence of the original chromosome can be determined. Not only can biologists now do such things (which in itself is amazing), but they can do it fairly cheaply. Hence the surge of newly-available data representing DNA sequences.

When biologists decide to sequence an entire genome, they separate the task into sequencing each of the distinct chromosomes that make up the genome. Then for each chromosome, they construct a *physical map*. By techniques well beyond this discussion, they determine an ordered sequence of short strings $S_1, S_2, S_3, ...S_n$ (called *restriction sites*) that occur within the chromosome (with large intervals of unknown characters between the restriction sites). Furthermore, they are able to estimate, sometimes very accurately, the number of unknown characters that occur between the restriction sites. Then the problem of sequencing the genome is partitioned into a set of smaller problems–filling in the unknown fragments.

Occasionally, multiple maps of the same chromosome may exist. In these cases, it may be possible to form a more detailed composite map. In the process, most known sequences of DNA can be assigned to one of the smaller unknown regions. In others, the exact interval containing a specific sequence of DNA may be unknown (e.g., it might only be possible to state that the sequence occurs somewhere within three contiguous fragments).

To actually determine the sequence of a fragment, biologists take many copies of it, chop them into smaller fragments that can be sequenced, and then look for overlaps in the short sequences to reconstruct the sequence for the original longer fragment. The methods used to assemble the sequence of an unknown part of a restriction map can in principle be scaled up to allow assembling the sequence of an entire chromosome. This allows one to avoid the intermediate step of mapping the chromosome. Currently, such an approach (called *shotgun sequencing*) is practical only for fairly small chromosomes.

A database for managing the accumulation of information about the sequences that make up a genome must be able to accurately represent at least maps, restriction sites, and known sequences.

The second part of the database problem is to record knowledge about the meaning of the sequences. This is intrinsically a far more complex problem, since the structure imposed on the data by necessity reflects only the current understanding. This will change radically as new insights occur, possibly causing major restructuring of at least sections of the interpretation.

Already, a great deal is known beyond just sequences of DNA. We know that sections of DNA are copied into strings in a second alphabet (RNA), which are then used to build proteins (which are strings in yet a third alphabet). Much of the actual function of the cell is achieved by interactions between proteins. Our knowledge is incredibly sketchy; in some cases, the exact mechanisms are well understood, while in others only the vaguest theories exist. In short, we are in the initial stages of this most incredible piece of detective work.

1.4.2 Levels of Data

Over the next 3–5 years, there will be a major effort to organize the data being accumulated by the biologists. Much of this data corresponds to sequences of DNA. Ways must be found to merge the output of numerous labs into a consistent resource from which information can be easily extracted. To understand exactly how this might occur, it is useful to think of the data in at least two subdivisions:

1. We will call the data relating directly to management of the known DNA sequence data the *core data*. This aspect of the database is required just to keep track of which sections of distinct genomes have successfully been determined.

2. A far more complex category of data relates to interpretation of information encoded in genomes. These data will be required to establish a computational framework to support the efforts of biologists as they gradually unravel the secrets stored in DNA.

Figure 1.4 depicts an Entity-Relationship model for the core data.
A brief description of a minimal relational representation of the core data shown in Figure 1.4 would be as follows.

genome A genome is the set of chromosomes for some particular organism. The genome for a simple bacterium contains a single chromosome, while a human genome includes 46 chromosomes. Here we use the term genome to refer to an abstraction, the collection of sequence information for a type of organism (rather than the sequences for a specific individual of that type). Thus, we speak of "the genome of *E. coli*", rather than the genome of a specific strain of *E. coli*. We will represent a genome by the relation

`genome(Organism).`

`Organism` is the unique identifier of a species for which sequence data is being maintained.

For example,

`genome(ecoli).`

strain For any specific organism, sequences from multiple strains must be managed within the single evolving database. We represent such strains by the relation

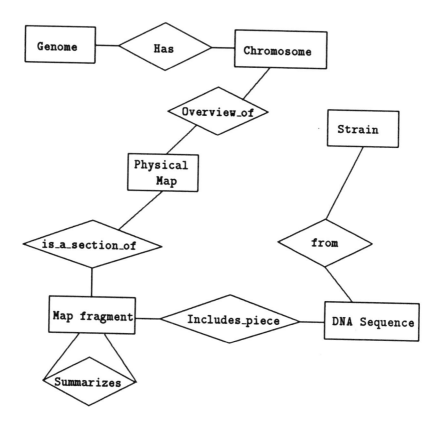

Figure 1.4: Core Data ER Diagram

```
strain(Organism,Strain).
```

Strain uniquely identifies one of a set of strains for a given organism. For example,

```
strain(ecoli,mg1655).
```

chromosome Physically, a chromosome is a single molecule of DNA. Here, we use the term abstractly. For example, we will speak of the "the *E. coli* chromosome", and by that we will refer to what is known about the *E. coli* chromosome (not the sequence of the DNA from a specific strain). Here we will represent the chromosome by

```
chromosome(Organism,ChromosomeId).
```

ChromosomeId uniquely designates the DNA molecule for the particular organism. For example, "chromosome 19" might be used to designate which of the human chromosomes was being represented.

For example,

```
chromosome(ecoli,'E. coli chromosome').
```

physical map A physical map is the ordered list of restriction sites of a chromosome, or part of a chromosome. It is defined as follows:

```
physical_map(PhysMapId,Organism,Chromosome).
```

PhysMapId is a unique identifier. For example,

```
physical_map(kohara,ecoli,'E. coli chromosome').
```

physical map fragment A physical map is built from an ordered set of physical map fragments, each of approximately determined length and containing a portion of the ordered list of restriction sites. We represent a map fragment as

```
map_fragment(FragmentId,MinLength,MaxLength).
```

The lowest level of a physical map is a list of such fragments. The relationship of physical map fragments to the map is implemented with

```
fragment_in_map(PhysMapId,FragmentId,PositionNumber).
```

For any section of the physical map, one can define overlapping sets of map fragments. The relationship between physical map fragments is given by

```
fragment_composed_of(FragmentId1,PositionNumber,
                     FragmentId2).
```

One use of the physical map is to keep track of which areas of a chromosome have known sequence values. During the initial stages of a sequencing project, there are very few known sequences; as data become available, they are placed on the map, and the entire chromosome is gradually filled in. When a sequence can be accurately associated with a map fragment, it is done so with this relationship:

`sequence_in_fragment(FragmentId,SequenceId).`

For example, suppose we know a section of the physical map, and that sequence 8781 occurs somewhere in this region. We represent this information as shown below. The *map_fragment* entities list each fragment in the order it appears on the map; the *fragment_composed_of* relations give the list of nearest neighbor relationships; and the *sequence_in_fragment* relationships place each known sequence on the map.

For example, suppose that we had a section of the map in which the following was known:

`agatct..<1780-1790 char>..ggtcg..<1540-1620 char>..gggtct`

Further, suppose that we know that sequence 8781 occurs somewhere in this region. We would propose to represent this as

```
map_fragment(1,6,6).
map_fragment(2,1780,1790).
map_fragment(3,5,5).
map_fragment(4,1540,1620).
map_fragment(5,6,6).
map_fragment(6,3337,3427).
fragment_composed_of(6,1,1).
fragment_composed_of(6,2,2).
fragment_composed_of(6,3,3).
fragment_composed_of(6,4,4).
fragment_composed_of(6,5,5).
sequence_in_fragment(1,1741). % seq 1741 is agatct
sequence_in_fragment(3,1748). % seq 1748 is ggtcg
sequence_in_fragment(5,1743). % seq 1743 is gggtct
sequence_in_fragment(6,8781).
```

DNA sequence A sequence of DNA is a string in the alphabet a,c,g,t. Such strings will be kept in two distinct forms. One represents a sequence actually reported from a biological laboratory, while the second represents a composite sequence formed from a set of shorter sequences. The composite sequences are frequently called "virtual sequences". We represent these two distinct types of sequences with the the same relation

`sequence(SequenceId,String).`

The connection between a virtual sequence and the short sequences from which it is composed will be represented by a relationship of the form

`virtual_from_short(Vid,Vposition,ShortId,ShortPos,Length).`

For example,

```
sequence(1326,[a,c,t,t,a,a]).          % short sequence
sequence(1327,[a,a,g,t,c,g,c]).        % short sequence
sequence(1328,[t,t,a,a,g,t,c,g,c]).    % virtual seq

virtual_from_short(1328,0,1326,2,4).
virtual_from_short(1328,0,1327,2,5).
```

The relationship between strains and sequences is implemented as

`strain_sequence(Organism,Strain,SequenceId).`

Sequencing projects will start producing massive amounts of data over the coming years. The core database that we have described can be used to record progress. However, it does not adequately structure the data to make it truly useful to biologists. To understand what we mean, suppose that you were aware of a magnificent blueprint of a wonderful office building. Further, suppose that you could painstakingly gain access to small pieces of the complete blueprint. The core database would correspond to recording exactly what pieces had been acquired and which were still missing. It would say nothing about the contents of the pieces that had been acquired. In reality, you would be interested in the sections of the document that described complete subunits. The white spaces between descriptions would tend to be ignored, except as they allowed you to assemble the complete picture.

A genome is similar to such a blueprint. The sections that describe complete functional units are called 'genes'. A living cell is an amazingly complex environment in which chemical reactions sustain life. As new substances are required, sections of the blueprint are used to govern their manufacture, much the way the blueprint of a building would be used to guide the construction of specific sections. Indeed, there are little machines in each cell that are used to manufacture molecules called proteins. The blueprint includes detailed instructions on how to manufacture every protein required to maintain the existence of the cell, as well as instructions on how to build the cell itself. Life is sustained by chemical reactions that require the proteins manufactured according to the blueprint. Sequences of such reactions, called *pathways*, are used to transform energy and materials into useful forms. Understanding exactly how these pathways sustain life, and how the blueprint supports the activities of these pathways, is one of the most exciting scientific goals of modern biology.

For a database to be useful to modern biologists, it must record more than just the raw sequence data. It must also include information relating to the genes represented by such data, the chemical reactions catalyzed by those gene products, and the reaction pathways that embody the basic activity of life. It is this additional structure that represents an information resource of real utility to the biologist. The ER diagram shown in Figure 1.5 imposes a minimal version of this additional structure:

A sketch of these additional entities would go as follows.

gene A gene is a section of the blueprint (i.e., a chromosome) that describes a single functional unit. We will represent a gene with the relation

gene(GeneId,RoleOfTheGene).

We will need more relations to describe exactly when the gene is used (that is, under what conditions the gene is "expressed"). In addition, much of the critical information about the gene is conveyed in its relationships to other entities. The gene is embodied in a particular instance of an organism (e.g., a single *E. coli* cell) as a sequence of DNA. However, distinct individuals might have slightly altered versions of the gene, due to mutations. Hence, when we relate the entity "gene" to actual DNA sequences, we must record the set of known variations. Each variation is called an "allele". The most common version is called "the wildtype allele". We represent this relationship of the gene to sequence data with

gene_allele(GeneId,SequenceId,WildType)

WildType will be "true" or "false". If the position of the gene on a physical map is known, then

gene_physical_map(GeneId,PhysMapId,Location)

is used to record the data.

gene feature A gene, like a section of a blueprint, may be composed of subunits. In the case of a blueprint, the description of a single room would include

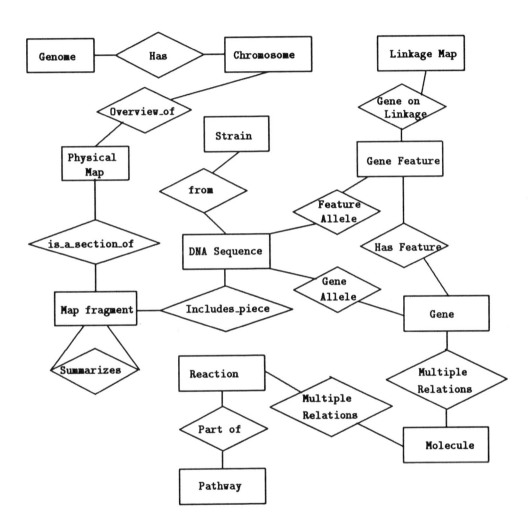

Figure 1.5: Extended ER Diagram

doors, windows, and mouldings. Similary, a gene has subunits that play distinct roles. These subunits we call "gene features". There are numerous types of subunits, the details of which go beyond the scope of this discussion. We will represent such features with

`gene_feature(GeneId,FeatureId,RoleOfTheFeature).`

and connect it to its alleles with

`gene_feature_allele(GeneId,FeatureId,SequenceId,WildType).`

gene family Occasionally, data are associated with a set of genes. This can occur when genes are related to each other in some way. For example, some genes are always turned on as a group. In other cases, researchers have hypothesized that several genes are likely to have evolved from a common ancestor. To represent such sets, we use

`gene_family(GeneFamilyId,TypeOfSet).`

and the relationship

`gene_in_gene_family(GeneId,GeneFamilyId).`

molecule Since the entire functioning of the cell depends on interactions between different types of molecules (DNA molecules, RNA molecules, proteins, etc.), we will need to include data describing these molecules. The level of representation can be fairly abstract, or it can go into a myriad of details. Early implementations will include a fairly modest amount of detail, while research over the next several decades will be required to fill in information about the structure and function of many of the molecules.

reaction When biologists speak of the "function of a gene", they normally mean the role that the product produced from the gene plays in chemical reactions. Enormous amounts of data exist describing exactly how different molecules interact under specified conditions. For now, we will think of a reaction as occurring between four classes of molecules: substrates, products, enzymes, and effectors. The minimal data that we need to encode includes

`reaction(ReactionId,KineticParameters,ThermodynamicParameters)`

and the relationship

`molecule_in_reaction(MoleculeId,ReactionId,RoleType).`

reaction pathway A reaction pathway is a set of reactions that together are viewed as a group. We represent such pathways with

```
pathway(PathId,DescriptionOfFunction,
        KineticParameters,ThermodynamicParameters)
```

and

`pathway_reaction(PathId,ReactionId1,ReactionId2)`

where we view the pathway as a set of "arcs" connecting the different reactions that participate in the process.

linkage map A good idea of the position of genes on a chromosome can be determined through indirect measurements. In particular, biologists have carefully studied recombination frequencies to determine which genes occur in close proximity. This information has been used to construct linkage maps. The basic data in such maps can be represented with

`linkage_map(LinkageMapId,Organism,Chromosome,Resolution)`

and the relationship

`gene_on_linkage_map(GeneId,LinkageMapId,Location)`

In this short description, we have indicated how one might begin to construct a database to support genetic research. Over the next two to four years, integrated databases encompassing the components that we have described will be made. These will form the starting point for research that will take place over decades. Our goal has not been to offer a complete design, but rather to suggest an approach towards producing such a design.

1.4.3   Implementing the Database

The entity-relationship diagram given above represents a fairly limited set of data items that, put into a single coherent framework, would represent a significant asset to currently practicing molecular biologists. This original database would then be expanded (both in term of the number of occurrences of the original entities and the number of different classes of entities). Logic programming offers a convenient vehicle for imposing a coherent representation. It is our hope that such a platform will offer the following benefits:

- It offers a representation that is completely independent of any specific database implementation. It is a straightforward task to translate existing sources of data into standard Prolog format from their present representations (which range from 80-character card-image files to relational databases in a variety of commercial systems).

- It is trivial to write small Prolog programs to convert sections of the database into whatever format is required by anyone using another representation.

- It provides a marvelous framework for logic programming advocates to study one of the most interesting applications of computers in modern science.

There are three central issues that must be addressed in a reasonable fashion for such an implementation to be of use:

- It must be possible to offer reasonable indexing to the predicates that implement the relational view. That is, simple first-argument indexing (which is offered by most Prolog systems) is inadequate.

- It must be possible to isolate the user of such a database from changes such as extending the set of attributes associated with an entity or adding new entities.

- It must be possible to point to a commercially available Prolog system that is capable of managing the amount of raw data that currently exists.

The last two points can be adequately handled by techniques that are well-known within the logic programming community, and the first point can be satisfactorily addressed in any of several ways.

Indexing on Multiple Arguments   Access to databases frequently requires reasonable discrimination on other than the first argument. Standard database systems are normally implemented by creating inversions on other attributes. These can easily be implemented within Prolog. For example, suppose that the relation *sequence_in_fragment* is implemented as

```
sequence_in_fragment(FragmentId,SequenceId).
```

For example,

```
sequence_in_fragment(2,1748).
```

might be used to state that sequence 1748 occurs in map fragment 2. We might very well have to access queries of the form

```
?- sequence_in_fragment(2,Seq).
```

which will work well using first-argument indexing. On the other hand, we need to also support queries like

```
?- sequence_in_fragment(Fragment,1748).
```

which would be used to locate fragments that contain sequence 1748. This is easily
done by defining *sequence_in_fragment/2* as

```
sequence_in_fragment(FragmentId,SequenceId) :-
    (nonvar(FragmentId) ->
        sequence_in_fragment_data(FragmentId,SequenceId)
    ;
        (nonvar(SequenceId) ->
            sequence_in_fragment_index(SequenceId,FragmentId)
        ;
            sequence_in_fragment_data(FragmentId,SequenceId)
        )
    ).
```

where *sequence_in_fragment_data/2* contains the facts that represent the relation,
and *sequence_in_fragment_index/2* is an implementation of the inversion on the second attribute. A slight modification to this code would work efficiently for cases in
which the relationship included attributes other than the keys of the related entities.
In good Prolog implementations, the above code will not generate any unnecessary
choice points, and it does offer adequate discrimination for our purposes.

Isolating the User from Changes in the Database   One major concern facing anyone writing software that must access data from a database is to isolate
the software from changes in the structure of the database. This becomes a major
concern when a substantial investment is required to produce and maintain the software. The major structural changes that are required for a database involve adding
more relations (due to adding more entities and relationships) or adding attributes
to existing relations (due to a desire to expand the data associated with entities
and relationships). In almost any reasonable database system, the introduction of
new entities and relationships is straightforward. It may require some effort by a
database administrator to actually load the new data items into the database, but
that is required in any event. The addition of new relations to the database should
not produce changes in user software.

Occasionally, it will be necessary to support new attributes for existing entities
and relationships. One could always avoid such a change by introducing a new
relation that would contain only the required key along with the added attributes.
This is a practical approach in many cases. On the other hand, given a Prolog

implementation, there is also a trivial approach to supporting such additions quite
naturally. Suppose that a relation

```
r(Attr1,Attr2,...Attrn)
```

should be extended by adding a new attribute *attr*. This is achieved easily by
reorganizing the database to include the extended relation

```
r(Attr1,Attr2,...Attrn,Attr)
```

and deleting the original relation. To maintain compatability with existing software,
the rule

```
r(Attr1,Attr2,...Attrn) :- r(Attr1,Attr2,...Attrn,Attr).
```

is added.

An alternative approach is to prepare from the beginning for the addition of
attributes to existing entities and relationships. This can be done by writing the
application programs that access the database so that all references to attributes
are through access predicates. Let us suppose that in the example above, `Attr1`
is the attribute of the relation `r(Attr1,...,Attrn)` that serves as the uniquely
identifying key. The most straightforward way to access, say the third attribute of
the instance of `r` with `Attr1` equal to `key`, would be invocation in application code
of the goal

```
r(key,_,Attr3,_,...,_).
```

If a new attribute is added to `r`, then all calls of this form must be modified.

The access predicate approach creates a separate predicate for each attribute,
whose purpose is to access that attribute. Such a predicate would look like

```
attribute(Attr1,Attr3) :- r(Attr1,_,Attr3,_,...,_).
```

The arity of `r` is hidden from the application program by the access predicates,
which are the only part of the system that must be changed when new attributes
are added.

An alternative to access predicates that provides the same insulation of users
and user programs from the structure of the data in the database is the "binary
relations" approach. Here, the relation `r` is *replaced* by a set of binary relations
`r1, r2, r3, ...`, where the first argument of `ri` is the key field of `r` and the second
argument is `attri`. For example we replace

```
book(Refnum,Title,Authorlist,Publisher,Keywordlist).
by
book_title(Refnum,Title),
book_authors(Refnum,Authorlist),
book_publisher(Refnum,Publisher),
and
book_keywords(Refnum,Keywordlist).
```

This makes it even easier to add new attributes to an entity or relationship, since
no existing code will have to be modified. The cost is in the increased size of the
database.

Supporting the Required Volume   While the power and elegance of logic programming have been widely accepted, there has been some concern about whether
or not Prolog implementations of databases are practical. A number of points
should be made in this regard:

- Many existing databases can be easily handled by existing commercial implementations of Prolog. While enormous databases command a great deal
  of attention, the vast majority of databases are of modest size. For example,
  consider a "personnel database"; what percentage of companies have over
  1000 employees? In fact, existing commercial systems running on workstations (which can hold at least 32-64 megabytes of memory for a relatively
  modest price) can support transaction rates well above more conventional
  disk-based systems.

- In the short range, the ability to interface commercial Prologs to existing relational database systems offers a practical way to handle substantial databases.

- The software development for even fairly small systems frequently takes place
  over 3-5 years. In such a context, some attempt should be made to distinguish
  current limitations from intrinsic limitations. That is, "Is Prolog intrinsically
  inefficient as a database manager?" Our belief is that logic programming
  will, in a fairly short time, become a dominant theme within the database
  community (it already commands far more attention than people would have
  thought possible even 5 years ago). Better implementations will make it clear
  that most limitations are not, in fact, intrinsic.

Finally, we would like to point out one particularly trivial approach that has
allowed us to experimentally handle fairly large amounts of genetic data. In the

case of genetic data, much of the actual storage space is consumed by long sequences
(or text comments relating to these sequences), while complex queries are based on
other attributes. For example, the query

> Approximately what percentage of chromosome 14 for humans has been
> sequenced?

requires a fairly complex computation accessing data from a number of entities and
relationships. It does not, however, require accessing the actual strings of known
DNA sequences (assuming the lengths of such strings are known without examining
the actual characters in the string). We have implemented a predicate

`external_storage(ListOfAtomicElements,Ref)`

that is called with exactly one argument instantiated. When called with the first
argument instantiated to a list of atomic data items, it copies them into external
memory (in our implementation onto a disk file) and binds the second argument
to an integer that acts as a reference to the data. On the other hand, when called
with the second argument instantiated, it reconstructs the list and binds the first
argument.

We represent the entity *genetic_sequence* using two relations–one containing all
attributes except the actual string of characters, and a second that accesses the
string. For example,

```
sequence(SequenceId,String) :-
    sequence_data(SequenceId,Ptr),
    external_storage(String,Ptr).
```

where *sequence_data/2* is a relation constructed when the database is loaded. This
trivial technique is easily implemented on most commercial Prolog systems using
a C interface, and it provides the required capacity without impacting the user's
software (the user need not be aware that a predicate like *sequence_data/2* has been
defined).

1.5   Summary

In this brief tutorial, we have presented a methodology for implementing databases.
Essentially, we advocate

- begin by developing an entity-relationship diagram that establishes the overall
  structure of the database,

- fill in the details by constructing a relational representation of the entities and relationships, and

- implement the relational representation in Prolog.

In addition, we have argued that the current developments in molecular biology make it an ideal application area to demonstrate the utility of this approach. We believe that the systems that evolve in molecular biology over the next few years will include numerous entities and, perhaps, hundreds of relations. Attempts to formulate a coherent view of these growing masses of information represent one of the most interesting problems in the field of database design. Success would offer a framework to address the truly fundamental issues now being investigated by biologists. We believe that logic programming will ultimately play an instrumental role in this developing investigation. Only time will tell whether or not our assessment is accurate.

1.6   Background

We urge the reader to read some of the better guides available. In particular, we highly recommend the following four sources:

1. *The Cartoon Guide to Genetics* [GW83] by Larry Gonick and Mark Wheelis, is one of the best pieces of tutorial writing available. It covers an amazing amount of material in an extremely pleasant format.

2. "Is the Genetic Code Arbitrary?" by Douglas Hofstadter appears in the book *Metamagical Themas* [Hof85], a collection of Hofstadter's articles. It is a beautiful summary of what is meant by "the genetic code".

3. Chapter XVI in *Godel, Escher, Bach* [Hof79] by Douglas Hofstadter contains a slightly more complete exposition.

4. "Mapping Our Genes" is a report that was prepared for Congress by the Office of Technology Assessment [Ass88]. It contains a good tutorial that covers issues relating directly to "mapping the human genome". It also includes information relating to the significance of the current genetics projects.

Chapter 2

PREDITOR : A Prolog-based VLSI Editor

Peter B. Reintjes

Microelectronics Center of North Carolina
3021 Cornwallis Road
Research Triangle Park
North Carolina, 27709

2.1 Introduction

Prolog is well suited to the implementation of Computer Aided Design tools for Very Large Integrated Circuits, or VLSI CAD. The declarative nature of electronic circuit descriptions leads to natural definitions of many CAD problems, and the logical variable has properties analogous to those of an electrical connection. In addition, Prolog's implicit database provides a convenient mechanism for creating tools sensitive to changing technology rules and design constraints.

Modern VLSI CAD systems span a rich diversity of design technologies including silicon compilation, logic synthesis, symbolic design, mask layout, gate arrays, and standard-cell place-and-route systems. In all of these areas new algorithms and new representations are being developed. But while many tough problems have been solved by experimental software, the production quality tools in the hands of designers are still quite primitive. One reason for this is that the implementation of a complex system of VLSI CAD tools presents several difficult software engineering problems.

The system described here accepts the diversity of VLSI CAD as a fact of life and strives to provide a uniform environment in which a designer can take advantage of different design styles. Although PREDITOR is basically a Prolog re-implementation of ideas from existing CAD systems, the gains of this modest implementation have been twofold.

- The source code is an order-of-magnitude smaller than implementations in imperative languages such as C, and readability is improved by the declarative aspects of Prolog.

• Implementing a basic CAD capability in a logic programming environment creates a solid foundation for more advanced work in Intelligent CAD.

The most common criticism of software developed in Prolog is the performance penalty paid for this level of abstraction. However, advances in Prolog compilation together with the emergence of high-performance workstations have made some of these arguments obsolete. Although some CAD algorithms run between 2 and 4 times slower than their counterparts in C, the interactive response of the editor is comparable to a similar program written in C.

2.2   Overview

2.2.1   Design Representation

The first component of this Prolog-based VLSI CAD system is a multi-lingual translator for hardware description languages. This translator can exist either as the stand-alone program AUNT (*A Universal Netlist Translator*), or as the database support sub-system of PREDITOR. AUNT currently supports reading and writing circuit descriptions in eight languages. This translation is achieved by constructing a common logical form from the circuit descriptions.

With AUNT as the language handling sub-system of Preditor, many issues of design representation and interchange formats can be ignored by the designer. The common format, the Logical Form Language (LFL), was arrived at empirically. The LFL is simply the set of Prolog terms required to represent all information in the superset of the supported hardware description languages. As support for different languages is added, the LFL may be modified to accommodate new features. Because the editing system operates only on the LFL built by the AUNT subsystem, it is largely independent of any specific circuit description language.

The database is constructed of primitive terms representing electronic components and collections of these components which form complex circuits, or *cells*. Complex hierarchical circuits are defined by treating other, simpler circuits as components. Thus, a digital inverter circuit contains transistor, wire, and contact primitives, as does a transmission gate circuit. A shift-register circuit contains *instances* of inverter and transmission gate circuits as sub-circuits.

The following terms represent the transistor, wire, and contact components.

```
TRANSISTOR:   tran(Name,Type,Point,Mods,S,G,D,Ext)
WIRE:         wire(Name,Layer,Width,PList,Net,Ext)
CONNECTION:   contact(Name,Type,Point,Mods,Net,Ext)
```

The term for the transistor contains a unique identifier (**Name**), the transistor **Type**, its location (**Point**), its width, gate-length, and orientation (**Mods**), the names of the nodes connected to the transistor's source (**S**), gate (**G**), and drain (**D**), and an extension field to hold information which does not fit in the other fields (**Ext**). Not all of this information is available from every circuit description language. For example, not all circuit languages assign individual unique names to each transistor. In this case, the **Name** argument would remain uninstantiated.

Circuits are represented as *cell/5* facts in the database.

```
cell(Name,Elements,Nets,Pins,BBox).
```

A circuit, or *cell*, contains a list of circuit elements in **Elements**. In practice these lists contain from 10 to 50 items and so a more complex data structure has not been necessary. Some of the objects in **Elements** represent basic electrical components such as the transistors, wires, or contacts. But the element list may also contain a special object representing an *instance* of another circuit.

```
instance(Name,Cellname,Mods,Connections,Matrix,Ext).
```

This structure is analogous to the hierarchy found in software, where a parameterized algorithm appears as a subroutine (the cell), and a subroutine call (the instance) causes the algorithm to execute in a certain context. Like a program, a circuit design is defined by a particular *cell/5* fact which is the equivalent of a main program routine. All of the other cells in the database will appear as instances under this top-level cell.

Each *instance/6* within a parent circuit has location and orientation information which specifies its relative placement within that circuit. Like the arguments of a subroutine, this information specifies the context for this particular instance of the prototype cell.

Once the translator has transformed the circuit design into Prolog clauses, small-scale Prolog programs can be written by the designer to answer questions about the design. For example, the following will determine the number of transistors in a particular circuit.

```
?- [user].
transistors(Name,Number) :-
    cell(Name,Elements,_,_,_),
    bagof(T,(member(T,Elements),functor(T,tran,_)),Ts),
    length(Ts,Number).
end_of_file.
```

```
?- transistors(multiplexor,Number).
Number = 12
yes.
```

Once *transistors/2* has been written, a predicate can be written to determine which circuit has the greatest number of transistors.

```
most_transistors(Cellname,Transistor_Count) :-
    bagof(count(Number,Name),transistors(Name,Number),List),
    sort(List,SList),
    append(_,[count(Transistor_Count,Cellname)],SList).
```

A query of the form ?-most_transistors(Cell, Number) will unify Cell and Number with the name and number of transistors of the largest circuit.

Below, a somewhat more useful predicate finds pairs of electrical nodes in a cell which are electrically connected although they have distinct names. The *nn/2* terms link the textual names of electrical nodes in the circuit description language with uninstantiated variables representing the electrical connection. Every object with an electrical connection to a particular node will have a connection variable unified with that node's second argument.

```
shorted(Cellname,Name1,Name2) :-
    cell(Cellname,_,Nodes,_,_),
    member(nn(Name1,Net1),Nodes),
    member(nn(Name2,Net2),Nodes),
    not(Name1 == Name2),
    Net1 == Net2.
```

If the circuits in the database follow the convention that power supply nodes are named **power** and **ground**, the query ?- shorted(Cell,power,ground). will search the database for cells with shorted power supply connections.

2.2.2 Graphical Display

The second component of the system is a graphical display system which supports four visualization and editing levels. These levels are: documentation (unrestricted pictures and text), schematic, symbolic, and layout. Thus, a single program gives the designer access to all four levels of abstraction. The visualization and editing subsystem is composed of predicates for the display, selection and identification of the design objects.

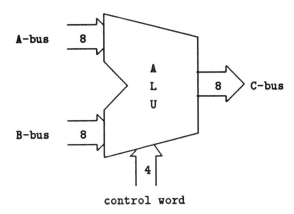

Figure 2.1: Documentation

The highest level of design can be described as the creation of an uninterpreted picture representing a "documentation-level" visualization of a circuit. Such a picture is an arbitrary collection of lines, filled or unfilled polygons, and text.

The next highest level is the schematic level. The graphical objects at this level consist of a set of logic symbols (nor, and, inverter, transmission gate) with connection points. This is similar to the documentation level except that the primitive objects are logic gates, logic blocks (such as adders or flip-flops), transistors, and wires instead of lines, polygons and text. Furthermore, the schematic representation contains additional semantic information about connectivity between components. Schematic representations are said to be technology independent because the same schematic could describe a circuit implemented in CMOS, nMOS, or Bi-polar technology.

The next level is the symbolic layout level. Here the objects are stylized transistors, wires, contacts, and pins placed on an evenly spaced grid. This level of description is identical to that found in the MULGA and VIVID^{TM} symbolic layout systems. The primitive objects in a symbolic description are generally *technology specific*. For example, a symbolic design in CMOS technology is quite different from an nMOS design because they have different materials and transistor types. A symbolic design is *design-rule independent*, however, since the exact size and spacing of the components is not specified. Symbolic layout descriptions are converted to physical layouts with exact dimensions by compaction programs.

As in the schematic level, wires at the symbolic layout level are described by a

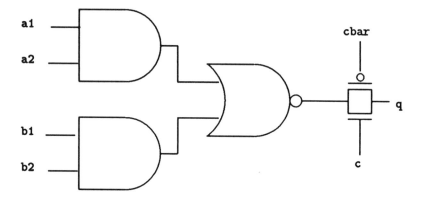

Figure 2.2: Schematic

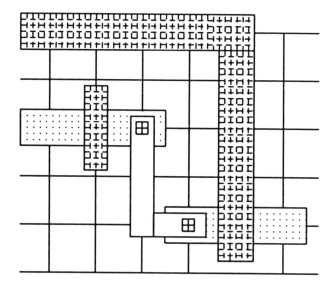

Figure 2.3: Symbolic

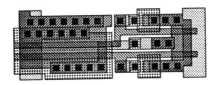

Figure 2.4: Physical Layout

list of points. However, unlike schematic wires and transistors, symbolic objects have associated parameters which give the relative size of the physical layout object which will be generated by the compactor.

The physical layout level differs from the three previous levels in that the coordinate system within the cell corresponds to the actual physical dimensions of the patterns on the integrated circuit processing mask. A user-specified scale factor determines the correspondence between physical dimensions in the circuit and the display-grid scale. Whenever the user is performing operations inside the perimeter of the physical layout cell, all coordinates are specified in physical dimensions. Just as the symbolic designs were technology specific, physical layouts are technology and design-rule specific.

The schematic and symbolic views of these circuits are the essential structural representations and are completely contained in the *cell/5* facts. If documentation or layout descriptions exist for a cell, these will appear in the database as separate *cell/6* facts, with the extra argument indicating how to interpret the components in the structure.

2.2.3   Editing

After building a database from the textual circuit descriptions and providing a display system, the next component will allow the user to perform edit operations on the objects in the database, and see these changes on an interactive display.

Stated in logic programming terms: the editing system is a meta-interpreter which, when given a command and a database, will produce a new database and a stream of graphics commands.

The database consists of a collection of *cell/5* facts which contain individual circuit descriptions, a *preditor_defs/8* fact which contains default values for the objects created by the editor, and a *preditor_state/3* fact which contains information

about the current state of the editor. Any or all of these predicates may be changed
during an edit operation.

For example, if a designer is editing the cell **adder** but then moves the cursor
over a neighboring cell **register** and deletes a transistor, the following changes
will occur in the editor:

- The *preditor_state/3* fact will be changed to reflect that the current cell being
edited is **register** instead of **adder**.

- The *preditor_defs/8* fact will be updated to represent the fact that the current edit
object is a transistor of the type deleted.

- The *cell/5* fact corresponding to the **register** circuit will have the selected transistor removed from its list of components.

- The transistor will be erased from the screen.

The top-level of the editor is the *interact/0* predicate. This predicate repeatedly gets a command from the user, performs the command on the database with
menu_op/1, and then fails back to *repeat* unless the command was the atom **quit**.
A quit command corresponds to a *menu_op/1* clause which does nothing, but then
the *interact/0* predicate will be completed successfully.

```
interact :-
    set_defaults,
    repeat,
        pick(Command),
        menu_op(Command),
    Command = quit,
    !.
```

Setting the default values for the editor state includes reading a startup file and/or
prompting the user for the name of the first circuit to edit. This information goes
into a global structure called *preditor_state/3*.

```
preditor_state(vcell(VCell,V_BBox),
               ecell(Cell,Instance,E_BBox),
               matrix(A,B,C,D,E,F)).
```

In general, the cell being viewed and the cell being edited are different. To allow
the designer to edit a circuit in context, Preditor will be viewing a parent cell

(*vcell/2*) which contains the edit cell (*ecell/3*) as a sub-circuit. The third argument
in *preditor_state/3* is a matrix which maps the coordinates in the design space to
the graphic display.

The predicate *menu_op/1* is the dispatch table for the different menu operations.
If the user did not select a menu item, the argument will be the atom "**field**",
indicating that the cursor was in the work area. In this situation, *menu_op/1* will
call the *edit/0* predicate discussed in section 2.5.

```
menu_op(field)    :- edit.
menu_op(zoom)     :- zoom(in).
menu_op(unzoom)   :- zoom(out).
menu_op(display) :-
    preditor_state(vcell(Cell,_),_,_),
    plot_cell_hierarchy(Cell,matrix(1,0,0,1,0,0)).
    .
    .
    .
menu_op(quit).
```

2.3 The Coordinate System

A concrete VLSI representation such as a mask layout is little more than a specification of geometric relationships. For this level of description, the primary role of
the database is to maintain spatial information. Even a more abstract view of an
electrical network such as a schematic depends upon component positions and the
location of connecting lines. In fact, at all levels of description in PREDITOR, the
common requirement is the need to represent spatial relationships.

Along with the database requirement for spatial information, there is an extensive need for geometric computations. Approximately 20% of the goals in the
PREDITOR program involve mapping geometric representations from one coordinate system to another. Three typical CAD problems are given below, together
with brief descriptions of how they are solved with coordinate transformations.

- "Determine which object in a complex hierarchy the user has selected with the
  cursor". *The bounding boxes of each sub-circuit on the screen are transformed to
  screen coordinates and compared with the cursor location to identify which circuit
  the cursor is over. A new matrix relating the screen coordinates to the coordinates
  INSIDE the circuit is used to transform the cursor location to a point inside the*

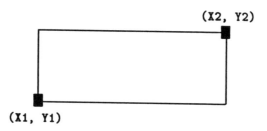

Figure 2.5: Information in a box/5 term

circuit. This circuit is then searched recursively for any sub-circuits or objects which lie under the transformed cursor location.

- "Plot a layout rectangle on the screen". *The corner points of a term representing the layout rectangle,* box(X1,Y1,X2,Y2,Color), *must be transformed and oriented using a matrix which relates the coordinates in the subcell to the display screen.*

- "Find the interconnection points of all sub-circuits in a cell." *This operation requires lists of all points on the perimeters of subcells. These points are transformed from each sub-circuit's coordinates into the parent cell coordinates. The points which coincide when transformed to the parent cell are then checked for interacting electrical components.*

Many operations in an interactive CAD system deal with the display and manipulation of objects in a two dimensional plane. The editing operations performed by the user are based upon the interactions between objects in this plane, as are circuit extraction and design rule checking. If we establish a uniform system of two-dimensional transformations over the universe of objects in the CAD system, other aspects of the system are greatly simplified. The *transform/3* predicate is defined to transform any VLSI object, including points, transistors, menu items, lists of objects, and any other compound objects containing spatial information.

2.3.1 The Transformation Matrix

The coordinate mapping transformation uses a nine element transformation matrix to transform points and objects in a two-dimensional space. The values of three elements of this matrix are always fixed, so we only need to maintain six of

$$[TX \quad TY \quad 1] = [X \quad Y \quad 1] \begin{bmatrix} A & B & 0 \\ C & D & 0 \\ E & F & 1 \end{bmatrix}$$

Figure 2.6: Coordinate Transformation

$$Translation : \quad [X' \quad Y' \quad 1] = [X \quad Y \quad 1] \begin{bmatrix} 1 & 0 & 0 \\ 0 & 1 & 0 \\ T\_x & T\_y & 1 \end{bmatrix}$$

$$Rotation : \quad [X' \quad Y' \quad 1] = [X \quad Y \quad 1] \begin{bmatrix} \cos(\Theta) & -\sin(\Theta) & 0 \\ \sin(\Theta) & \cos(\Theta) & 0 \\ 0 & 0 & 1 \end{bmatrix}$$

$$Scaling : \quad [X' \quad Y' \quad 1] = [X \quad Y \quad 1] \begin{bmatrix} S\_X & 0 & 0 \\ 0 & S\_Y & 0 \\ 0 & 0 & 1 \end{bmatrix}$$

Figure 2.7: Transformation Components

these values. The expression `transform(X&Y,TX&TY,matrix(A,B,C,D,E,F))` can be read as *The point (X, Y) is transformed with the matrix(A,B,C,D,E,F) to get the point (TX,TY)*. This expression defines the matrix operation in Figure 2.6.

This transformation may relate the location of an object in the design space to its display screen coordinates. The transformation matrix can best be understood by considering the individual components of two-dimensional transformation in Figure 2.7.

The **&** operator is simply a combiner operator which defines the data structure containing the two coordinates of a point. If a Prolog system does not allow operator definitions, every occurrence of `X&Y` in the program could be changed to `point(X,Y)`. The first clause of the predicate *transform/3* defines the point transformation.

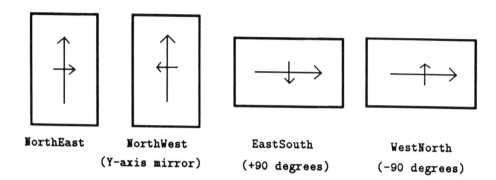

Figure 2.8: Four of Eight Orientations

```
transform(X&Y,TX&TY,matrix(A,B,C,D,E,F)) :-
    TX is A*X + C*Y + E,
    TY is B*X + D*Y + F.
```

The following clauses define the transformation for all VLSI objects in terms of this point transformation. The *box/5* term is used to represent physical layout features, defined as a rectangular region of a particular material.

```
transform(box(X1,Y1,X2,Y2,D),box(RX1,RY1,RX2,RY2,D),Matrix) :-
    !,
    transform(X1&Y1,NX1&NY1,Matrix),
    transform(X2&Y2,NX2&NY2,Matrix),
    min(NX1,NX2,RX1), max(NX1,NX2,RX2),
    min(NY1,NY2,RY1), max(NY1,NY2,RY2).
```

Note that the relationship between the lower-left and upper-right corners is maintained with *min/3* and *max/3*. The relative positions of the lower-left and upper-right corners is a form of orientation information.

Some objects, such as transistors, instances, and gates have structures which depend upon a more general notion of orientation. Eight orientations are possible when four 90-degree rotations are combined with the two operations of mirroring about the X or Y axis. The default, North-East orientation, is represented by a northern major axis and an eastern minor axis. A 90-degree clockwise rotation of this orientation results in the East-South orientation, with major axis east and minor axis south.

The *orien_matrix/2* predicate relates a four-element matrix to each of the eight orientations. This smaller orientation matrix corresponds to the rotation sub-matrix of the general transformation matrix.

```
orien_matrix(ne, or_matrix( 1, 0, 0, 1)).
orien_matrix(es, or_matrix( 0,-1, 1, 0)).
orien_matrix(sw, or_matrix(-1, 0, 0,-1)).
orien_matrix(wn, or_matrix( 0, 1,-1, 0)).
orien_matrix(en, or_matrix( 0, 1, 1, 0)).
orien_matrix(se, or_matrix( 1, 0, 0,-1)).
orien_matrix(ws, or_matrix( 0,-1,-1, 0)).
orien_matrix(nw, or_matrix(-1, 0, 0, 1)).
```

In the following clause, the transistor's location point is transformed, and then its orientation matrix is transformed to get a new matrix (and corresponding orientation).

```
transform(tran(N,T,Pt,mods(Or,Wid,Len),S,G,D,Ext),
    tran(N,T,NPt,mods(NOr,Wid,Len),S,G,D,Ext),Matrix) :-
    !,
    transform(Pt,NPt,Matrix),
    orien_matrix(Or,Or_Matrix),
    transform(Or_Matrix,New_Matrix,Matrix),
    orien_matrix(NOr,New_Matrix).
```

A *wire/5* contains a list of points as well as information about the wire width and material. A transformed wire is simply a wire with a transformed point list.

```
transform(wire(N,L,W,Plist,N,E),wire(N,L,W,TPlist,N,E),Matrix) :-
    !,
    transform(Plist,TPlist,Matrix).
```

The transformation of a list of objects is just a list of the transformed objects. This simple clause recursively handles lists-of-lists.

```
transform([Obj|T],[TObj|TT],Matrix) :-
    !,
    transform(Obj,TObj,Matrix),
    transform(T,TT,Matrix).
```

$$\begin{bmatrix} Na & Nb & 0 \\ Nc & Nd & 0 \\ Ne & Nf & 1 \end{bmatrix} = \begin{bmatrix} Ca & Cb & 0 \\ Cc & Cd & 0 \\ Ce & Cf & 1 \end{bmatrix} \begin{bmatrix} Ea & Eb & 0 \\ Ec & Ed & 0 \\ Ee & Ef & 1 \end{bmatrix}$$

Figure 2.9: Matrix Transformation

The next two clauses implement matrix multiplications. The variables have the prefixes C, E, and N, to emphasize the use of this operation in creating new environment matrices when editing sub-cells. The local matrix of a circuit instance (C) is multiplied by the current environment matrix (E), to get a new environment (N).

```
transform(matrix(Ca,Cb,Cc,Cd,Ce,Cf),matrix(Na,Nb,Nc,Nd,Ne,Nf),
        matrix(Ea,Eb,Ec,Ed,Ee,Ef)) :-
            !,
            Na is Ca*Ea + Cb*Ec,
            Nb is Ca*Eb + Cb*Ed,
            Nc is Cc*Ea + Cd*Ec,
            Nd is Cc*Eb + Cd*Ed,
            Ne is Ce*Ea + Cf*Ec + Ee,
            Nf is Ce*Eb + Cf*Ed + Ef.
```

An "orientation matrix" is simply the four-element submatrix which defines an orientation without translation.

```
transform(or_matrix(Ca,Cb,Cc,Cd),or_matrix(Na,Nb,Nc,Nd),
        matrix(Ea,Eb,Ec,Ed,_,_)) :-
            !,
            Na is Ca*Ea + Cb*Ec,
            Nb is Ca*Eb + Cb*Ed,
            Nc is Cc*Ea + Cd*Ec,
            Nd is Cc*Eb + Cd*Ed.
```

The base case of the list transformation is the same as for all non-geometric objects since nothing needs to be done. All such objects are handled by the last clause.

```
transform(Obj,Obj,_).
```

2.3.2 Hierarchy Flattening

An important use of the *transform/3* predicate is to "flatten" or remove hierarchy from a cell. The following predicates implement a circuit flattener which recursively copies objects from subcells into the coordinate system of the parent cell. The use of definite clause grammar syntax produces a particularly concise definition of hierarchy flattening.

The *flatten_prims/3* predicate is used to transform circuit elements to screen coordinates for plotting and also for finding global placement to detect when circuit elements touch or violate design rules.

```
flatten_cell(Cellname,Matrix,Flat) :-
    flatten_cell(Cellname,Matrix,Flat,[ ]).

flatten_cell(Cellname,Matrix) -->
    {cell(Cellname,Prims,_,_,_)},
    flatten_prims(Prims,Matrix).

flatten_prims([ ],_) --> [ ].
flatten_prims([instance(_,Cell,_,_,IMat,_)|Ps],Matrix) -->
    !,
    { transform(IMat,NewMatrix,Matrix) },
    flatten_cell(Cell,NewMatrix),
    flatten_prims(Ps,Matrix).

flatten_prims([P|Ps],Matrix) :-
    [Obj], {transform(P,Obj,Matrix)},
    flatten_prims(Ps,Matrix).
```

2.4 The Graphical Interface

The graphics subsystem is a set of C subroutines which control an X-windows graphics interface and appear as Prolog predicates through a foreign function interface. Predicates are defined which initialize the graphics display, set the current color, and draw primitive shapes such as lines and rectangles. Cursor control predicates allow setting various cursor styles, including stretchable lines for drawing wires and complex cursors such as logic symbols for schematic editing.

The colors available for drawing are the basic material layers of VLSI layout,

```
draw_prim(con(_,Type,X&Y,_, _, _)) :-
    graph_layer(Type),
    LLX is X - 0.2,
    LLY is Y - 0.2,
    URX is X + 0.2,
    URY is Y + 0.2,
    graph_rect(LLX,LLY,URX,URY).
```

Figure 2.10: Display Code and Resulting Image of a Contact

including the colors which represent MOS-diffusion and polysilicon, as well as miscellaneous colors for menu labels and backgrounds.

```
avail_colors([ select, well,  contact, vss,    vdd,
               via,    glass, metal,   metal2, thinox,
               pdiff,  ndiff, poly,    yellow, white,
               blue,   mark,  black,   green,  tan ]).
```

Predicates which are linked to foreign functions have the prefix *graph_*, such as *graph_layer/1* for setting the current color, *graph_rect/4* for drawing a rectangular region and *graph_text/3* for printing text strings.

2.4.1 Drawing Predicates

Predicates with the prefix **draw_** are higher level graphic routines to display menus or VLSI objects by calling the **graph_** predicates. For example, the clauses of *draw_prim/1* are defined to display the primitive VLSI objects.

The simplest of the VLSI objects is the connection primitive, or contact, which is represented by a small square. Since the plotting predicate doesn't need the identification or electrical information in the *con/6* term, these arguments appear as anonymous variables.

Transistors are more complex, having different orientations, widths, and materials, as shown figure 2.11. The gate regions are drawn in black and the source and drain regions are white. The second clause of *draw_prim/1* computes the width of the device, sets the color for the source and drain regions, and then calls *draw_transistor/5* which uses the orientation to select the order of arguments for *draw_transistor/6*.

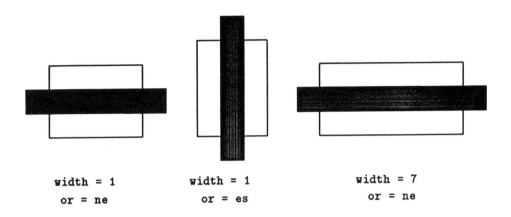

width = 1   width = 1   width = 7
or = ne   or = es   or = ne

Figure 2.11: Transistors

```
draw_prim(tran(_,Type,X&Y,_,mods(Or,Wid,_), _,_,_, _,_)) :-
    !,
    DrainWidth is  (Wid/2) - 0.2,
    GateWidth  is 0.25 + DrainWidth,
    graph_layer(Type),
    draw_transistor(Or,X,Y,DrainWidth,GateWidth).

draw_transistor(Orientation,X,Y,DeltaW,DeltaG) :-
    memberchk(Orientation,[ne,nw,se,sw]),
    draw_transistor(X,Y, 1.5, DeltaW, 0.25, DeltaG).

draw_transistor(_,X,Y,DeltaW,DeltaG) :-
    draw_transistor(X,Y, DeltaW, 1.5, DeltaG, 0.25).

draw_transistor(X,Y,DDX,DDY,DGX,DGY) :-
    DX is X - DDX, DY is Y - DDY,
    SX is X + DDX, SY is Y + DDY,
    graph_rect(DX,DY,SX,SY),
    GX1 is X - DGX, GX2 is X + DGX,
    GY1 is Y - DGY, GY2 is Y + DGY,
    graph_layer(poly),
    graph_rect(GX1,GY1,GX2,GY2).
```

Additional *draw_prim/1* clauses exist for layout rectangles, symbolic and schematic wires, pins, and instances.

The predicate *plot_cell_hierarchy/2*, which displays an entire hierarchical design, can now be defined. The following goal will plot the hierarchical cell named **adder**. Since the display coordinates correspond to the coordinates in the top-level cell, we specify a transformation matrix corresponding to a north-east orientation with no translation.

```
?- plot_cell_hierarchy(adder, matrix(1,0,0,1,0,0)).
```

The implementation of *plot_cell_hierarchy/2* must take the four different views of the circuit into account. For example, if a circuit is defined in the database as a *gate/1*, its schematic representation will always be displayed.

```
plot_cell_hierarchy(Cell,Matrix) :-
    gate(Cell),
    !,
    plot_schematic(Cell,Matrix).
```

If the cell is not defined as a gate, we may still display it in schematic form if the following conditions are met.

• The current display mode is **schematic**.

• The cell is the top-level display cell.

• The cell is a leaf cell. That is, it is non-hierarchical and contains only primitive circuit elements such as transistors and wires.

```
plot_cell_hierarchy(Cell,Matrix) :-
    current_mode(schematic),
    preditor_state(vcell(Cell,_),_,_),
    is_leaf(Cell),
    !,
    plot_schematic(Cell,Matrix).
```

The remaining clause displays the primitive elements within the cell. This operation is potentially recursive because one of these primitives may be an instance of a cell, for which we call *plot_cell_hierarchy/2* with the appropriate display matrix.

```
plot_cell_hierarchy(Cell,Matrix) :-
    cell(Cell,Ps,_,_,_),
    plot_primitives(Ps,Matrix).
```

Clauses in *plot_primitives/2* are defined for the end of the list, instance primitives, and low-level circuit elements. When an instance is encountered, five distinct display modes are considered by *plot_mode/4*. These five modes are the four basic display modes described earlier plus the default representation of a sub-circuit as a labeled rectangular region, as shown in figure 2.13.

```
plot_primitives([ ],_).
plot_primitives([INST|Ps],EMatrix) :-
    INST = instance(IN,Cell,imods(_,_,_,_,_,_,Mode),_,IMat,_),
    !,
    transform(IMat,New_Matrix,EMatrix),
    plot_mode(Mode,IN,Cell,New_Matrix),
    plot_primitives(Ps,EMatrix).
```

Leaf primitives are transformed and then displayed with *draw_prim/1*.

```
plot_primitives([P|Ps],Matrix) :-
    transform(P,DisplayPrim,Matrix),
    draw_prim(DisplayPrim),
    plot_primitives(Ps,Matrix).
```

If the mode of the instance is *instance*, it calls *draw_instance/3* which just displays a rectangular region of the proper size with the instance name inside. If the mode is layout, schematic, or documentation then the appropriate display routine is called. The documentation and layout display routines will look for parallel *cell/6* clauses which contain alternate views for the corresponding *cell/5* terms. If the mode is symbolic then *plot_mode/4* makes a recursive call to *plot_cell_hierarchy/2*. Figure 2.12 summarizes the characteristics of the five display modes.

```
plot_mode(instance,InstName,Cell,Matrix) :-
    draw_instance(InstName,Cell,Matrix).
plot_mode(layout,_,Cell,Matrix) :-
    plot_layout(Cell,Matrix).
plot_mode(schematic,_,Cell,Matrix) :-
    plot_schematic(Cell,Matrix).
plot_mode(documentation,InstName,Cell,Matrix) :-
    plot_documentation(InstName,Cell,Matrix).
plot_mode(symbolic,_,Cell,Matrix) :-
    plot_cell_hierarchy(Cell,Matrix).
```

Display Mode	Coordinate System	Hierarchy Displayed	Description Required
Default	virtual	no	none
Documentation	virtual	no	drawing
Symbolic	virtual	yes	symbolic
Schematic	virtual	yes	symbolic
Layout	physical	no	mask

Figure 2.12: Five Display Modes for a Sub-circuit Instance

```
draw_instance(IName, Cell , Matrix) :-
    cell(Cell,_,_,_, Bbox),
    transform(Bbox,bbox(X1,Y1,X2,Y2),Matrix),
    erase(X1,Y1,X2,Y2),
    graph_layer(black),
    graph_line_rect(X1,Y1,X2,Y2),
    TextX is  X1 + ((X2 - X1)/2),
    TextY is  Y1 + ((Y2 - Y1)/2),
    graph_text(TextX,TextY,IName).
```

adder_1

Figure 2.13: Code and Display Output of *draw_instance/3*

The *draw_instance/3* predicate is the default, non-hierarchical view of a circuit instance. This predicate draws a rectangle the size of the named cell with the instance name inside.

2.4.2 Interactive Graphics

Menus are defined in normalized units for a 1000X1000 point screen, and then mapped to the actual graphic device coordinates inside the foreign function interface.

Two distinct coordinate systems are understood by the interface. The predicate *menu_window* sets the coordinate system to the above mentioned menu coordinates, while *restore_window* sets the coordinate system to the design space. The user sets the scale for the design space with the windowing commands.

The main editing menu specifies each menu name, a color for the menu text, the rectangular dimensions of the menu item (*X1,Y1,X2,Y2*), and a color for the menu item background.

```
menu(edit,[
    m(zoom,    black, 280, 40, 400, 120, tan),
    m(unzoom, black, 280,  0, 350,  40, yellow),
    m(display,white, 400, 40, 620, 120, black),
    m(write,   black,  0,  0, 110,  60, green),
    m(quit,    white,  0, 60, 110, 120, black),
    .
    .
    .
    m(route, black,410,  0, 460,  40,blue)]).
```

Similar menus for schematic and the documentation are also compiled into the database. The central part of the schematic menu is shown here.

```
menu(schematic,[
    m('OR',      black, 700,  0, 800,  30, grey),
    m('AND',     black, 800, 90, 900, 120, grey),
    m('adder',   black, 800, 60, 900,  90, white),
    m('NAND',    black, 800, 30, 900,  60, yellow),
    m('Xgate',   black, 800,  0, 900,  30, tan),
    m('NOR',     black, 900, 90,1000, 120, tan),
    m('Inverter',black,900, 60,1000,  90, yellow)]).
```

The *display_menu/0* predicate can be called at any time to redisplay the current menu. It simply displays the menu indicated by *current_mode/1*. Once the menu window is set, *display_menu/1* takes a list of menu items and draws a rectangle of the specified background color, determines the correct size of the menu text, and prints the menu name in the specified text color for each item.

```
display_menu :-
    current_mode(Mode),
    menu(Mode,M1),
    menu_window,
    erase_screen,
    display_menu(M1),
    restore_window.
```

The following input predicates are defined to get information from the mouse. Several predicates with the prefix **get_** have been defined to simplify the programmer's view of getting point and rectangular regions. These predicates call the foreign function *graph_await_event/4* which returns the cursor position and mouse button information.

- *get_box/4* gets two points while echoing a changing rectangular cursor.

- *get_point/2* returns the X and Y position of a mouse-button hit.

- *get_point/3* returns X, Y, and which button was pressed.

- *get_point_quan/2* same as above with X,Y data quantized to integers.

- *get_point_quan/3* same as above with button information.

The following routines do not wait for user input but merely "look-up" the data from the last interaction. This is useful because one can change coordinate systems and then get the last point in units of the new coordinate system, even though the original mouse hit was made while in the old coordinate system.

- *get_last_point/2*

- *get_last_point/3*

- *get_last_point_quan/2*

- *get_last_point_quan/3*

An arbitrary object can be drawn on the screen in the special highlight color and then be "captured" by the *graph_cursor_capture/4* predicate. This causes a region of the screen to be copied into a bit-map which is then continuously redisplayed at the current cursor position. Thus, a drawing such as a logic–gate symbol becomes a cursor and follows the user's mouse until a button is pressed.

2.5   The Editor

2.5.1   Edit Operations

Preditor is designed to work with a three-button mouse. In nearly all cases, these three buttons will be associated with the operations of deleting a circuit element,

left	middle	right
DELETE	INSERT	IDENTIFY

Figure 2.14: Mouse-Button Functions

inserting a circuit element, or identifying a circuit element without modifying the
database.

Generally, if the DELETE button is pressed when the cursor is over a primitive
VLSI object, that object will be removed from the database. However, there is one
situation in which this action will not cause a deletion. During complex operations
which require multiple button hits, such as inserting a wire by specifying a sequence
of points, or designating a region of the screen with a box cursor, the left button
temporarily takes on the role of an ABORT function. In this situation, the left
button can be pressed to abandon any complex operation and return to the basic
editing mode.

The middle button triggers the INSERT operation. When it is pressed, a copy of
the current object, as specified by *preditor_defs/8*, will be inserted into the circuit
at the cursor location.

The right button is the IDENTIFY function. When a circuit primitive is selected
with this button, its characteristics become the current default characteristics of
the system. In other words, IDENTIFY uses the specified object to update the
preditor_defs/8 fact. Thus, an IDENTIFY operation on a transistor followed by an
INSERT at some other location will add a copy of the identified transistor to the
database at the new location.

An IDENTIFY performed over a subcell which is not being edited will direct
the editor to begin editing that subcell by updating *preditor_state/3*. This subcell
instance will be highlighted momentarily to indicate that it has become the current
edit cell.

If a cell contains only leaf elements (transistors, wires, contacts, and pins), an
insertion inserts the current leaf element type as specified by the last object IDEN-
TIFIED, DELETED, or selected from the menu. If a cell contains instances, there
are two possible behaviors of the INSERT operation. If the designer performs the
INSERT over an instance in the current cell, the editing system makes that cell
the current editing cell, essentially going down into the hierarchy until it reaches a

leaf-cell and inserts the primitive in that cell. If the designer performs the insert over a region with no instances, a instance insertion is initiated.

A pseudo-code description of the calling sequence described above is shown here:

```
edit :-
    change edit hierarchy?,
    !,
    operate.
edit :-
    insert sub-circuit.

operate :-
    get Button,
    do_operation(Button).

do_operation(left) :-
    pick_objects(Objs),
    delete(Objs).
do_operation(middle) :-
    insert.
do_operation(right) :-
    redefine current object (IDENTIFY).

delete([ ]) :-
    perform area delete.
delete(Objs) :-
    preference(Objs,Object),
    delete Object.

insert :-
    insert wire.
insert :-
    insert transistor.
insert :-
    insert contact.
    .
    .
```

In this section we are concerned with the calling sequence under the *operate/0* goal, which performs the edit operation on the current cell. The hierarchical operations handled by *edit/0* are discussed in a later section.

The *matrix/6* term in *preditor_state/3* represents the transformation required to display the components of the current cell. That is, it is the matrix which maps the coordinates of the cell currently being edited onto the graphics screen. The inverse of this matrix is required to determine where the cursor (given in screen coordinates) is positioned in the coordinate system of the design.

```
operate :-
    preditor_state(_,ecell(Cell,_,_),Matrix),
    cell(Cell,Ps,_,_,_),
    current_hit(Point,Button),
    invert(Matrix,IMatrix),
    transform(Point,NewPoint,IMatrix),
    do_operation(Button,NewPoint,Cell,Ps,Matrix).
```

The three clauses for *do_operation/5* perform an insertion, deletion, or an identify operation.

We begin with the insertion clause, which adds an instance of the current object into the current edit cell. The first goal in the body of this clause creates a new primitive list containing the new object, the next goal displays this new object, and the third goal updates the global state of the editor.

```
do_operation(middle,Point,Cell,Ps,Matrix) :-
    insert(Ps,NewPs,Point,Prim),
    plot_primitives([Prim],Matrix,Cell),
    make_new(Cell,NewPs).
```

The next clause performs the DELETE operation:

1. Identify all primitives which touch a selected point

2. Identify which primitive is to be deleted.

3. Erase the identified primitive from the screen (goals 3-5).

4. Create a new primitive list with the primitive removed.

5. Update the *cell/5* clause with the new primitive list.

```
do_operation(left,Point,Cell,Prims,Matrix) :-
    pick_prims(Prims,Point,Selected_Prims),
```

```
        delete(Selected_Prims,Prims,DeletedPrims),
        plot_mode(erase),
        plot_primitives(DeletedPrims,Matrix,Cell),
        plot_mode(draw),
        remove(DeletedPrims,Prims,NewPrims),
        make_new(Cell,NewPrims).
```

The *make_new/2* predicate is simply:

```
make_new(Cell,NewPrims) :-
        retract(cell(Cell,          _,Net,Pins,BB)),
        assert( cell(Cell,NewPrims,Net,Pins,BB)).
```

Identify is similar to delete except it merely *identifies* the selected primitive and uses its characteristics to define the current primitive type. The *preference/2* predicate is also called by *delete/3* to select a single primitive from the set returned by *pick/3*. The *flash/2* predicate causes the selected object to be highlighted briefly on the graphics display. The *make_current/1* call changes the global default characteristics to match those of the selected primitive and also moves down in the circuit hierarchy if the primitive is an instance.

```
do_operation(right,Point,_,Ps,Matrix) :-
        pick_prims(Ps,Point,Selected_Prims),
        preference(Selected_Prims,Prim),
        flash(Prim,Matrix),
        make_current(Prim).
```

If the current primitive is defined as *wire*, then the insert will prompt the user for a series of wire points. If the resulting point list has more than one point, a wire of the appropriate type is inserted in the list. Note that while wires and transistors can be inserted at the front of the primitive list, contacts must be appended to the end, to ensure that they are drawn last during display. This is because contacts are small and would be rendered invisible if a large object was drawn over them.

```
insert(Prims,[Wire|Prims],Wire) :-
        preditor_defs(wire,_,Lay,Wid,_,_,_,_),
        get_wire_points(Lay,Wid,Pt,Plist),
        length(Plist,L),
        L > 1,
        !,
        Wire  = wire(_,Lay,Wid,Plist,_,_).
```

```
insert(Ps,[D|Ps],Pt,D) :-
    preditor_defs(tran,Ty,_,_,DW,DO,_,_),
    D = tran(_,Ty,Pt,mods(O,W,1),_,_).

insert(Ps,NewPrims,Pt,C) :-
    preditor_defs(con,_,_,_,_,_,ConType,_),
    C = con(_,ConType,Pt,_,_,_),
    append(Ps,[C],NewPrims).
```

If a DELETE operation is performed over open space in either a leaf-cell or co-mposition-cell, the first argument to *delete/3* will be the empty list. This is how an *area delete* operation is initiated. This operation then allows the user to specify a rectangular region, from which all circuit elements will be removed. Thus, a delete operation will do one of the following:

- Perform an area delete operation (with normal user interaction).

- Abandon the area delete operation (as directed by the user).

- Perform the normal operation of deleting a single primitive.

These three functions define the three clauses of the *delete/3* predicate.

```
delete([ ],Prims,DeletedPrims) :-
    area_pick(Prims,DeletedPrims),
    !.

delete([ ],Prims,[ ]) :-
    !,
    write('Area delete abandoned'),nl.

delete(Prims,_,[Prim]) :-
    preference(Prims,Prim),
    make_current(Prim).
```

When the user indicates a point on where several primitives overlap, a selection criteria must decide which primitive is to be acted upon. Currently we define the selection function as follows:

If the user selects a point over the gate of a transistor, the transistor is selected, regardless of what other primitives share the same location. Otherwise, a contact is the preferred primitive. After that, a pin would be selected. The lowest precedence

*primitive is the wire. This is because wires cover many grid points, making it easy
to select a point where the wire does not overlap another primitive. Failing all
of the above selection criteria, we simply pick the first primitive from the list of
candidates.*

The selection criteria is crucial to streamlining user interaction. Previous systems required the user to cycle through the candidate primitives and select the
desired one. It can be seen that the above selection criteria allows nearly all items
to be selected (deleted) with a single interaction, since contacts never occur over
transistor gates, and pins rarely occur over contacts.

```
preference(Primitives, Selection) :-
    current_prim(CP),
    functor(CP,CPF,_),
    member(Pref,[tran,con,pin,CPF,_Anything]),
    member(Selection,Primitives),
    functor(Selection,Pref,_).
```

The first call to *member/2* generates the preferences and the following *member/2*
searches for the desired primitive.

Not only can the selection function be stated concisely in Prolog, but by making
the selector available as a separate relation we can insure that the behavior of the
identify and delete operations will be consistent. This compact coding of a complex
relationship does bring up the issue of time and space efficiency (it may create
unused choice points in *member/2* and is highly non-deterministic). Fortunately,
our context is that of a failure driven loop which spends most of its time waiting
for the user and can reclaim memory easily.

The *pick_prims/4* predicate collects the primitive elements in a cell which were
under the cursor. In order to delete a primitive, we need to collect all of the
candidates for the deletion with this predicate and then ask *preference/2* to select
the single item to be deleted. The *location/2* predicate succeeds for primitives
which reside at a single point, such as a contact or transistor while *location_line/2*
succeeds if the point lies on any line segment defined by a list of points.

```
pick_prims([ ],_,[ ],[ ]).

pick_prims([P|PT],Point,NewPT,[P|STail]) :-
    location(P,Point),
    !,
    pick_prims(PT,Point,NewPT,STail).
```

```
pick_prims([Wire|PT],Point,NewPT,[Wire|STail]) :-
    functor(Wire,wire,_),
    arg(4,Wire,Plist),
    location_line(Point,Plist),
    !,
    pick_prims(PT,Point,NewPT,STail).

pick_prims([Instance|PT],Point,[Instance|NewPT],STail) :-
    Instance = instance(_,Cell,_,_,M,_),
    cell_bboxes(BBoxes),
    bbox_member(Cell&bbox(X1,Y1,X2,Y2),BBoxes),
    preditor_state(_,_,Matrix),
    new_matrix(M,Matrix,NM),
    invert_matrix(NM,NMI),
    transform(Point,NPt,NMI),
    inside(NPt,bbox(X1,Y1,X2,Y2)),
    !,
    pick_prims(PT,Point,NewPT,STail).

pick_prims([P|PT],Point,[P|NewPT],STail) :-
    pick_prims(PT,Point,NewPT,STail).
```

If no objects were under the cursor during the delete operation, PREDITOR initiates an AREA-DELETE operation. The predicate to select all primitives which lie in a specified area is called *area_pick/2*. It divides the primitives in the current cell into two groups; those inside and those outside the selected area.

```
area_pick(InsidePrims,OutsidePrims) :-
    preditor_state(_,ecell(Cell,_,_),Matrix),
    cell(Cell,Ps,_,_,_),
    invert_matrix(Matrix,IMatrix),
    write('Enter Area to be Deleted'), nl,
    get_box_quan(A,B,C,D),
    transform(bbox(A,B,C,D),PickArea,IMatrix),
    area_sweep(Ps,InsidePrims,OutsidePrims,PickArea).
```

Below, a simple version of *area_sweep/4* separates out the primitives which are inside the selected area. In the production version of PREDITOR, this predicate has an

additional clause to break wires which cross the selected area boundary. These
newly created wire fragments are then divided between the Inside and Outside
lists.

```
area_sweep([ ],[ ],[ ],_).
area_sweep([P|Ps],[P|Inside],Outside,Box) :-
    inside(P,Box),
    !,
    area_sweep(Ps,Inside,Outside,Box).
area_sweep([P|Ps],Inside,[P|Outside],Box) :-
    area_sweep(Ps,Inside,Outside,Box).
```

2.5.2   Hierarchy Control

We saw the *make_current/1* predicate called from the IDENTIFY operation. This is
the primary mechanism for changing current location of the editor in the hierarchy.
If this predicate is given the name of a cell, it will make this cell the top level cell
for viewing (*vcell/2*) and editing (*ecell/3*), unless it already *is* the current cell, of
course.

```
make_current(Cell) :-
    preditor_state(vcell(Cell,_),ecell(Cell,_,_),_),
    !.

make_current(TopCell) :-
    cell(TopCell,_,_,_,BBOX),
    !,
    abolish(preditor_state,3),
    assert(preditor_state(vcell(TopCell,BBOX),
                    ecell(TopCell,void,BBOX),
                    matrix(1,0,0,1,0,0))).
```

When called with a primitive object, *make_current/1* changes the default definitions
in *preditor_defs/8* to reflect the characteristics of the new object.

```
make_current(con(_,Type,_,_,_,_)) :-
    !,
    retract(preditor_defs(  _,T,L,W,DW,Or,   _,N)),
    assert( preditor_defs(con,T,L,W,DW,Or,Type,N)).
```

When *make_current/1* is called with an *instance/6*, the instance cell becomes the new edit cell. A new coordinate system is established and the previous editor state is pushed onto the stack.

```
make_current(INST) :-
    INST = instance(IName,Cell,_,_,IMatrix,_),
    !,
    preditor_state(VCELL,ECELL,Matrix),
    transform(IMatrix,NewMatrix,Matrix),
    cell(Cell,_,_,_,CellBBox),
    transform(CellBBox,TransBBox,NewMatrix),
    asserta(preditor_state(VCELL,ecell(Cell,INST,TransBBox),
                           NewMatrix)),
    plot_instance(IName,Cell,NewMatrix).
```

The inverse of pushing the editor state down into an instance in the design hierarchy is popping to a higher level in the design by restoring the previous editor state. Note that the state is only inspected if the the state indicates that we are at the top-level, insuring that we never *retract* the top level editing state.

```
top_level :-
    preditor_state(vcell(Cell,_),
                   ecell(Cell,void,_),
                   matrix(1,0,0,1,0,0)).
pop_state :-
    top_level,!.
pop_state :-
    retract(preditor_state(_,_,_)).
```

2.5.3   The Editing Loop

We can think of an editor as an interpreter which modifies its database under the direction of user commands. The *repeat/fail* construction in the top-level *interact/0* predicate has the virtue of being particularly efficient in Prolog implementations that lack garbage collection.

```
interact :-
    set_defaults,
    repeat,
        pick(Command),
        menu_op(Command),
    Command = quit,
    !.
```

When *pick/1* is called, either a menu item name is returned in `Command`, or the atom "field" is returned and `current_hit(Button,X,Y)` is asserted to record the position and mouse button pressed. If a menu item was not selected, *menu_op/1* will call *edit/0* and the location of the cursor will indicate one of the following:

- A point inside the current edit subcell was hit: continue editing.

- A point outside all instances was hit while editing a lower level cell: transfer editing control to the parent cell.

- A point outside all instances was hit while editing the top-level cell. This signifies an instance insertion unless the top-level cell is a leaf cell, having only low-level primitives, in which case the operation is a low-level primitive insert.

- A point was selected on an subcell other than the current edit subcell: make the selected subcell the current edit cell.

An insert operation will insert an *instance/6* if the current cell is a composite cell but the insert operation did not take place over one of its instances. Therefore, it should *not_insert_instance/2* if it is in a leaf cell (e.g. one without instances) or if the selected point was inside the bounding box of an instance in the cell.

```
not_insert_instance(Pt,Ps) :-
    not memberchk(instance(_,_,_,_,_,_),Ps)
    ;
    in_instance(Pt,Ps,_).
```

When inserting a "pin" at the top of the hierarchy, it goes directly to the *operate/0* goal, without affecting the edit hierarchy.

```
edit :-
    current_hit(_,middle),          % Inserting
    preditor_defs(pin,_,_,_,_,_,_,_), % a pin
```

```
    top_level,                         % In the Top Cell ...
    !,
    operate.
```

If not inserting a pin, and the conditions are not right for an instance insertion, the next clause may move the edit hierarchy down into a sub-cell of the current cell with *maybe_deeper/2*, before calling *operate/0*.

```
edit :-
    get_hit_and_state(Pt,Cell,BBOX),
    in_or_on(Pt,BBOX),
    cell(Cell,Ps,_,_,_),
    not_insert_instance(Pt,Ps),
    !,
    maybe_deeper(Cell,Ps),
    % OPERATE ON WHATEVER LEVEL WE ARE AT NOW (N or N-1)
    operate.
```

This may be a simple operation in a top-level leaf cell.

```
edit :-
    top_level,
    preditor_state(_,ecell(Cell,_,_),_),
    is_leaf(Cell),
    !,
    operate.
```

The third clause is invoked if the designer is in a composition cell (a cell containing instances) and hits the insert button while the cursor is not over of any instances. This initiates an insertion of a sub-circuit instance of the name currently on the Cell menu. A separate menu operation allows the user to select this name.

```
edit :-
    current_hit(_,middle),
    !,
    instance_insert.
```

At this point any delete operation should proceed without affecting the editor state or design hierarchy.

```
edit :-
    current_hit(_,left),
    !,
    operate.
```

If none of the above conditions were met, we need to move up in the design hierarchy and reconsider our position. The next clause will pop the state to get into the current cell's parent. Ultimately, the recursive call to *edit/0* may lead us back down into the design hierarchy via another instance.

```
edit :-
    pop_state,
    !,
    edit.
```

The following test was called by *edit/0* to identify a leaf-cell.

```
is_leaf(Cell) :-
    cell(Cell,Ps,_,_,_),
    not memberchk(instance(_,_,_,_,_,_),Ps).
```

If the right button (IDENTIFY) was hit, and the current cell contains an instance at this point, we will go down a level in the hierarchy. Note that we do not want to transfer the hierarchy into any cell designated as a *gate/1*.

The *turn_on_instance/2* predicate instantiates the **Mode** variable in the instance to indicates that the contents of this instance are to be displayed. The value of **Mode** will be either **schematic**, **layout**, **symbolic**, or **documentation** depending upon the definition of *current_mode/1*.

```
maybe_deeper(Cell,Ps) :-
    current_hit(Pt,_),
    in_instance(Pt,Ps,Instance),
    arg(2,Instance,CellName),
    not gate(CellName),
    !,
    preditor_state(_,_,Matrix),
    flash(Instance,Matrix),
    turn_on_instance(Cell,Instance),
    make_current(Instance).

maybe_deeper(_,_,_). % Succeeds in general
```

Non-determinism is used in an interesting way in the predicate *instance_insert/3* as the *repeat/fail* loop updates and echoes the cursor. If the user presses the `right` mouse button, it fails back to *member/2* which selects a new orientation. Thus, the user can easily preview and examine the different orientations of an instance before placing it. Only when the user has pressed the `middle` (insert) or the `left` (delete or abandon) buttons will it leave the loop.

The predicate *graph_set_input/1* specifies the conditions under which the input predicate will return the cursor location. After the call to graph_set_input(b), *graph_await_event/4* will return only in the event of a button press. When placing a sub-circuit in a design, we want a ghost image of the circuit instance to follow the movement of the cursor around the screen until the user places it. The goal **graph_set_input(mb)** specifies that *graph_await_event/4* should return the cursor position if either the mouse is moved or a button is pressed. Thus, `Event` is instantiated to either **mousemoved** or **buttonhit** by *graph_await_event/4*. With this input mode, the predicate *track_cursor/3* re-displays the ghost image of the circuit, which is really just a special cursor, whenever the mouse is moved, and then finally succeeds when a mouse button is pressed.

```
track_cursor(Button,X,Y) :-
    repeat,
      graph_await_event(Event,Button,X,Y),
      graph_redraw_cursor(X,Y),
    Event = buttonhit,
    !.

instance_insert(Cell,IName,bbox(X1,Y1,X2,Y2)) :-
    H is Y2 - Y1,
    W is X2 - X1,
    % ECHO IS A BOX THE SIZE OF THE NAMED CELL
    graph_set_input(mb),
    repeat,
        member(Or,[ne,se,nw,sw,wn,es,ws,en,ne]),
        instance_cursor(Or,W,H),
        track_cursor(Button,X,Y),
        graph_erase_cursor,
    Button \== right,
    !,
    graph_set_input(b),
    (Button = left -> true   % ABANDON
```

```
    ;   perform_insert(Cell,IName,X,Y,H,W,Or)
).
```

The predicate *perform_insert/7* adds the new sub-circuit instance to the cell being edited. The appropriate *cell/5* clause in the database and the editor state information in *preditor_state/3* are updated during this operation. With this predicate, the single most complex operation of the editor culminates by updating the database.

```
perform_insert(middle,Cell,IName,X,Y,H,W,Or) :-
    preditor_state(_,ecell(Parent,_,_),_),
    cell(Parent,Ps,PNet,PPin,PBox),
    I = instance(IName,Cell,imods(X&Y,Or,11,1,h,0,_),_,_,[ ]),
```

This newly created instance must have a transformation matrix computed from its position (**X&Y**) and orientation (**Or**). The call to *get_matrix/1* will instantiate the fifth argument of the *instance/6* to the correct *matrix/6* term.

```
    get_matrix(I),
```

Update the *cell/5* in the database to include the new instance. Then display the instance on the screen.

```
    retract(cell(Parent,    Ps, PNet,PPin,PBox)),
    assert( cell(Parent,[I|Ps],PNet,PPin,NewPBox)),
    plot_primitives([I],PM),
```

The bounding box of the parent cell may have expanded to accommodate the new instance. This information is required globally as editor state information *preditor_state/3*.

```
    HX is X + W, HY is Y + H,
    adjust_bbox(PBox,bbox(X,Y,HX,HY),NewPBox),
    retract(preditor_state(V,ecell(Parent,XX,        _),PM)),
    asserta(preditor_state(V,ecell(Parent,XX,NewPBox),PM)).
```

In addition to edit operations which directly modify the design, there are menu operations which allow the designer to position and scale the graphical view of the design. The **zoom(in)** function prompts the user for a box and zooms in on that segment of the work area.

```
zoom(in) :-
    preditor_state(vcell(Cell,_),_,_),
```

```
    get_box_quan(A,B,C,D),
    erase_screen,
    set_workspace(Cell,A,B,C,D),
    plot_cell_hierarchy(Cell,matrix(1,0,0,1,0,0)).
```

The zoom(out) function enlarges the viewing area by approximately a factor of 2.

```
zoom(out) :-
    preditor_state(vcell(Cell,bbox(A,B,C,D)),_,_),
    Height is D - B,
    Width is  C - A,
    max(Height,Width,Max),
    NA is integer(A-(Max/3+2)), NB is integer(B-(Max/3+2)),
    NC is integer(C+(Max/3+2)), ND is integer(D+(Max/3)+2),
    erase_screen,
    set_workspace(Cell,NA,NB,NC,ND),
    plot_cell_hierarchy(Cell,matrix(1,0,0,1,0,0)).
```

2.5.4   Alternate Implementation

The basic personality of the editor is described in a few hundred lines of Prolog. By personality, we mean the way it responds to user interactions and modifies the database. By changing this part of the editor, an editing system with a completely different "feel" could be created. This section contains a proposal for the next-generation personality for Preditor.

Among the obvious advantages of using Prolog to implement an editor is the ability to backtrack gracefully, undoing all of the effects of an operation. Using traditional programming languages, a robust "undo" facility requires extra effort to implement and careful attention to preserve the integrity of the database. Unfortunately, Preditor does not exploit this aspect of Prolog semantics. There is no user-level "UNDO" facility in the editor because we use *assert/1* and *retract/1* to update the database after every operation. This could be remedied by structuring the editor on a recursive, rather than iterative model.

To implement an "UNDO" 'function, the *edit/3* clause below is written so that selecting the undo menu will cause the recursive edit to fail over the previous successful operation. Complex *edit objects* are defined to replace the database in the iterative model and the logical editor takes an edit object EO_1 as input, and produces the edit object EO_2 as output.

```
logical_edit(EO_1,EO_2) :-
    get_operation(Action),
    edit(Action,EO_1,EO_2).

edit(quit,EO,EO).

edit(undo, _, _)  :- !, fail.

edit(Action,EO_1,EO_N) :-
    perform(Action,EO_1,EO_2),
    get_operation(Next_Action),
    %  A failure of the following call to edit/3 occurs
    %  on 'undo' and will cause this clause to fail.
    edit(Next_Action,EO_2,EO_N).
```

When 'undo' causes a failure over the operation, we retain information about it for
forward traversal (undoing the undo).

```
edit(Action,EO_1,EO_2) :-
    assertz(action(Action)),
    get_operation(Next_Action),
    edit(Next_Action,EO_1,EO_2).
```

In performing the specified action, the failure of *call/3* is reported, but *perform/3*
will always succeed. The *call/3* predicate is a DEC-10 library routine which adds
the second and third arguments to the term **Action** and invokes *call/1*.

```
perform(Action, EO_1, EO_2) :-
    call(Action,EO_1,EO_2),
    !.

perform(Action,EO,EO) :-
    report_failed_operation(Action).
```

Since the **undo** operation causes the information about the action to be saved,
we can implement a **forward** operation which will re-do the last undo operation.
This **forward** command will execute the undone commands in the same order that
they were originally executed. This operation will fail unless it was preceded by at
least one **undo**.

```
edit(forward,EO_1,EO_2) :-
    retract(action(Command)),
    edit(Command,EO_1,EO_2).
```

In addition to a simple mechanism for "undoing" operations, the representation of user operations as Prolog terms leads to a simple model of user interactions. Every action corresponds to a callable term, where the last two arguments are the edit object before and after the operation. Collections of these terms can be combined in command sequences (macros), and once these sequences are consulted or compiled, they will be available to the *call/3* goal in the *edit/3* predicate. The user can experiment at length with these created sequences since the arbitrarily deep undo operations are guaranteed to restore the previous state of the system.

With the savestate feature found in most Prolog systems, the state of the CAD system can be continuously maintained over different editing sessions, and the necessity of writing out and re-reading design representations is avoided. Thus, in spite of the overhead associated with Prolog execution, the time to start up the system on a large design can be considerably less than a CAD system which must re-parse circuit descriptions when beginning a session.

While the savestate feature is not an exclusive characteristic of Prolog systems, and is not itself a logic programming concept, when combined with features of logic programming systems it gives Prolog several advantages over other programming languages.

- *The savestate feature can allow the user to begin execution of the saved editing system and immediately "UNDO" the operations performed at the end of the previous editing session.*

- *A savestate of an editing session with a number of operations followed by an equal number of "UNDO" operations becomes an instant tutorial program, which can be given "FORWARD" commands to step through the operations performed during the initial session. No code needs to be written to support the tutorial mode, it is a natural consequence of the editor semantics.*

If we employ recursion to implement an editor, save its state over many editing sessions, and retain the option of backtracking over all commands executed, we might expect to run into an impractical storage requirement. But in fact, the resulting state may not be too large. In the editing system, program growth occurs on user interactions, placing a realistic limit on the problem size. If we assume that a designer can perform an edit operation every ten seconds, and that he keeps this pace up for an eight-hour day, we have an upper bound of 3,000 operations in a full day of editing. A six month project could include 500,000 edit operations. Given that half of these operations create objects no larger than 128 bytes, the resulting editor state will require a maximum of 65 megabytes of data and state information. This editor state would actually contain and have accessible every operation and state transition made by the editor over the entire six-month design period. While this is a large data requirement by today's standards, it is not impossibly large.

While it is possible to imagine an editing system which retains all of this information, this is probably an unnecessary level of generality. For reasons of practicality, we can take the comparison between our edit interpreter and a Prolog meta-interpreter further, and add a "commit" operation which is essentially a meta-level cut. The commit operation will *assert/1* the edit object, fail back over the entire recursive editing session and then begin the edit recursion with the retracted edit object. Space can be reclaimed when this commit is performed, but then no previous operations can be undone.

Traditional editing systems often have problems with database integrity which can be easily avoided in a Prolog implementation. For example, many editing systems allow command sequences to be defined as user macros. If such a sequence consists of several legal commands followed by an illegal one, the editor may execute the legal steps and then fail on the illegal one, leaving the database in a partially modified state which may be difficult for the user to interpret or recover from. However, it is a natural consequence of the recursive Prolog editor that if any part of a composite action fails, the entire action will fail, leaving the "database" unchanged.

2.6   Conclusion

The decision to use Prolog as a CAD implementation language is based on much more than the usual considerations of selecting a general purpose high-level programming language. The semantics of Prolog directly address significant aspects of the CAD problem. This paradigm is well suited to the task of reading different design representations, representing complex technology-specific information, and providing a high level of user-programmability as well as a database query system. In addition, Prolog seems particularly well suited to the representation of circuit connectivity.

All of the major components of the AUNT hardware description translation problem have compact and clear implementations in Prolog. The PREDITOR editing system is described in less than five thousand lines of code, and implements a fully hierarchical editing system for symbolic and physical VLSI layouts as well as schematics and documentation drafting. The editing system was able to take advantage of the relational and backtracking mechanisms of Prolog in surprising ways.

The net result has been a consistent ten-fold reduction in source code size with considerably expanded capability when compared to traditional CAD tool implementations. Further, because the resulting system defines a deductive database on the design data, it provides natural framework for the exploration of intelligent CAD.

2.7   Background

For a good introduction to VLSI design, see *Introduction to VLSI Systems* by Mead and Conway [MC80] and *Principles of CMOS VLSI Design: A Systems Perspective* by Weste and Eshraghian [WE85].

The symbolic layout abstraction in the PREDITOR/AUNT system was based on the MULGA system developed at AT&T Bell Laboratories [Wes81] and one of its descendants, the VIVID System, developed at the Microelectronics Center of North Carolina [RRD85].

A complete discussion the two-dimensional coordinate transformation can be found in chapter four of *Principles of Interactive Computer Graphics* by Newman and Sproull [NS73].

An early version of the graphical interface used by PREDITOR was developed by Bruce Smith at MCNC.

The hierarchy flattening predicate, which takes advantage of Prolog's definite clause grammar syntax, was suggested by Richard O'Keefe.

Several people have worked on the specification and verification of hardware with logic. A good example is Mike Gordon's work with higher-order logic [Gor85].

The appropriateness of using Prolog for Electronic CAD has previously been demonstrated in the work of William Clocksin and Miriam Leeser at Cambridge University [CL86, Clo87].

As part of the Aquarius Project at the University of California at Berkeley a system of Prolog-based tools has been developed for the specification and synthesis of VLSI circuits [Des87, BCMD87].

A brief description of the *Electric* CAD program, which includes a Prolog sub-system for specifying circuits, can be found in *Computer Aids for VLSI Design* [Rub87].   Some of the ideas in the *AUNT* translation system [Rei87] came from Prolog-based natural language systems. In particular, the use of the term *LFL* was inspired by [McC86].

The software engineering aspects of this project are described in [Rei88].

Chapter 3

Assisting register transfer level hardware design: A Prolog Application

Paul J. Drongowski

Computer Engineering and Science
Case Western Reserve University
Cleveland, Ohio 44106, USA
(216) 368-5028
E-Mail: pjd@alpha.ces.CWRU.Edu

Abstract

Due to the overwhelming complexity of VLSI systems, designers are turning to higher level notations and abstractions for the description of hardware systems. This paper briefly describes the graphical hardware design language **Gdl** and the application of Prolog to the analysis of designs expressed in Gdl at the register transfer level. Issues of representation, implementation and the use of Prolog in combination with procedural languages are addressed.

3.1 Introduction

Designers and toolbuilders often separate the design of a computer system into five levels of abstraction: architecture, organization, switching (logic), electrical, and geometric (physical fabrication plan.) We are interested in supporting design at the organization level using a register transfer notation. This level of design consists of register transfer events (assignments), the scheduling of those events, the system datapath, and in the case of a very large scale integrated (VLSI) system, the chip floor plan. Our long term goal is a "sketchpad" to assist system architects and organization level designers to create a design, estimate the speed, space and power complexity of the system (without extensive simulation), and transform the design to one that better fits the engineering specification for the system.

[0]This work was supported in part by the Semiconductor Research Corporation (contract 87-DJ-092), the National Science Foundation (grant DMC85-08362), the Microelectronics and Computer Technology Corporation, and the Cleveland Advanced Manufacturing Program (Ohio Edison Program.)

We have constructed two prototype systems using a graphical hardware design language (Gdl) and interactive editing tools for the creation and modification of a design expressed in Gdl. Both prototypes use procedural languages for graphics programming and interaction, and Prolog for design analysis. Differences between the two tools include incremental versus "on demand" analysis, overall program structure and internal design representation.

This chapter is a summary of experiences in constructing the prototypes and concentrates on the use of Prolog. We begin with a brief description of Gdl followed by a characterization of the two prototypes. Design trade-offs are addressed. Next, the algorithms used in this application are presented. The paper concludes with a commentary and a description of future work.

3.2   Graphical Design Language

The Graphical design language, **Gdl**, separates engineering concerns into *behavioral, structural* and *physical* domains. Three distinct, but interrelated notations are provided (Gdl/b, Gdl/s and Gdl/p) which address each of these domains. [DBR+88, Dro85b] In VLSI technology, system performance very much depends upon the physical partitioning of the system. For example, off-chip and long-wire signals have especially long delays due to increased wire capacitance. The signal delays can be reduced by exploiting physical locality (i.e., placing critical path components and modules near each other.) In order to assist the designer, one must capture and use spatial information about the chip partition and floor plan to estimate system performance. Gdl provides this capability. [Dro85a, Dro83] The LOGOS, SARA and ADAS design systems are similar to Gdl, but do not address the physical aspects of a system design. [GBK72, HR72, RBK72, Ros72, Est85, F+85b, F+85a]

Gdl/b is a graph schema based upon Petri Nets and the work of Karp and Miller. [Pet81, KM69] Figure 3.1 contains an example behavior graph which describes the fetch and execute loop of a small computer. Note that a graph is composed of places (circles), transitions (bars) and arcs as in a conventional Petri Net graph. Each transition is annotated with the register transfers (assignments) which will be performed when the transition fires. A place may be annotated with a verification assertion that must hold whenever one or more tokens occupy the place.

The conventional Petri Net firing rule has been modified in order to describe conditional control flow. A transition is fireable if all the input places of a transition are marked and the *enabling condition* for the transition is **true**. Thus, two or more transitions may be in conflict as long as the enabling conditions guarantee that only

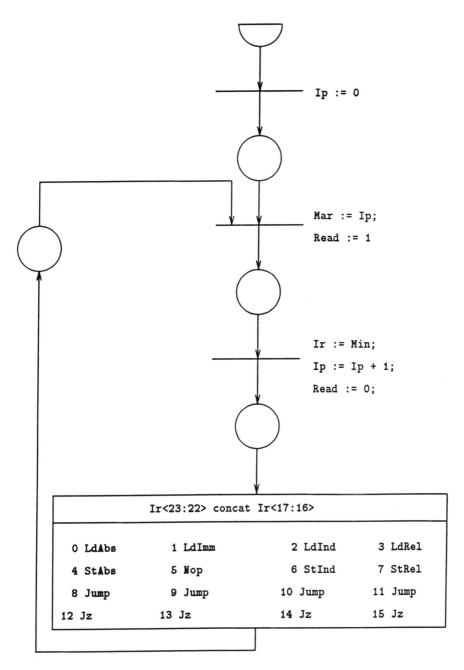

Figure 3.1: Example Behavior Graph

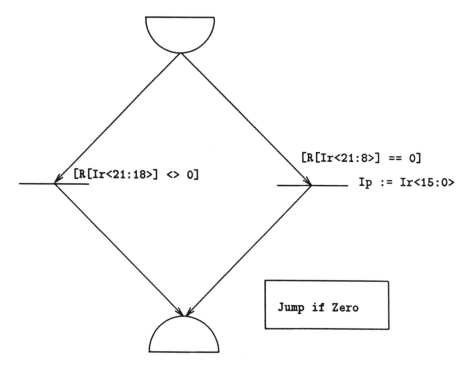

Figure 3.2: Subnet with Conditional Control Flow

one of the transitions will be fireable. If no enabling condition is provided by the designer, it is assumed to be **true**. An example of a graph with conditional control flow appears in Figure 3.2. Enabling conditions directly correspond to hardware datapath conditions which must be sensed by the control element.

The behavioral description can be decomposed hierarchically through subnet call and definition constructs (Figure 3.2.) *Subnets* are single entry - single exit graphs that begin with an entry place (at the top of the editing window) and end with an exit place (at the bottom.) *Case* and *select* constructs permit the convenient specification of multi-way flow branches in addition to the simple subnet *call*. The case implements an indexed dispatch to one of several subnets while a select is generalized to any enabling condition for selection. The case box in Figure 3.1 decodes the operation and addressing mode fields of the machine instruction.

The behavior graph must eventually be evaluated by a set of hardware resources commonly known as the machine datapath. The datapath is drawn in the **Gdl/s** block diagram notation (Figure 3.3.) The notation is the conventional hierarchical

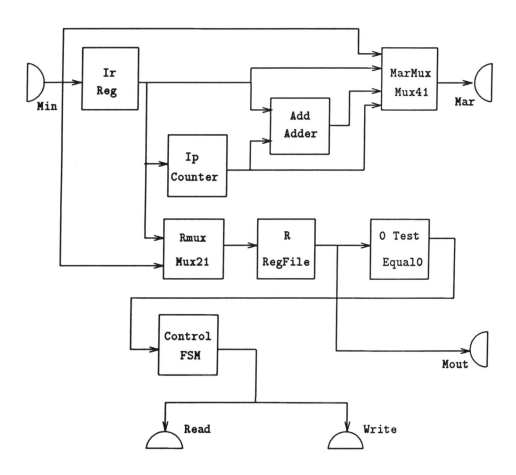

Figure 3.3: Example Structure Diagram

one that designers expect – module and component instance blocks, connection ports, named external interface ports and connections. A module may be decomposed further into its constituent parts while a component is an atomic design object (i.e., a leaf node at the bottom of the structural design hierarchy.) Any condition appearing in a Gdl/b enabling condition must be available as a named connection in the block diagram. The components and connection structure of the Gdl/s diagram must also be directly capable of performing assignments in the behavior graph. For example, to perform the register transfer:

R = S + T

there must be three register components, R, S and T, where S and T are connected to the inputs of an adder (or some component capable of addition), and the output of the adder is connected to register R.

Physical design information is captured in hierarchical Gdl/p floor plans. Every module has a drawn to scale floor plan showing the placement and size of module and component instances. We assume that the structure and physical planning hierarchies are identical. Component instances require parameter values indicating the number of bits per word and number of words per device. This information is needed to compute the overall bounding box of component, its overall delay, current consumption and power dissipation.

3.3 Two Implementations

Two different experimental design systems were constructed: CGDP and Agent. Both systems provide interactive, graphical editing using a multi-window approach. Figures 3.1, 3.2 and 3.3, for example, are screen images from Agent.

3.3.1 CGDP

One of the goals of CGDP was incremental design analysis. For example, when the designer adds or removes a component, CGDP analyzes the Gdl design and determines if any errors were introduced. Thus, CGDP operates as an interactive syntax directed editor for Gdl. We also wanted to add performance oriented routines to evaluate the speed, space and power complexity of the design and to suggest changes to the engineer. Since much of design is a heuristic activity, we decided on a rule-based implementation of the "assistant." The natural fit between Prolog and rule-based systems led to the selection of Prolog.

CGDP was constructed for Apollo workstations using the Domain Dialog package for user interaction and a mixture of C and C-Prolog code. CGDP consists of

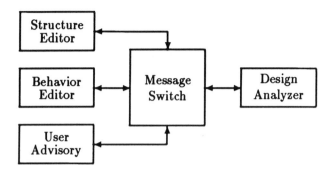

Figure 3.4: CGDP System Structure

five processes: one process each for the behavior and structure editors, the message switch, a user advisory window and the analyzer (Figure 3.4.) (Physical design is not handled in CGDP.) The multiprocess implementation permitted a clean separation of concerns, the use of C language and Apollo Domain Dialogue for graphics programming, and the use of Prolog for the rule-based analyzer. The analyzer is a set of rules executing on a modified C-Prolog interpreter. The normal terminal input mechanism of the interpreter was changed to accept messages through the Apollo Domain mailbox facility. Thus, analyzer directives appear to be regular, top-level C-Prolog goals and "commands." When the designer makes a change to the behavior graph or structure diagram, the change is communicated to the analyzer by the message switch. Output from the analyzer is displayed in a third window by the user advisory process again via the message switch.

Overall, this scheme had several disadvantages. Incremental analysis was not found to be particularly useful after using CGDP since designs are usually in an inconsistent state and the stream of advisory notes were either identifying rather obvious inconsistencies or just plain annoying (or both.) An "analysis on demand" mode eventually was added. Further, the editors and anlayzer had to maintain their own parallel design databases. Much of the Prolog code (2500 lines total) was devoted to design management (creating, removing or changing objects.) Coupled with the extra overhead of process context switching, very little actual benefit was gained through the multiprocess implementation.

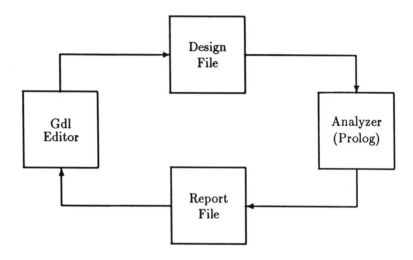

Figure 3.5: Agent System Structure

3.3.2   Agent

The development of the second prototype design environment, **Agent**, started in February 1988. Based upon the CGDP experience, we did not seek to support incremental analysis. However, we did want to support physical design (floor planning), rule-based analysis and a more flexible structure for student projects. (There is a steep learning curve for new project members. Since the department has abundant numbers of Sun workstations, that machine was selected for the platform.)

Agent was built using the Sun Network Extensible Window System (NeWS) for user interaction and graphics, C language for graphics code and Sicstus Prolog for analysis. C was selected for the Gdl editor to recoup the effort invested in the CGDP editing code. As this is an experimental system in an academic environment, we decided not to mix languages *a la* CGDP, but to write the Gdl design database to a file in the form of ground clauses or "facts." This separation permits other investigators to independently construct Prolog-based analytical tools without a lot of extra baggage (e.g., knowing the internal Agent design data structure, event handling and graphics mechanisms, etc.)

The structure chosen for Agent is shown in Figure 3.5. The Gdl editor and the analyzer communicate via two files: the design file and the report file. To keep the Prolog infrastructure at an absolute minimum, the design file consists of a set of ground clauses which are consulted into the analyzer. The report file is a text file containing error messages, performance estimates, etc. to be read by the editor and presented in dialog boxes.

The structure led to an interesting separation of function between the Gdl editors and Prolog analyzer as well as a few tricks. The use of ground clauses as the intermediate representation meant that no Prolog code was required to read and parse the design file. The editor produces the design in Prolog "fact" format without difficulty while taking the care to quote identifiers and operators working around the syntax for variable names and operators. We knew that eventually the analyzer would examine the register transfer expressions and preferred to perform the parsing with a DCG. Since lexical analysis is necessary and is laborious in Prolog, expressions are tokenized on output by Agent. This proved to be a good division of labor – facile implementation of the parser in Prolog and execution efficiency during lexical analysis. Figure 3.6 is the intermediate representation of the subnet "Main" appearing in Figure 3.1.

Object names are always a critical issue in the design of CAD databases. Each of the Gdl notations supports hierarchical design through subnets in Gdl/b, modules and components in Gdl/s and nested partitions and components in Gdl/p. We chose to identify a design object by a "concatenation" of the parent module name, parent subnet name (if necessary) and finally a symbol to identify the object uniquely within its parent. For example, unique identifiers are required for places and transitions within a subnet. These names are formed by concatenating a "t" or "p" with the X-Y screen position of the object. By including this identifier in the report file with the module name, subnet name and message string, the editor can display the module or subnet in question, highlight the appropriate place or transition and display the advisory message. For consistency, we have placed the parent module, subnet and unique identifier first in all object relations.

3.4   Design Relations

The intermediate design representation is a relational one. There is one relation per Gdl object, thirteen relation types in all. Figure 3.7 is the template for the Gdl transition relation. Transition objects may be one of four types: regular, case, select or subnet call. By folding all four types of transition object into a single relation, the graph walking code can be generalized and significantly simplified. Entries, exits and regular places are also folded into a single place relation for the same reason. Arcs, however, are differentiated into prearcs and postarcs because

```
subnet('Move','Main').
place('Move','Main',px240y32,entry,['[','True',']']).
place('Move','Main',[ ],exit,[true]).
transition('Move','Main',tx240y128,regular,
  ['[','True',']'],
  ['IR',':=','MIN',';','IP',':=','IP','+',1,';','Read',':=',0]).
transition('Move','Main',tx240y64,regular,
  ['[','True',']'],
  ['MAR',':=','IP',';','Read',':=',1]).
transition('Move','Main',tx240y192,case,
  ['[','IR','<',23,':',22,'>','concat','IR','<',17,':',16,'>',']'],[ ]).
casebind('Move','Main',tx240y192,15,'JZ').
casebind('Move','Main',tx240y192,14,'JZ').
casebind('Move','Main',tx240y192,13,'JZ').
casebind('Move','Main',tx240y192,12,'JZ').
casebind('Move','Main',tx240y192,11,'JUMP').
casebind('Move','Main',tx240y192,10,'JUMP').
casebind('Move','Main',tx240y192,9,'JUMP').
casebind('Move','Main',tx240y192,8,'JUMP').
casebind('Move','Main',tx240y192,7,'STREL').
casebind('Move','Main',tx240y192,6,'STIND').
casebind('Move','Main',tx240y192,5,'STIMM').
casebind('Move','Main',tx240y192,4,'STABS').
casebind('Move','Main',tx240y192,3,'LDREL').
casebind('Move','Main',tx240y192,2,'LDIND').
casebind('Move','Main',tx240y192,1,'LDIMM').
casebind('Move','Main',tx240y192,0,'LDABS').
place('Move','Main',px240y160,place,['[','True',']']).
place('Move','Main',px240y96,place,['[','True',']']).
place('Move','Main',px48y160,place,['[','True',']']).
prearc('Move','Main',px240y160,tx240y192).
postarc('Move','Main',tx240y128,px240y160).
prearc('Move','Main',px240y96,tx240y128).
postarc('Move','Main',tx240y64,px240y96).
prearc('Move','Main',px240y32,tx240y64).
postarc('Move','Main',tx240y192,px48y160).
prearc('Move','Main',px48y160,tx240y64).
```

Figure 3.6: Design File Representation of "main"

transition/6

transition(Module, Subnet, TrId, TrType, TrCondition, TrAssign)

Module	Parent module
Subnet	Parent subnet
TrId	Unique identifier within subnet
TrType	One of {regular, case, select, call}
TrCondition	Enabling condition (list of tokens)
TrAssign	Assignments (list of tokens)

Figure 3.7: Transition Relation

the graph walking algorithms need to quickly find the input and output arcs of the graph transitions.

Finally, the transition relation contains the tokenized list form of the associated enabling condition and assignments. The tokenized lists are translated to a prefix form before analysis using the techniques outlined in Chapter 23 of Sterling and Shapiro. [SS86] A register transfer statement is represented as a 4-tuple:

[Destination, LeftSource, Operator, RightSource]

For unary operators, the **LeftSource** field has the value **empty**. Sources and destinations are 4-tuples of the form:

[Name, WordIndex, HighBit, LowBit]

The special name **empty** denotes a syntactic field which was not explicitly assigned a value. The subsections that follow describe the major Gdl object relations.

3.4.1 Modules and Subnets

A Gdl design is organized into a hierarchy of modules. The Gdl/s description of a module shows the module and component instances which comprise the module, any external communication ports and the connections between the instances and interfaces.

The *module* relation (Figure 3.8) declares a symbolic name for a module definition and indicates the kind of physical package which contains the module. Possible package types include:

```
module/2

  module(Module, Package)

  Module     Symbolic name for module
  Package    Package (onchip, chip, board, etc.)

subnet/2

  subnet(Module, Subnet)

  Module     Parent module (symbolic name)
  Subnet     Parent subnet
```

Figure 3.8: Module and Subnet Relations

- *Onchip.* The module will appear on the surface of a chip. No special interface circuitry is provided.

- *Chip.* The module will be a separately packaged chip. External interface ports must be implemented using bonding pads and interface circuitry (drivers, hysteresis, static protection, etc.)

- *Board.* The module will be a printed circuit board. External interface will be implemented as board edge connectors.

The *subnet* relation (Figure 3.8) establishes a child-parent relationship between the subnet *SubnetName* and the module *ModuleName*.

3.4.2 Behavioral Representation

The primary behavioral object relations are *place, transition, prearc* and *postarc*. All relations begin with the name of the module and subnet to which the object belongs.

Every *place* has a unique identifier within its parent subnet (Figure 3.9.) The symbolic identifier is formed by concatenating the letter "p" with the X-Y screen position of the place. (This assumes that screen objects do not overlap.) A place may be an **entry**, **exit** or regular **place** as specified by the **PlaceType** field. The verification assertion is a tokenized form of the textual assertion associated with the place. The *Assertion* is a list of quoted tokens such that syntactic problems

place/5 - Gdl/b graph place

place(Module, Subnet, PlaceId, PlaceType, PlaceAssertion)

Module	Parent module (symbolic name)
Subnet	Parent subnet
PlaceId	Unique identifier within parent subnet
PlaceType	One of {entry, exit, place}
Assertion	Verification assertion (tokenized list)

Figure 3.9: Place Relations

with capitalized identifiers and special delimiter sequences (predefined operators) are avoided.

Transition relations have a similar form (Figure 3.7.) In this case, four types of transition object are available: regular, case, select and call. Graph walking is simplified by having exactly one representation (relation) each for transitions and places since transitions must follow places and places must follow transitions. Special cases can still be identified by placing a constant value into the type field, thereby forcing the selection of a particular rule, e.g.,

transition(Module, Subnet, _, select, _, _).

Instead of an assertion, the transition relation has two token lists – the enabling condition and register transfer assignments.

The representation of the case and select constructs requires another relation type, the *casebind*, as shown in Figure 3.10. This relation associates a condition value (case only) and subnet call name with a case or select. The transition identifier specifies the parent case or select.

When analyzing a graph, one often needs to find the transition which is fed by a place, or the places which are fed by a transition. The *prearc* and *postarc* relations give this information and define the graph topology (Figure 3.11.) The place and transition identifiers specify the head and tail of the arc. The division of arcs into the pre and post categories should also assist simulation, i.e., finding fireable transitions and advancing tokens after firing.

```
casebind/5

  casebind(Module, Subnet, TrId, CondValue, BoundSubnet)

  Module       Parent module
  Subnet       Parent subnet
  TrId         Case/select parent transition identifier
  CondValue    Case condition value (nil for selects)
  BoundSubnet  Subnet to be called for CondValue
```

Figure 3.10: Case and Select Dispatch Relation

```
prearc/4 - Arc leading into transition (input arc)

  prearc(Module, Subnet, PlaceId, TrId)

  Module       Parent module
  Subnet       Parent subnet
  PlaceId      Input place
  TrId         Destination transition

postarc/4 - Arc leading from transition (output arc)

  postarc(Module, Subnet, TrId, PlaceId)

  Module       Parent module
  Subnet       Parent subnet
  TrId         Source transition
  PlaceId      Output (destination) place
```

Figure 3.11: Arc Relations

`moduleinstance/3`

   `moduleinstance(Module, Instance, Defn)`

Module	Parent module
Instancee	Name of module instance
Defn	Name of module definition

`componentinstance/3`

   `componentinstance(Module, Instance, Defn)`

Module	Parent module
Instance	Name of component instance
Defn	Name of component definition

Figure 3.12: Module and Component Instance Relations

3.4.3 Structural Representation

The structural representation chosen here is rather conventional. The two relations *moduleinstance* and *componentinstance* define the constituent (sub)modules and components of a module. An instance relation gives a unique (within the parent module definition) name to the instance and the name of its definition. The definition name must refer to either a component or another Gdl module definition.

Component instances may have several attribute - value definitions as specified in a *componentattribute* relation. The attribute name may be any symbolic identifier and the value may be any atomic Prolog constant value.

All modules and components have interface ports. There are two types of ports in a Gdl/s description – external interface ports within an object definition and ports that appear at the site of an instance (Figure 3.14.) Port objects are not created on an instance by instance basis. The instancing of a port is implicit in the instancing of the parent object. Thus, a port is defined once in the parent and is dynamically "instantiated" when necessary.

An interconnection between two ports is captured in a *connection* relation (Figure 3.15.) The end of a connection is specified by the instance name of the component (module) and one of its port names.

`componentattribute/4`

`componentattribute(Module, Instance, Attribute, Name)`

`Module`	`Parent module`
`Instance`	`Component instance name`
`Attribute`	`Attribute name`
`Value`	`Attribute value`

Figure 3.13: Component Attribute/Value Definition

`port/4`

`port(Module, Instance, PortName, PortId)`

`Module`	`Parent module`
`Instance`	`Name of a component/module instance or parent module/component`
`Port`	`Name of interface port (symbolic name)`
`PortId`	`Port identifier`

Figure 3.14: Port Definition Relation

`connection/5`

`connection(Module, FromInstance, FromPort, ToInstance, ToPort)`

`Module`	`Parent module`
`FromInstance`	`Name of component/module (signal source)`
`FromPort`	`Port identifier at end of connection`
`ToInstance`	`Name of component/module (signal sink)`
`ToPort`	`Port identifier at other end of connection`

Figure 3.15: Connection Relation

```
placement/7

placement(Module,Instance,TransX,TransY,Rotate,MirrorX,MirrorY)
```

Module	Parent module
Instance	Component or module instance name
TransX	X offset from module origin
TransY	Y offset from module origin
Rotate	Angle of rotation (degrees)
MirrorX	Mirror along X-axis if true
MirrorY	Mirror along Y-axis if true

Figure 3.16: Placement Information

3.4.4 Physical Representation

The placement of a module or component instance within a module floor plan is given by its *placement* relation (Figure 3.16.) The actual size (bounding box) of a component must be computed from its parameters as given by a series of attribute - value pairs.

3.4.5 Components

The design system depends upon a library of predefined, well-characterized standard circuit cells. A component is described using six relations. The *component* relation defines a particular component prototype giving its symbolic name, whether it is combinational (**fnl**), has storage capability (**memory**), performs a data routing function (**switch**) or is a controller (**control**.) A component also belongs to a category that defines the interdependence or independence of signal delays within a one or two dimensional array of like components.

In order to perform graph analysis such as datapath covering, we need a list of the intrinsic operations performed by each component. This information is present in the *comp_ops* relation (Figure 3.17.)

Component delay values are given in the *comp_delay* relation. The analyzer uses a simple delay model. All components have some fixed switching delay time. This is the usual notion of worst case signal propagation delay time through the component indepenent of output loading. Fan-out or loading effects are modelled using the **Load** factor. If the delay is further affected by chaining (e.g., ripple carry

```
component/3

  component(Name, Type, Category)

  Name      Name of component definition
  Type      One of {fnl, memory, switch, control}
  Category  One of {bit_indep, bit_linear, bit_array}

comp_ops/2

  comp_ops(Name, Ops)

  Name      Name of component definition
  Ops       List of instrinsic operation names
```

Figure 3.17: Component Definition Relations

```
comp_delay/5

  comp_delay(Name, Height, Width, Load, Switch)

  Name      Name of component definition
  Height    Height portion of delay (nanoseconds)
  Width     Width portion of delay (ns)
  Load      Effective of load on delay (ns)
  Switch    Basic component switching time (ns)
```

Figure 3.18: Component Delay Relation

in an adder), the **Height** and/or **Width** factors will further increase the delay. The rules below,

```
compute_delay(Module, Instance, Load, Delay) :-
  componentinstance(Module, Instance, Definition),
  componentattr(Module, Instance, 'Height', Height),
  componentattr(Module, Instance, 'Width',  Width),
  component(Definition, _, DelayType),
  delay_is(DelayType, Definition, Load, Height, Width, Delay).

delay_is(bit_indep, Definition, Load, _, _, Delay) :-
  comp_delay(Definition, _, _, FLoad, FSwitch),
  Delay is (FLoad * Load) + FSwitch.

delay_is(bit_linear, Definition, Load, _, Width, Delay) :-
  comp_delay(Definition, _, FWidth, FLoad, FSwitch),
  Delay is (FLoad * Load) + FSwitch + (FWidth * Width).

delay_is(bit_array, Definition, Load, Height, Width, Delay) :-
  comp_delay(Definition, FHeight, FWidth, FLoad, FSwitch),
  Delay is (FLoad * Load) + FSwitch
    + (FWidth * Width) + (FHeight * Height).
```

will compute the delay for a component instance. The first rule retrieves the height, width and delay type attributes of the component instance. One of the last three rules (**delay_is**) will be executed to compute the delay depending upon the delay type of the component.

The height and width specified in the *comp_space* relation must be multiplied by the number of bits and/or words in a component instance to determine the overall bounding box or total area of the instance (Figure 3.19.) This information is retrieved, of course, from the appropriate component attribute relations, such as,

```
componentattribute('Move', 'IP', 'Width', 16).
componentattribute('Move', 'IP', 'Height', 1).
```

Current consumption and power dissipation values for a component instance must also be multiplied by the number of bits and words in the instance.

```
comp_space/3

    comp_space(Name, Width, Height)

    Name     Name of component definition
    Width    Size in horizontal dimension (microns)
    Height   Size in vertical dimension (microns)

comp_current/2

    comp_current(Name, Current)

    Name     Name of component definition
    Current  Component current consumption (mA)

comp_dissipation/2

    comp_dissipation(Name, Dissip)

    Name     Name of component definition
    Dissip   Component power dissipation (mW)
```

Figure 3.19: Component Physical Characteristics

3.5   Algorithms and Code

The algorithms used in the analyzer can be separated into three major categories.

- *Consistency checks.* Errors to be detected and reported include references to an undefined subnet, a missing entry or exit place in a subnet, a transition connected to a transition, a place connected to a place, a dangling arc, a missing component or port, a missing transfer path, an unused component or port, and an unconnected port or component. These checks are generally performed by applying a predicate to all occurences of an object type. For example, the rules in Figure 3.20 are applied to all pre- and postarcs to see if any arc is dangling (unconnected at either end), if a transition is connected to a transition or if a place is connected to a place.

- *Structure and expression walking.* The structure diagram must be traced to find and estimate the critical delay through the datapath. An interesting variation of this problem is datapath covering (functional sufficiency.) Here the analyzer must simultaneously walk an assignment expression and the structure graph, assigning data operations to combinational components and verifying that the components and connections are sufficient to perform the assignment. Switch components such as multiplexers complicate the process as any one of the alternative inputs can supply the value of a subexpression. High fan-out makes this a potentially slow process.

- *Hierarchy expansion and walking.* While walking a behavior graph or structure diagram, the analyzer must often enter another subnet or module block. Power estimation, for example, requires the analyzer to expand and walk the hierarchy accumulating current consumption and heat dissipation values as it goes.

Prolog proved to be a good language for rapidly prototyping our analytical routines. The statement of certain rules, like those that govern the allowable connections between transitions and places, have a clarity in Prolog which becomes obscured by pointers, structures and excessively detailed list handling code in C. This is definitely a strength of the logic programming style. Pattern matching was used extensively to detect and handle special cases. The rule in Figure 3.21 attempts to map an assignment of the form `Dest := Dest + 1` into an intrinsic "increment by one" counting register operation. Procedural code to identify such special cases is comparatively obtuse.

```
% An arc must have a transition or place at either end.

body_of_arc_loop(Module, Subnet, From, To) :-
  transition(Module, Subnet, From, _, _, _),
  place(Module, Subnet, To, _, _),
  !.

body_of_arc_loop(Module, Subnet, From, To) :-
  place(Module, Subnet, From, _, _),
  transition(Module, Subnet, To, _, _, _),
  !.

% The next two cases may be errors, but at least the arc
% is not dangling!

body_of_arc_loop(Module, Subnet, From, To) :-
  place(Module, Subnet, From, _, _),
  place(Module, Subnet, To, _, _),
  !,
  print_error_message('Place connected to another place.'),
  offending_object(Module, Subnet, 'place', From),
  offending_object(Module, Subnet, 'place', To).

body_of_arc_loop(Module, Subnet, From, To) :-
  transition(Module, Subnet, From, _, _, _),
  transition(Module, Subnet, To, _, _, _),
  !,
  print_error_message('Transition connected to another transition.'),
  offending_object(Module, Subnet, 'place', From),
  offending_object(Module, Subnet, 'place', To).

body_of_arc_loop(Module, Subnet, From, To) :-
  print_error_message('Dangling arc (from/to.)'),
  offending_object(Module, Subnet, 'arc', From),
  offending_object(Module, Subnet, 'arc', To).
```

Figure 3.20: Report Arc-related Errors

```
% Treat increment by 1 as an intrinsic operation
trace_rt_path(M,S,[assign,[Dest,_,_,_],['+',[Dest,_,_,_],1]]):-
    componentinstance(M, Dest, Defn),
    component(Defn, _, _),
    comp_ops(Defn, OpList),
    member('incr', OpList).
```

Figure 3.21: Handling Increment as a Special Case

3.5.1 Register Transfer Parsing

This section presents the Prolog code for register transfer parsing. It uses the parsing techniques described in Chapter 23 of Sterling and Shapiro. [SS86] The top-level of the parser is invoked through a call to *compile_rt* where the first argument is bound at call time to the token list to be parsed (Figure 3.22.) The second argument should be a variable to which the resulting Polish prefix code will be bound.

The parser is separated into two steps. During the first step, the input statements are parsed and a prefix structure of the register transfer assignments is produced. The second step invokes a set of encoding rules that will take the structure to the equivalent Polish prefix list form.

The first rule in the Definite Clause Grammer (DCG) for register transfer statements handles a list of assignments where the transfers are separated by a semicolon. The next rule begins the parse for transfers of the form:

destination-register := expression.

If the parse is successful, the clause will return a prefix structure whose functor is **assign** with the Prolog prefix structure for the destination register and expression. (Although we chose to map this structure to a nested list of prefix expressions, the intermediate Prolog prefix structure could have been used directly in our analytical code.)

Expression parsing code appears in Figure 3.23. Note that most of this code consists of operator definitions. It is really quite easy to add new hardware operators to the language.

Data source and sink syntax rules are given in Figure 3.24. A register (or memory element) is identified by its instance name optionally followed by a word index or bit field selector. Thus, the following register references:

```
/********************************
 * Register transfer compile rule *
 ********************************/

compile_rt(Tokens, Code) :-
  rt_list(Structure, Tokens, [ ]), !,
  encode_rt(Structure, Code).

/***************************************************
 * DCG for a list of register transfer statements *
 ***************************************************/

rt_list( (RT ; RTs) )   --> rt_statement(RT), other_rts(RTs).

other_rts( (RT ; RTs) ) --> [';'], rt_statement(RT), other_rts(RTs).
other_rts( void )       --> [ ].

/**************************************
 * DCG for register transfer statements *
 **************************************/

rt_statement(assign(X,E)) --> destination(X), [':='], expression(E) .
```

Figure 3.22: Register Transfer Parsing Top-level

```
expression(X)            --> ex_term(X) .
expression(X)            --> ['('], expression(X), [')'] .
expression(expr(Op,X))   --> prefix_op(Op), ex_term(X) .
expression(expr(Op,X,Y)) --> ex_term(X), infix_op(Op), expression(Y) .

infix_op('+')   --> ['+'] .
infix_op('-')   --> ['-'] .
infix_op('*')   --> ['*'] .
infix_op('/')   --> ['/'] .
infix_op('mod') --> ['mod'] .
infix_op('div') --> ['div'] .

infix_op('and')    --> ['&'] .
infix_op('or')     --> ['|'] .
infix_op('xor')    --> ['xor'] .
infix_op('nand')   --> ['nand'] .
infix_op('nor')    --> ['nor'] .
infix_op('concat') --> ['concat'].

infix_op('asl') --> ['asl'] .    % Arithmetic
infix_op('asr') --> ['asr'] .
infix_op('asl') --> ['<<'] .
infix_op('asr') --> ['>>'] .
infix_op('lsl') --> ['lsl'] .    % Logical
infix_op('lsr') --> ['lsr'] .
infix_op('rol') --> ['rol'] .    % Rotate
infix_op('ror') --> ['ror'] .

infix_op('eql') --> ['='] .
infix_op('neq') --> ['<>'] .
infix_op('lss') --> ['<'] .
infix_op('leq') --> ['<='] .
infix_op('gtr') --> ['>'] .
infix_op('geq') --> ['>='] .

prefix_op('not') --> ['not'] .
prefix_op('neg') --> ['neg'] .
```

Figure 3.23: Expression Parsing and Operators

```
R
R[5]
R[Index]
R<7:5>
R<0>
R[3]<15:12>
```

are permitted by the language syntax. The parse ends with register sources, sinks and integer constants – the primary terms of a Gdl/b expression. The same expression syntax is also used in enabling conditions and place assertions.

The rest of Figure 3.24 contains the rules for mapping the Prolog prefix structure to an equivalent prefix list form. Naturally, the expression rules are recursive. The catch-all rule:

```
encode(X,X).
```

guarantees that the encoding process will succeed even for unknown or erroneous structures produced in the presence of parse errors.

3.5.2   Datapath Sufficiency

In this section we present the Prolog code for performing missing transfer path analysis. *detect_missing_path*, the top-level goal, takes as its arguments the symbolic name of the parent module, the subnet name, the transition identifier and prefix list form of the register transfers associated with the transition (Figure 3.25.) If a missing path is discovered, an error message is displayed containing the module and subnet names and transition identifier. The message can be reformatted into a dialogue box message by the Gdl behavior editor. *detect_missing_path* will iterate through a list of transfers and analyze each one in turn.

The procedure for analyzing datapath sufficiency (covering) is straightforward. The code begins at the destination register (the left hand side of the assignment) and works back to the data source registers. [1] The algorithm essentially compares the expression with the datapath structure, making a match between register names and instances, between expression operators and combinational components, and between the data dependencies in the expression with structural interconnections.

The implementation is pattern driven. Each clause head specifies the prefix expression which is handled by the rule body. In Figure 3.25, for example, the rules attempt to cover increment (decrement) by one expressions by the intrinsic

---

[1] Ports and memory elements are handled identically. Thus, we will not explicitly refer to these kinds of elements in this discussion.

```
/***************************************
 * Register sources/sinks and constants *
 ***************************************/

destination(sink(X,W,H,L))
  --> identifier(X), word_index(W), bit_field(H,L) .
ex_term(source(X,W,H,L))
  --> identifier(X), word_index(W), bit_field(H,L) .
ex_term(number(X))
  --> integer_term(X) .

word_index(W)     --> ['['], ex_term(W), [']'] .
word_index(empty) --> [ ] .

bit_field(H,L) --> ['<'], integer_term(H),
                   [':'], integer_term(L), ['>'] .
bit_field(H,H) --> ['<'], integer_term(H), ['>'] .
bit_field(empty,empty) --> [ ].

identifier(X)   --> [X], {atom(X)} .
integer_term(X) --> [X], {integer(X)} .

/********************************************
 * Translate from intermediate to list form *
 ********************************************/

encode_rt((RT ; RTs),[ERT|ERTs]) :- encode(RT,ERT),
                                     encode_rt(RTs,ERTs).
encode_rt(void, [ ]).

encode_enable(enable(E), [EE]) :- encode(E, EE).
encode_assert(assert(E), [EE]) :- encode(E, EE).

encode(assign(X,E), [assign,EX,EE]) :- encode(X, EX), encode(E, EE).
encode(expr(Op,X), [Op,EX]) :- encode(X, EX).
encode(expr(Op,X,Y), [Op,EX,EY]) :- encode(X, EX), encode(Y, EY).

encode(source(X,W,H,L), [X,EW,H,L]) :- encode(W, EW).
encode(sink(X,W,H,L), [X,EW,H,L]) :- encode(W, EW).
encode(number(N), N).
encode(void,[ ]).
encode(X,X).
```

Figure 3.24: Sinks, Sources and Prefix Encoding

```
/*****************************************
 * Trace path from destination to sources *
 *****************************************/

% Given a module name, transition identifier and list of
% register transfers, check for missing transfer paths.

report_missing_path(_, _, _, [ ]) :- !.

report_missing_path(Module, Subnet, Tid, [RT|RTs]) :-
  trace_rt_path(Module, Subnet, RT),
  report_missing_path(Module, Subnet, Tid, RTs).

report_missing_path(Module, Subnet, Tid, [RT|RTs]) :-
  print_error_message('Missing transfer path.'),
  offending_object(Module, Subnet, 'transition', Tid),
  report_missing_path(Module, Subnet, Tid, RTs).

% Treat increment by 1 as an intrinsic function.

trace_rt_path(M, S, [assign,[Dest,_,_,_],['+',[Dest,_,_,_],1]]) :-
  componentinstance(M, Dest, Defn),
  component(Defn, _, _),
  comp_ops(Defn, OpList),
  member('incr', OpList).

% Treat decrement by 1 as an intrinsic function.

trace_rt_path(M, S, [assign,[Dest,_,_,_],['-',[Dest,_,_,_],1]]) :-
  componentinstance(M, Dest, Defn),
  component(Defn, _, _),
  comp_ops(Defn, OpList),
  member('decr', OpList).

% Trace the paths for a single register transfer assignment.

trace_rt_path(M, S, [assign,[Dest,_,_,_],Expr]) :-
  connection(M, X, _, Dest, _),
  trace_back(M, S, X, Expr).
```

Figure 3.25: Begin Trace from Destination Register

counting register operations incr (decr.) If an expression of the form:

destination := destination + 1

is encountered, the rule body will try to find the operation incr among the intrinsic operations in the definition of the *destination* register. The last rule in Figure 3.25 initiates the general trace back procedure for expressions. A connection is required between the input of the destination register and the hardware that computes the value of the expression.

Trace back rules are given in Figures 3.26 and 3.27. They perform a depth first exploration of the datapath using the register transfer expression as a guide. The first three rules succeed when a constant, memory element or port is encountered which successfully terminates the search. In the case of a switch component such as a multiplexer, all paths leading into the component must be explored since any one of the paths can produce the needed subexpresison. The rule in Figure 3.28 performs the fan-out search from the switch component. The last two rules handle dyadic and monadic operators. There must be a component at that point in the datapath which is capable of performing the specified arithmetic or logical operation (i.e., the operation is in the set of intrinsic operations for the component.) A connection must exist from the component to the circuitry producing its argument values.

Two analytical deficiencies remain. The trace back routine for dyadic operators does not handle commutivity. This requires information in the component library about the commutivity of intrinsic operations. Next, it is possible that two or more assignments within the same list of transfers will be allocated to the same connections and combinational components – a resource conflict. Resource conflicts may also occur when two assignments in concurrent execution paths use the same circuitry simultaneously. Clearly, this algorithm is more complex than simple sufficiency and may require additional net theory as well.

3.5.3   Current and Power Estimation

Current and power estimation is an example of an analytical procedure which must walk through the module-component hierarchy (Figure 3.29.) The main clause, *print_estimates*, calls an "inner" routine, *print_estimate*. This routine is called twice – once to compute and display current consumption and once to compute and display power dissipation. The *estimate* code actually walks the structural hierarchy summing values over the constituent modules and components.

```
% If the expression is a numeric constant, then terminate
% the trace with success.

trace_back(_, _, Inst, N) :- number(N).

% If the instance name matches the name of a source variable
% (register or port) then we have succeeded.

trace_back(M, _, Inst, [Inst,_,_,_]) :-
  componentinstance(M, Inst, Defn),
  component(Defn, memory, _), !.

trace_back(M, _, Inst, [Inst,_,_,_]) :- port(M, _, Inst, _), !.

% If the instance is a switch component, then explore all
% incoming paths to the switch.

trace_back(M, S, Inst, Expr) :-
  componentinstance(M, Inst, Defn),
  component(Defn, switch, _), !,
  findall(X, connection(M, X, _, Inst, _), BackList),
  trace_list(M, S, BackList, Expr).

% If the expression is dyadic and the operator is in the
% set of intrinsics for the instance, then trace the right
% and left paths.

trace_back(M, S, Inst, [Op,Left,Right]) :-
  componentinstance(M, Inst, Defn),
  component(Defn, fnl, _),
  comp_ops(Defn, OpList),
  member(Op, OpList), !,
  connection(M, ILeft, _, Inst, _),
  trace_back(M, S, ILeft, Left),
  connection(M, IRight, _, Inst, _),
  trace_back(M, S, IRight, Right).
```

Figure 3.26: Trace Expression and Datapath

% If the expression is monadic and the operator is in the
% set of intrinsics for the instance, then trace the one
% incoming path.

```
trace_back(M, S, Inst, [Op,Source]) :-
  componentinstance(M, Inst, Defn),
  component(Defn, fn1, _),
  comp_ops(Defn, OpList),
  member(Op, OpList), !,
  connection(M, ISource, _, Inst, _),
  trace_back(M, S, ISource, Source).
```

Figure 3.27: Trace Monadic Expression and Datapath

% Trace back to each instance in the argument list. This is
% used for switch elements with several incoming paths.

```
trace_list(_, _, [ ], _) :- fail.
trace_list(M, S, [X|L], Expr) :-
  trace_back(M, S, X, Expr) -> true ; trace_list(M, S, L, Expr).
```

Figure 3.28: Fan-out from a Switch Element

```
print_estimates(Module) :-
  print_estimate(current, Module, ' mA '),
  print_estimate(power,   Module, ' mW ').

print_estimate(Property, Module, Unit) :-
  estimate(Property, Module, Estimate),
  printstring('The estimated '), write(Property),
  printstring(' of module '), write(Module),
  printstring(' is '), write(Estimate), write(Unit), nl.

estimate(Property, Module, Estimate) :-
  estimate(Property, Module, 0.0, Estimate).

estimate(Property, Module, Sum0, Sum) :-
  findall(Mod, moduleinstance(Module, Mod, _), Mods),
  sum_over_modules(Mods, Property, Sum0, Sum1),
  findall(Comp, componentinstance(Module, Comp, _), Comps),
  sum_over_components(Comps, Module, Property, Sum1, Sum).

sum_over_modules([ ], _, Sum, Sum).
sum_over_modules([Mod|Mods], Property, Sum0, Sum) :-
  estimate(Property, Mod, Value),
  Sum1 is Sum0 + Value,
  sum_over_modules(Mods, Property, Sum1, Sum).

sum_over_components([ ], _, _, Sum, Sum).
sum_over_components([Comp|Comps], Module, Property, Sum0, Sum) :-
  compute_property(Property, Module, Comp, Value),
  Sum1 is Sum0 + Value,
  sum_over_components(Comps, Module, Property, Sum1, Sum).
```

Figure 3.29: Current and Power Estimation

```
/****************************************
 * Compute component current consumption *
 ****************************************/

compute_property(current, Module, Instance, Current) :-
  componentinstance(Module, Instance, Definition),
  componentattr(Module, Instance, 'Height', Height),
  componentattr(Module, Instance, 'Width',  Width),
  comp_current(Definition, Factor),
  current_is(Factor, Height, Width, Current).

current_is(Factor, 0, 0, Current) :-
  printstring('Height and width are zero.'),
  Current is 0.

current_is(Factor, 0, Width, Current) :-
  Current is Factor * Width.

current_is(Factor, Height, Width, Current) :-
  Current is Factor * Width * Height.

/****************************************
 * Compute component power dissipation *
 ****************************************/

compute_property(power, Module, Instance, Power) :-
  componentinstance(Module, Instance, Definition),
  componentattr(Module, Instance, 'Height', Height),
  componentattr(Module, Instance, 'Width',  Width),
  comp_dissipation(Definition, Factor),
  power_is(Factor, Height, Width, Power).

power_is(Factor, 0, 0, Power) :-
  printstring('Height and width are zero'),
  Power is 0.

power_is(Factor, 0, Width, Power) :-
  Power is Factor * Width.

power_is(Factor, Height, Width, Power) :-
  Power is Factor * Width * Height.
```

Figure 3.30: Code to Compute Component Current and Power

3.6   Commentary

Prolog is quite suitable for the analysis of hardware designs especially as the level of abstraction moves away from gates toward higher level hardware description languages. As mentioned earlier, Prolog is a good environment for rapidly constructing prototype tools. This is due primarily to the declarative style, the program execution mechanism (backtracking and pattern matching are implicit) and the easy resolution of graph connections and names. For example, a recursive descent parser for register transfers as written in C language required about 300 lines of code. The Prolog DCG-based parser is about 75 lines and the grammar is clearly expressed as productions. The algorithms for datapath sufficiency require 102 lines of Prolog versus roughly 180 lines of C. The C code does *not* include several hundred lines of ancillary functions for component library management, handling bus connectivity, etc. Thus, the actual total code count should be adjusted upwards to be completely fair to Prolog!

3.7   Background

More information about register transfer level synthesis and design can be found in either of two tutorial articles by Alice Parker, Michael McFarland and Raul Camposano. [Par84, MPC88] The goal of research in this area is to raise the level of design abstraction to a very "high level." Hardware engineers no longer have the time to design one transistor or one gate at a time. Further, the complexity of modern hardware systems requires the development of a precise statement of the intended behavior. Of course, these high level descriptions must be mapped to the usual gate or transistor level implementations and thus, our interest in synthesis.

One would ultimately like the expressive power of a formal specification language coupled with the creative and economically effective synthesis skills of a human engineer. We have been actively developing a collection of heuristics for register transfer level synthesis. One such experiment, a translator from a subset of the C language to the supporting datapath, was constructed in Prolog. We found the Prolog statement of the the synthesis process to be more understandable than an equivalent synthesizer in C. [Boy89] Future work here includes the specification of signalling behavior, inward synthesis from the interface specification and the implementation of a rule-based assistant. We will continue to work in Prolog.

Other work in progress at Case includes a set of "back-end" tools for Agent – a translator from Gdl to the DoD VHSIC Hardware Description Language (VHDL)

:t tool set for VLSI design. The VHDL translator
in, we have found Prolog to be quite suitable for

Chapter 4

Developing a Portable Parallelizing Pascal Compiler in Prolog

Eran Gabber

Computer Science Dept.
School of Mathematical Sciences
Tel–Aviv University
Tel–Aviv 69978, Israel
E-Mail: eran@MATH.TAU.AC.IL

Abstract

The Portable Parallelizing Pascal Compiler (PPPC) is a research compiler written in Prolog, which compiles serial application programs written in a Pascal based language into a portable and efficient parallel code. The PPPC compiler extracts parallelism from the user program using global data flow analysis and generates code for VMMP[Gab89] (A Virtual Machine for MultiProcessors), which is a portable software environment running on diverse multiprocessors. PPPC optimizes the generated code and performs an accurate prediction of multiprocessor speedup using the target machine cost table. PPPC is fully automatic and does not require any user directives or assistance.

PPPC can be ported easily to other target multiprocessors by updating the target cost table and porting the virtual machine (VMMP).

This article describes PPPC operation, algorithms and the generated parallel code. PPPC implementation is explained with emphasis on Prolog constructs used. Some representative code excerpts from PPPC implementation are shown. The article concludes by a discussion of the Prolog features which were found most useful for the implementation.

4.1 Introduction and Background

Current high performance MIMD multiprocessors offer a price/performance advantage over conventional uniprocessors. The most important MIMD architectures today are shared memory multiprocessrs (such as Sequent Balance[TGF88]) and message passing multiprocessors[AS88].

Most multiprocessor application programs today are explicitly parallel, meaning that the target machine services are directly accessed. This approach produces an efficient code but requires much programming effort. Moreover, the resulting code must be rewritten in order to port it to a different multiprocessor. See the paper by Karp and Babb II[KB88] for further examples.

Good software development tools are the key to the effective use of multiprocessors. These tools should simplify the task of writing and debugging efficient parallel programs and eliminate the necessity to rewrite the code for different target machines. The ultimate software development tool for multiprocessors should make them as easy to use as current uniprocessors while fully exploiting their power.

One approach to solve the multiprocessor software development problem is to employ a parallelizing compiler, which converts a serial user application program written in a conventional high level language into a highly efficient parallel code. There are currently several parallelizing compilers, which generate parallel code from a FORTRAN serial program, e.g. PTRAN[BCF+88, ABC+87] and Parafrase[PKP86]. These compilers perform an extensive control and data dependence analysis in order to identify potential execution parallelism. However, these compilers are limited to shared memory multiprocessors.

PPPC (Portable Parallelizing Pascal Compiler) is a research parallelizing compiler, which produces an explicitly parallel C code for VMMP[Gab89] from serial programs written in a subset of Pascal. PPPC differs from the above parallelizing compilers by emphasizing compiler and code portability in exchange for less extensive parallelization efforts. Although PPPC uses a relatively simple parallelization algorithm, it produces highly efficient code for various application programs as described in section 4.3.6.

We decided to implement PPPC in Prolog, because we felt that Prolog provides the necessary symbolic manipulation capabilities. In retrospect, this was a fortunate decision, because it saved us much development time and allowed us to experiment with different versions of the parallelization algorithm. The specific Prolog features found useful in the implementation are described in section 4.5.

Prolog has been used previously for developing compilers and parsers. In particular, Definite Clause Grammar (DCG) provides an effective tool to develop parsers. The books [CM87, chapter 9] and [SS86, chapter 16] describe DCGs in detail. Prolog can be also used to implement other compiler components, such as lexical analyzers, code generators and code optimizers. Sterling and Shapiro[SS86, chapter 23] describe a toy compiler for a structured language. Cohen and Hickey[CH87] provide numerous insights and techniques for implementing compilers in Prolog. PPPC implementation is more complicated than the above compilers because it performs more sophisticated data flow analysis and code transformations.

The rest of the article is organized as follows: Section 4.2 describes the two level structure of the parallelization tool. Section 4.3 describes PPPC operation, including the TAU–Pascal language, the parallelization algorithm, execution time prediction and code generation. Section 4.3 concludes by actual run time measurements of the generated code. Section 4.4 describes PPPC implementation in detail, including major components operation and data structures. Section 4.5 summarizes our experience with Prolog as an implementation language for prototype compilers.

4.2 PPPC Usage

The Portable Parallizing Pascal Compiler consists of two parts: the parallelizer (PPPC) and the virtual machine (VMMP[Gab89]). The parallelizer accepts a serial program written in a TAU–Pascal and generates an explicitly parallel C code for VMMP. The TAU–Pascal language is described in section 4.3.1. VMMP (A Virtual Machine for MultiProcessors) is a software package, which implements a common set of services on diverse target machines, including shared memory multiprocessors, message passing multiprocessors and uniprocessors. PPPC produces C code and not Pascal code, because VMMP currently supports only C programs. Figure 4.1 illustrates PPPC usage.

The separation of the parallelizer into a high level part (PPPC) and a low level part (VMMP) simplifies the design and enhances portability. In this way, the machine dependent task of parallelization extraction is performed by PPPC, while the specific details of the implementation are hidden inside VMMP. This two level structure resembles current high level language compilers, which consists of a front end and several back ends, one for each target. Moreover, the Virtual Machine code may be regarded as a common intermediate language, much like the intermediate language used between front end and back ends.

Although any VMMP application program will run on every target machine supported by VMMP, it will probably run inefficiently, because the efficiency of VMMP services is different on different targets. PPPC avoids this inherent inefficiency of portable code by tailoring the generated code to the specific target machine using the target *cost table*. The cost table contains the relative time to perform various computation and synchronization operations on that target.

VMMP is implemented as a subroutine library. VMMP services are activated by

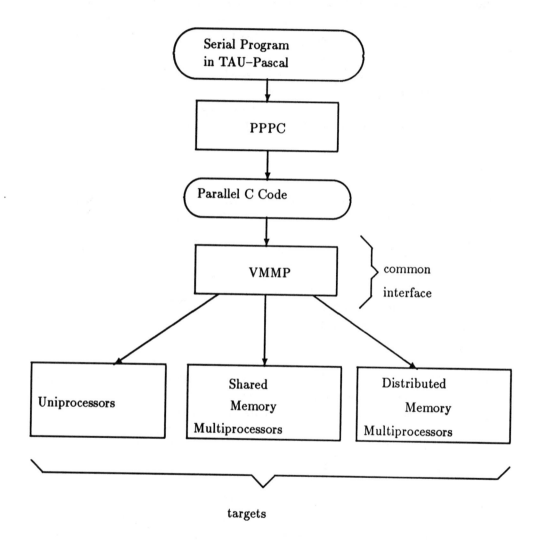

Figure 4.1: PPPC Usage

subroutine calls. The application program is compiled using the appropriate target machine C compiler and linked with the appropriate VMMP library. We save effort by using the existing C compilers to compile the VMMP application program. We may even use a vectorizing C compiler if available in order to vectorize the inner loops, while the parallelizer generated code to concurrentize the outer loops.

VMMP is currently implemented on UNIX uniprocessors (SUN3 workstations, IBM RT, National Semiconductor's VME532), on MMX[Gab88], an experimental shared memory multiprocessor developed at Tel–Aviv University, and on ACE[GFF89], an experimental shared memory multiprocessor developed at IBM Research and running MACH. VMMP implementation on a distributed memory (message passing) multiprocessor is planned.

4.3   PPPC Operation

PPPC creates an explicitly parallel code which executes in SPMD (Single Program Multiple Data) mode[FDP88, Jor87]. SPMD is a restricted form of parallel execution, in which the same program runs on all processors. The parallel sections of the SPMD program are executed by all processors running the same code but manipulating distinct parts of the common workload. The serial sections of the program are executed on a single processor. PPPC implements some serial sections by duplicating the computation on all processors (called *replicated computation*) in order to reduce synchronization overheads.

PPPC produces SPMD code because it can be generated by relatively simple techniques from parallel loops. Although SPMD code is less efficient than general parallel code, its performance is good for numerical algorithms, which manipulate large arrays of data.

This section is organized as follows. It begins by a brief introduction to TAU–Pascal, which is the input language for PPPC. A short introduction to VMMP services follows. The parallelization algorithm of **for** loops are described next, along with the algorithm for accurate run time prediction. PPPC will parallelize a **for** loop only if it both obeys the parallelization rules *and* the run time prediction indicates that parallel execution time is shorter than serial execution. The structure of the generated code is illustrated by a typical code fragment. The section concludes by some actual run time measurements of several application programs compiled by PPPC.

4.3.1   TAU–Pascal

TAU–Pascal (Tel–Aviv University Pascal) is a Pascal[Wir74] based language oriented for scientific computations. It is a subset of Pascal with several extensions for scientific computation.

TAU–Pascal extensions are: Zero assignment to compound data types is allowed, provided that all elements of the compound data type are numeric. Two new dyadic operators **min** and **max** are defined. They compute the minimum (or maximum) of their numeric operands. **min** and **max** may be used like any other arithmetic operators and their precedence is the same as relationship operators. The **min** and **max** operators shorten user code and simplify data flow analysis by eliminating an **if** statement.

4.3.2   VMMP Services

As noted earlier, PPPC generates parallel code which executed in SPMD[FDP88] (Single Program Multiple Data) mode. This section describes only the VMMP services requested by SPMD computations. Other VMMP services, especially those implementing dynamic tree computations, are described in [Gab89].

VMMP creates an initial process, which executes the user's main program. This process may spawn other processes using the **Vcrowd** service, which creates a *crowd* of cooperating processes running concurrently with the father process. The **Vwait** service forces the father process to wait for the termination of all its child processes in order to assure correct output results.

Crowd processes synchronize and communicate by the **Vcombine** operation, which combines partial results supplied by each of the crowd processes into a single global result. The global result is returned to all participating processes. **Vcombine** is used to share the results of a distributed computation between the crowd processes.

Crowd processes receive input and produce output using *shared objects*. Shared objects are named memory areas, which may be accessed only using VMMP services. They resemble shared memory variables with the advantage of easy implementation also on message passing multiprocessors. Shared objects are created and initialized by the **Vdef** service. The **Vset** service changes the value of a shared object and **Vget** retrieves the current value. Global and static variables are forbidden in VMMP application programs because they can not be implemented reliably on distributed memory multiprocessors.

4.3.3 Parallelization Rules

PPPC attempts to parallelize only **for** loops with independent iterations. A **for** loop is eligible for parallelization if and only if all the variables accessed inside the loop body belongs to one of the following categories, which do not cause any dependencies between loop iterations. PPPC does not perform more sophisticated tests as in PTRAN[ABC+87]. The variable categories are:

read only
> Read only variables are used inside the loop but not changed.

index
> Loop index variables are changed only by the loop control statement and not inside the loop body.

distributed
> Distributed variables are arrays that are changed in the loop, so that each iteration changes a different array element. In addition, each iteration may access only the array element it is updating and not any other element. For example:

```
for i := 1 to N do
begin
    v[i] := expression;
    ..... v[i] {used here}
end
```

> Current implementation identifies distributed arrays only by their first index, which must be a loop index variable. We don't handle more complex access patterns of distributed variables, because it is extremely difficult to assure that two general index expressions will produce different results in all iterations.

associative
> Associative variables are updated inside the loop by an associative and commutative operation, such as +,*, and, or, min, max. The value of the associative variables is not used elsewhere inside the loop except in its update operation. For example:

```
for i := 1 to N do
    sum := sum + expression;
```

The final value of associative variables may be computed at the end of all loop iterations by combining the partial values supplied by the participating processors. We ignore the effect of rounding errors, which may produce different answers depending on the evaluation order.

local

The values of local variables are used only in the same iteration which had set them. These variables are considered "local" to the loop, because their value is not passed between iterations. They do not cause any dependencies between iterations. For example:

```
for i := 1 to N do
begin
    v := expression;
    ... v is used here ...
end;
```

Other access patterns cause dependencies between loop iterations and inhibit loop parallelization.

The above simple rules are sufficient to parallelize many practical algorithms. See a more complicated nested loops example in section 4.3.5.

4.3.4   Run Time Prediction

Accurate run time prediction during compilation is essential to produce efficient parallel code. The run time prediction is used mainly to avoid generating parallel code where the synchronization and data distribution overhead is larger than the savings in computation speed. It is also used to compute the anticipated speedup.

The run time prediction is based on the target *cost table*, which contains the execution time of all constructs appearing in the serial program, such as arithmetic operations, array indexing, data movement, if overhead, loop test overhead, etc. The run time is expressed relative to the time needed for an integer addition. The cost table contains also the parameters for the cost functions of VMMP services. (see below).

The program run time is computed by the following method:

- The run time of a straight code sequence without loops or if statements is computed directly by summing the execution time of all constructs appearing in this code.

- The run time of an **if** statement is the arithmetic mean of the run time of its *then* and *else* parts plus the time to compute the **if** condition. We assume that the *then* and *else* parts have equal execution probability.

- The run time of a serial **for** loop is the product of the number of loop iterations by the loop body time. The number of loop iterations is computed exactly when both loop bounds are constants. Otherwise we use the default estimate of 25 iterations.

- The run time of a parallel **for** loop is the product of the loop body time by the average number of iterations executed on a single processor. We add to the product time needed to collect and distribute loop results.

- The run time of **while** and **repeat** loops is the product of the estimated number of iterations (25) by the sum of loop body time and loop condition time.

- The overhead of loop synchronization and most other VMMP services is computed by a formula:

$$\alpha + f(\#processors) \times (\beta + \gamma \times sizeof(data))$$

  Where α, β and γ characterize the specific operation. f is a function dependent on the target architecture.

The cost table is produced by a special program, which measures the time needed for the operations.

4.3.5   Code Generation

PPPC tries to parallelize the outermost program loop, which is both eligible for parallelization (checked by parallization rules) and reduce total running time (checked by run time prediction). Inner parallel loops are not recognized yet (no handling of nested parallelism). This section illustrates the code generation process by using a small code excerpt, which is typical to scientific programs. Most of the code generation details will be eliminated from the following discussion for clarity.

The following code excerpt is taken from a program for the solution of a system of linear equations $Ax = b$ by Jordan iterations. Each iteration computes a better approximation to the solution vector x by computing:

$new\_x_i = (b_i - \sum_{j \neq i} A_{i,j} x_j)/A_{i,i}$

```
4    var  a:array[1..N,1..N] of real;
5         b:array[1..N] of real;
6         x,new_x:array[1..N] of real;
     ...
10   repeat
11     error := 0;
12     for i := 1 to N do
13     begin
14       sum := 0;
15       for j := 1 to N do
16         sum := sum + a[i,j]*x[j];
17       new_x[i] := x[i]+(b[i]-sum)/a[i,i];
18       error := error max abs(b[i]-sum);
19     end;
20     x := new_x;
21   until error < EPS;
```

The nested loop structure in the above code excerpt is typical for scientific code. The outer **repeat** loop is inherently serial, while the inner **for** loops are parallel.

The **for** loop at line 12 is eligible for parallelization according to the rules of section 4.3.3. All of the variables accessed in the loop belongs to one of the permitted categories: i is **index**, sum and j are **local**, a and b are read **only**, new_x is **distributed** and **error** is associative.

PPPC produces SPMD code for executing the user program. It tries to reduce the parallel code overhead by *replicating* the execution of the outer serial loop in all processors using the same data and distributing the work of the inner parallel loops between the processors. In this way, the outer replicated loop does not require any synchronization nor data movements, because all processors execute the same outer loop code on the same data and getting the same results. Synchronization is required only at the end of the inner parallel loops in order to combine the partial results computed by the processors, so that all processors may proceed with the same results.

PPPC creates a crowd to compute the parallel loops. The loops code becomes the body of a new procedure, which will be executed by all crowd processes. PPPC replaces the parallel loop code by the following code:

```
Vdef(a); Vdef(b); Vdef(x)    Define input and output variables
Vcrowd(..., task, ...)       Create a crowd of processes
```

Vwait	*Wait for crowd termination*
Vget(x)	*Get results*

PPPC produces the following procedure body, which contains the code of the parallel loops. This procedure is executed concurrently by all processors. Note that the code of the outer replicated loop is not changed. Only parallel loop(s) inside the replicated loop are changed, so that each processor handles a different set of loop iterations and the processors share the same results at the end of the parallel loop(s). The routine **Vcrowd_part** computes the index boundaries of the slice belonging to the current processor. **l** and **h** are new variables containing the low and high bounds of the slice, respectively.

```
task(..)
{   variable declarations

    Vget(a); Vget(b); Vget(x)           Get input
    do {
        replicated loop body
        Vcrowd_part(N, 0, &l, &h);       compute my work slice
        for (i = l+1; i < = h+1; i++)
            parallel loop body
        Vcombine(error)                  combine loop results
        Vcombine(new_x)
        rest of replicated loop body - everybody got the same values
    while(!(error < EPS));
    Vset(x)                              Write result
}
```

In general, PPPC converts the parallel loop
for i := *low* **to** *high* **do** *body*
into code of the form:

Compute index range of my slice from the range [low .. high]
for(i = l; i <= h; i++)
    body;
Vcombine *(results);*

Where **l** and **h** are new variables containing the bounds of the loop slice.

Program	Data	MMX Processors			
		serial	2	3	4
Pi	Actual Speedup	1	2	2.99	3.99
	Pred. Speedup		1.99	2.99	3.99
MontePi	Actual Speedup	1	1.99	2.99	3.98
	Pred. Speedup		1.99	2.99	3.99
Mandel	Actual Speedup	1	1.93	2.88	3.71
	Pred. Speedup		1.96	2.88	3.76
Linear	Actual Speedup	1	1.91	2.65	3.31
	Pred. Speedup		1.81	2.57	3.26
Nbody	Actual Speedup	1	1.94	2.85	3.71
	Pred. Speedup		1.88	2.70	3.42
MM	Actual Speedup	1	1.88	2.75	3.60
	Pred. Speedup		1.93	2.81	3.62
CG	Actual Speedup	1	1.86	2.62	3.28
	Pred. Speedup		1.86	2.63	3.26

Table 4.1: Speedup Measurements

4.3.6 Speedup Measurements

Table 4.1 contains actual speedup measurement of several application programs compiled by PPPC and run on MMX[Gab88], an experimental shared memory multiprocessor containing 4 processors. The predicted speedup computed by PPPC is also presented. The actual speedup is given by $\frac{serial\ time}{parallel\ time}$.
Note: the speedup is computed relative to the serial execution time, which is obtained by running the C code generated without the parallelization step in PPPC. This C code is the direct translation of the TAU–Pascal serial program.

These measurements are encouraging, because the programs achieved a speedup of 3.28–3.99 on 4 processors, which is equivalent to 82%–100% efficiency (efficiency $= 100 \times \frac{speedup}{\#processors}$). Also the predicted speedup is very close to the actual speedup. The difference between them is usually 2%–3% and never more than 8%.

The application programs range from the trivial to the complicated. They represent a wide range of scientific code. Some of them are not trivial for parallelization by hand.

The application programs are: **Pi** computes the value of π by integration of the function $\sqrt{1-x^2}$. **MontePi** computes the value of π by Monte-Carlo integration. **Mandel** computes the Mandelbrot set. **Linear** solves a system of 250 linear equations in 250 unknowns by Jordan iterations. **Nbody** simulates the motion of 100 bodies in 3 dimensions using long range (gravitation) force. **MM** multiplies two 140 by 140 matrices. **CG** solves a system of 250 linear equations of 250 unknowns using the Conjugate-Gradient method.

4.4   Implementation

This section describes PPPC design decisions, components, data structures, algorithms and implementation details. The implementation follows closely the data structures and flow natural to the problem. The PPPC compiler implements many techniques developed for conventional high level language compilers. The reader should consult a general reference book on compiler design, such as "the dragon book" [ASU86], for further details.

This section is intended to provide enough information on the implementation to ease the development of similar compilers. The section begins by a description of the design decisions and the internal data structures. Each of the PPPC passes is described in detail, followed by some data on code size and execution time.

4.4.1   Design Decisions

The overall operation of PPPC was fixed before we started the PPPC implementation. In particular, the TAU–Pascal language, parallelization algorithms and the virtual machine level were all defined prior to the implementation.

We wanted to implement a prototype compiler quickly and to ensure that it will be easy to modify and experiment with. In order to achieve this goal, we decided that the prototype should consist of several independent passes with a clear interface definition and that it should use text files for all inter-pass communications. The separation into independent passes allowed us to change any of the passes independently from the others. The text file interface between the passes enables the passes to be implemented in different languages.

We decided to implement the PPPC front end by a combination of YACC[Joh75] and LEX[LS75] tools, because these tools can generate a compiler front end from a compact high-level description of the language syntax.

We decided to implement the rest of PPPC in Prolog, because Prolog can express complicated symbolic data manipulations clearly and concisely. Prolog also offers the flexibility needed for code experiments. The author had also some prior positive experience with high-level language processing tools written in Prolog. In retrospect, the decision to use Prolog was fully justified. See section 4.5 for more details.

4.4.2 PPPC Components

PPPC consists of four passes:

- **Front End**
  The front end reads the TAU–Pascal input and performs the syntax analysis.

- **Semantic Check**
  The semantic check pass reads the program parse tree and performs the semantic analysis.

- **Parallelizer**
  The parallelizer reads the program in the form of a typed parse tree and produces an optimized explicitly parallel program.

- **Code Generation**
  The code generation pass reads the program typed parse tree and emits the equivalent C code.

Figure 4.2 illustrates PPPC internal structure. The rectangles represent the compiler passes and the ovals represent intermediate data files. Note that the parallelizer pass is optional. If it is omitted, PPPC will translate TAU–Pascal to serial C without modifications. The output of PPPC is combined with **VMMP** run-time library to form an executable code, as shown in figure 4.1.

4.4.3 Data Structures

The most important data structure in PPPC is the program parse tree. It is generated by the front end and modified by subsequent passes. All passes but the first perform a series of parse tree traversals and modifications.

The parse tree is a recursive data structure represented by Prolog compound terms. The nodes in the parse tree are represented by simple terms (leafs) or compound terms (interior nodes). The terms in the parse tree have the general format of:

name(*source_line_no, [list_of_arguments]*)

For example, dyadic operators are represented by terms of the format:

op2(*source_line_no, [op_name, left_arg, right_arg]*)

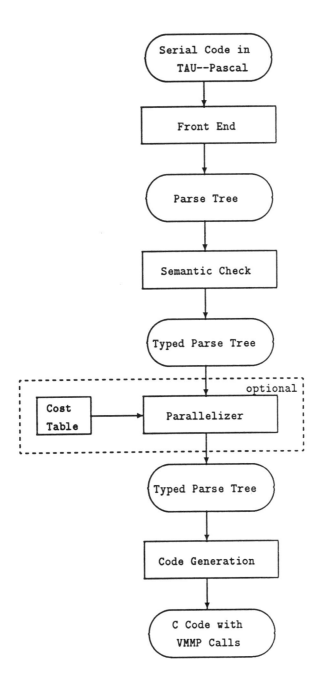

Figure 4.2: PPPC Components

The source line number is included in every term in order to produce the originating line number in the generated code and to provide more accurate error messages.

The typed parse tree is similar to the above parse tree, but it also contains the type of each expression as the third argument in each term. Some examples of parse trees are given in the next sections.

In addition to the parse tree, PPPC also creates some facts dynamically during computation in order to store information derived from the parse tree, such as symbol table entries. Other facts are generated to hold temporary results in order to avoid duplicate computations. The symbol table entries are passed along with the parse tree from the semantic check pass forward. See examples for such facts in sections 4.4.4 and 4.4.5.

4.4.4   Front End Pass

The front end performs the parsing and syntax checking of the input program. The lexical analyzer is written in LEX[LS75] and the parser is written in YACC[Joh75]. Both lexical analyzer and parser are a straight forward implementation of TAU–Pascal syntax definitions. The parser implements a limited recovery from syntax errors.

The following example illustrates the operation of the front end. Given the code excerpt:

```
5   if a > b then
6        c.re:= a+b
7   else c.im := 2.0*sin(a)
```

The front end will generate the following parse tree. We assume that a and b are reals. c is a record containing two **real** fields, re and im.

```
if(5,[
  op2(5,['>', id(5,'a'), id(5,'b')]),
  assignment(6,[ field(6, [id(6,'c'), id(6,'re')]),
      op2(6,['+', id(6,'a'), id(6,'b')])
  ]),
  assignment(7,[ field(7, [id(7,'c'), id(6,'im')]),
      op2(7,['*', fconst(7,'2.0'),
          fcall(7,[ id(7,'sin'), id(7,'a')])
      ])
  ])
])
```

])

The above example is an abbreviation of the actual parse tree, which contains more information on declarations and program structure. Note that all tree terms contain the corresponding source line number.

4.4.5   Semantic Check Pass

The semantic check pass reads the program parse tree and performs all semantic checks. It also builds the program symbol table, containing the type of each declared variable.

The semantic check pass first analyzes the declarations of constants, types and variables. Afterwards it traverses the program parse tree in order to assign type information to expressions. It first assigns type information to expression leaves (variables, constants and parameter-less functions) and then moves upwards to complete type information of interior nodes. Type clashes in interior nodes are identified by comparing the types assigned to the leaves with the expected operand types of the operation in the node.

The heart of the type check operation is the *check_expr/3* predicate. Here are some clauses from the *check_expr/3* predicate, which handle dyadic operations and field reference in records.

```
check_expr(op2(Line,[Op,L,R]),            /* Input:  expression */
      op2(Line,[Op,Left,Right],Type), /* Output: typed expression */
      Type) :-                        /* Output: expression type */
              check_expr(L,Left,T1),
              check_expr(R,Right,T2),
              check_op2(Line,Op,T1,T2,Type).
check_expr(field(Line,[R,id(_,Field)]),field(Line,[Record,Field],Type)
      Type) :-
              check_expr(R,Record,T),
              check_field_ref(Line,T,Field,Type).


/* Check dyadic operations */
check_op2(_,Op,T1,T2,Type) :- op2(Op,T1,T2,Type), !.
check_op2(Line,Op,_,_,integer) :-          /* Print error message */
              err(Line,'type clash at operator',Op).
/* Check field reference */
check_field_ref(Line,record([[Type,Ids]|_]),Field,Type) :-
              member(Field,Ids),!.
```

```
check_field_ref(Line,record([_|R]),Field,Type) :-
            check_field_ref(Line,record(R),Field,Type).
check_field_ref(Line,_,Field,integer) :-
            err(Line,'invalid field reference:',Field).


/* op2(Op, Left_type, Right_type, Result_type) is a table of valid */
/* operand types for each operator */
op2('+',integer,integer,integer).
op2('+',integer,real,real).
....
op2('<',integer,integer,boolean).
....
```

The output of this pass is a *typed* parse tree, which contains the type of each expression as the third argument in the term. This pass also outputs the symbol table as a series of facts, one for each declared variable.

For example, the semantic check pass will produce the following typed parse tree and symbol table entries given the parse tree of section 4.4.4:

```
if(5,[
    op2(5,['>',id(5,a,real),id(5,b,real)],boolean),
    assignment(6,[field(6,[id(6,c,record([[real,[re,im]]])),
                        re],real),
        op2(6,['+',id(6,a,real),id(6,b,real)],real)
    ]),
    assignment(7,[field(7,[id(7,c,record([[real,[re,im]]])),
                        im],real),
        op2(7,['*',const(7,'2.0',real),
            fcall(7,[sin,[id(7,a,real)]],real)
        ],real)
    ])
])
...
var(a,real).
var(b,real).
var(c,real).
```

4.4.6 Parallelizer Pass

This is the heart of the PPPC and the most complex part in the implementation. It reads a typed parse tree, extracts its parallelism using global data flow analysis and generates a typed parse tree of an equivalent explicitly parallel program. This pass contains six phases, which are executed in a sequential order: statement labeling, global data flow analysis, parallel loop detection, run time prediction, code transformation and cleanup.

Statement Labeling Phase This phase assigns a unique label to each statement in the parse tree. The statement label is a list of integers. It is used in the global data flow analysis. The label is built hierarchically, so that the label assigned to a compound statement is the prefix of all statement labels inside that compound statement. This property of the statement labels allows efficient tests of nesting/inclusion relationships between statement labels.

For example, consider the following code fragment. If the statement label of the **for** loop is l, then the labels of the internal statements will be as follows:

```
[1]          for i := 1 to N do
             begin
[1,1]           x := y/z;
[1,2]           if x > w then
[1,2,1]            y := x
[1,2,2]         else z := x
             end
```

Global Data Flow Analysis Phase This phase implements the iterative solution of *reaching definitions* equations described in [ASU86, chapter 10.5]. It collects all possible dependencies between statements which set (define) the value of a variable and the statements which reference that value. This data flow information is stored as a sequence of facts, one for each define/use statements pair. These facts look like:

reach(*variable_name, defining_statement_label, using_statement_label*).

For example, a part of the data flow information for the program excerpt of section 4.4.6 is as follows. Note that several dependencies are caused by passing variable values between iterations.

```
reach(x,[1,1],[1,2]).
reach(x,[1,1],[1,2,1]).
reach(x,[1,1],[1,2,2]).
reach(y,[1,2,1],[1,1]).
reach(z,[1,2,2],[1,1]).
```

Parallel Loop Detection Phase This phase marks all parallel loops based on the global data flow data. It performs a bottom up traversal of the parse tree and accumulates variable access information for each statement. The variable access pattern information is described by four lists: a list of all variables referenced in the statement, a list of variables changed in the statement, a list of variables changed by an associative operation of the form *var := var op exp*, where *op* is one of the associative operations of section 4.3.3, and a list of arrays referenced or changed in the statement. A variable may appear in the associative variables list only if it is not referenced or changed by any other statement in the same program block. Array references and changes are recorded both in the appropriate variable reference/change list and in the array reference list.

The information of a compound statement is computed by merging the information from its constituent statements. The merger of the associative variables lists may remove a variable if this variable is changed by different associative operators or if it is referenced or changed in the other statement.

The determination of parallel loops is based on the variable access pattern information. All of the variables referenced or changed in the loop must belong to one of the categories of section 4.3.3.

The code of the parallel loop determination is especially concise and clear, because it uses Prolog implicit backtracking. For example, the predicate *is_local/2* for checking a local variable is as follows:

```
is_local(V,L) :- /* Check if variable V is local in loop L */
  /* Variable set inside the loop */
  reach(V,S1,_),prefix(L,S1),
  /* Never use a value defined outside from inside the loop */
  not((reach(V,S2,U2),prefix(L,U2),not(prefix(Loop,S2)))),
  /* Never use a value defined inside the loop on the outside */
  not((reach(V,S3,U3),prefix(L,S3),not(prefix(L,U3)))),
  /* Never use a value defined in a previous iteration, */
  /* meaning that the use statement preceeds the definition */
  not((reach(V,S4,U4),prefix(L,S4),prefix(L,U4),not(before(S4,U4)))).
```

The predicates *prefix/2* and *before/2* are defined as expected on lists of numbers.

For example, consider the code excerpt of section 4.4.6, when the value of **x** is not
used outside loop [1]. In this case, the call is_local(x,[1]) succeeds, because all
three **reach** facts generated for **x** in the loop [1] obey the condition:

```
reach(x, S, U), before(S, U)
```

The variables **y** and **z** fail this condition.

Run Time Prediction   This phase computes the anticipated execution time of
the program using the algorithm of section 4.3.4. It performs one bottom up traversal of the parse tree to compute the serial and parallel run time along the way. The
run time of **for** loops is stored in facts for later use.

The run time prediction uses the target *cost table*, containing the relative cost
(execution time) of operations on the target machine. For example, a part of the
cost table for MMX[Gab88] multiprocessor is:

```
/* cost_op2(Operator, Left_operand_type, Right_operand_type, Cost) */
/* is the cost of Dyadic Operators */
cost_op2('+',integer,integer,1).
cost_op2('+',real,real,5).
cost_op2(and,boolean,boolean,1).

/* cost_op1(Operator, Operand_type, Cost) is the cost of Monadic */
/* Operators */
cost_op1('+',integer,0).
cost_op1('-',integer,1).
cost_op1('-',real,1).

/* Cost of Standard Functions */
cost_func(odd,10).
cost_func(sqrt,80).
cost_func(succ,1).
cost_func(sin,80).
```

The following code fragment contains the definition of the *cost_expr/2* predicate,
which computes the cost (execution time) of an expression.

```
/* cost_expr(Exp,Cost) computes the cost of the expression Exp */
cost_expr(id(_,_,_),0) :- !.
cost_expr(string(_,_,_),0) :- !.
cost_expr(const(_,_,_),0) :- !.
cost_expr(op2(_,[Op,L,R],_),Time) :- !,      /* Dyadic operations */
        cost_expr(L,Ltime),
        cost_expr(R,Rtime),
        arg(3,L,Ltype),
        arg(3,R,Rtype),
        cost_op2(Op,Ltype,Rtype,Otime),
        Time is Ltime+Rtime+Otime.
cost_expr(op1(_,[Op,L],Type),Time) :-        /* Monadic operations */
        cost_op1(Op,Type,Otime), !,
        cost_expr(L,Ltime),
        Time is Otime+Ltime.
cost_expr(index(_,[V,Ilist],_),Time) :- !, /* Array index */
        cost_expr(V,T1), !,
        cost_expr_list(Ilist,T1,Time).
cost_expr(field(_,[V,_],_),Time) :- !,       /* Record field */
        cost_expr(V,Time).
cost_expr(fcall(_,[Func,Args],_),Time) :-  /* Function call */
        cost_func(Func,Ctime),!,
        cost_expr_list(Args,Ctime,Time).

/* Compute cost of a parameter list. Add 1 cost unit to each */
/* parameter for pushing it onto the stack */
cost_expr_list([ ],T,T) :- !.
cost_expr_list([E|L],In,Time) :-
        cost_expr(E,T1), T2 is T1+1+In, !,
        cost_expr_list(L,T2,Time).
```

Code Transformation Phase   This phase locates the outermost *replicated loop* containing a parallel loop, so that the predicted parallel execution time of the replicated loop (including crowd creation/termination overhead) is less than the serial execution time. Such replicated loops are transformed into a crowd handling code, which is described in section 4.3.5. The replicated loop code is moved into the body of the crowd process. The parallel loops inside the replicated loop are modified to allow work distribution and sharing of results.

Cleanup Phase This phase removes the statement label information from the parse tree and eliminates superfluous variable declarations. Its output is a typed parse tree with the same format as the the output of the semantic check pass, so that the parallelizer pass may be omitted if desired.

4.4.7 Code Generation Pass

The code generation pass reads a typed parse tree and emits the equivalent C code. This pass performs one top down traversal of the parse tree and emits the C code along the way.

The code generator first produces all **typedef** declarations corresponding to the Pascal type declarations. Then it produces code for the main program and all other procedures. The procedure code starts with a prolog, followed by parameter declarations, variable declarations and the procedure body.

There are three predicates which generate the bulk of the C code: the *type_gen/2* predicate generates the type declarations, the *stmt_gen/2* predicate generates the code for statements and the *expr_gen/2* predicate generates the code for expressions.

Here are some clauses from the *stmt_gen/2* and *expr_gen/2* predicates.

```
stmt_gen(Tabs,if(Line,[Cond,Then,Else])) :-
        tabs_gen(Tabs),               /* Create proper indentation */
        write('if('), expr_gen(Cond,0), write('){'),
        line_gen(Line),               /* Line number comment */
        T1 is Tabs+1,                 /* Next nesting level */
        stmt_gen(T1,Then),
        tabs_gen(Tabs), write('} else {'), nl,
        stmt_gen(T1,Else),
        tabs_gen(Tabs), write('}'), nl.


/* expr_gen(Expr, Parenthesis_required) generates code for the */
/* expression. The code is surrounded by parenthesis if 2nd    */
/* parameter is 1. */
expr_gen(id(_,ID,_),_) :- write(ID).            /* Identifier */
expr_gen(const(_,Int,integer),_) :- write(Int). /* Integer */
....
expr_gen(Exp,1) :-                    /* Force parenthesis */
        write('('), expr_gen(Exp,0), write(')').
expr_gen(op2(_,[Op,L,R],_),0) :-
        expr_gen(L,1), op_gen(Op), expr_gen(R,1).
```

Part	Language	Source lines
front end	YACC+LEX+C	751
semantic check	Prolog	720
parallelizer	Prolog	†2064
code generation	Prolog	431
Total		3966

† expected to grow

Table 4.2: PPPC Components Source Size

...

```
/* op_gen(Operator) writes the equivalent operator in C */
op_gen('=') :- write('==').
op_gen('<>') :- write('!=').
op_gen('mod') :- write('%').
...
op_gen(Op) :- write(Op).   /* Default */

/* Generate a comment containing line number */
line_gen(Line) :- write(' /* '), write(Line), write(' */'), nl.
```

4.4.8 PPPC Implementation Statistics

PPPC was developed in 4 man months using a combination of Prolog, YACC[Joh75], LEX[LS75] and C. We expect that further developments will be easy and painless as the result of PPPC modularity and the use of Prolog. Table 4.2 describes the source size of the different parts of the PPPC.

PPPC execution times are rather slow, mainly because of the C-Prolog[Per84] interpreter we are using. We expect at least a factor of 3 improvement in execution time when we will use a Prolog compiler.

Table 4.3 contains the CPU consumption (user + system) of PPPC compilations on a CMOS IBM RT workstation. The CPU consumption is given for two application programs, **Pi** and **CG**. **Pi** is a simple program of 22 source lines and one parallel loop, **CG** is a complex program of 176 source lines with many parallel loops. All timing measurements are in seconds.

Part	Pi		CG	
	CPU	% of total	CPU	% of total
front end	0.1s	1.6%	1.1s	1.4%
semantic check	1.1s	17.2%	11.7s	15.0%
parallelizer	3.1s	48.4%	49.7s	63.5%
code generation	2.1s	32.8%	15.7s	20.1%
Total	6.4s	100%	78.2s	100%

Table 4.3: PPPC Compilation Time

4.5   Prolog as an Implementation Language

The Prolog language provides many advantages over procedural high level programming languages (e.g. C, Pascal) for writing prototype compilers and code transformation tools. The most important advantages we identified during the development of PPPC were:

- The Prolog unification mechanism offers a powerful pattern matching capability, which shortens the code considerably.

- Prolog programs access both facts and rules in the same way, so it is easy to compute some function by a combination of facts and rules. For example, a collection of facts may replace a complex rule during the development.

- Implicit backtracking and meta operations (e.g. *bag_of*) simplify the code for complex tests involving many inter-dependent factors.

- Prolog failure mechanism allows a routine to return an indication of an exceptional condition without the need for a special parameter and eliminates explicit tests for this condition.

- The dynamic typing shortens program code and supports *polymorphic* routines, which accept input of several types. For example, a single routine for calculating list length may be applied to a list of integers, a list of atoms, a list of lists, etc.

- Prolog provides built-in operations for reading and writing complex nested data structures to/from text files. These operations simplify the data transfer between components of a large system. For example, the data is transferred from one PPPC pass to the next by a single *write* or a simple output routine. A single *consult* reads the data in the next pass.

- Prolog interpreter allows quick fixes to the code and shortens program development cycle.

- Prolog contains powerful debugging facilities, which shorten debugging time.

Note: The last four services are supported also by other symbolic programming languages, such as Lisp.

We estimate that the Prolog implementation is about one third of the size of an equivalent compiler written in C with YACC and LEX. This estimate is based on an Ada subset compiler written by the author, which is comparable in complexity to PPPC, and requires about 12,000 source lines.

The only disadvantage we found in Prolog is the slow execution time (see table 4.3). This is the result of the inherent inefficiency of the C-Prolog interpreter. An optimizing Prolog compiler is expected to reduce the execution time substantially, so the execution time of Prolog programs will be closer to compiled languages such as C and Pascal.

4.6 Future Research

Future research in PPPC will concentrate on the following topics:

- Expand the TAU–Pascal language to improve support of regular grids, multigrids, irregular grids and data structures needed by physics particle simulations.

- Improve parallelization algorithms. Handle parallelization of grid access and row/column matrix operations.

- Port PPPC to a message passing multiprocessor.

4.7 Summary and Conclusions

PPPC is a research compiler written mostly in Prolog, which converts serial programs to a highly efficient parallel code. Our experience indicates that the Prolog language is well suited for developing similar research compilers. We found that we can easily express in Prolog the data structures and data manipulations natural to our problem. The Prolog code is significantly shorter, clearer and easier for experimentation than an equivalent code in a conventional high level language.

Chapter 5

ProMiX: a Prolog Partial Evaluation System

Arun Lakhotia[1] and Leon Sterling

Department of Computer Engineering and Science
Case Western Reserve University
Cleveland, OH 44106, USA
E-Mail: arun@cacs.usl.edu, leon@alpha.ces.cwru.edu

Abstract

ProMiX is a partial evaluation system for "full" Prolog. It is decomposed into three main modules: *kernel*, *driver*, and *knowledge base*. The kernel provides the partial evaluation engine. The other two modules "drive" and "control" this engine. The paper discusses the problems associated with each module and presents the solutions adopted in the system. The driver module and control knowledge are designed for using ProMiX as a compiler by specializing interpreters.

5.1 Introduction

Partial evaluation is now a well researched subject in the logic and functional programming research community. It is of interest to the Prolog world because it offers a practical solution to reduce the meta-level overhead in meta-programming. This is crucial in making meta-programming a viable method of programming for production quality programs.

In recent years several researchers have reported partial evaluation of complete Prolog. They have cited the problems in partially evaluating Prolog programs with cuts, extra-logical predicates, side-effecting predicates, and in terminating recursion. The solutions announced in the literature have mostly presented the abstract details without giving the implementation details.

---

[1] Current address: Center for Advanced Computer Studies, Lafayette, LA 70504

```
% solve(Goal)
solve(true):-!.
solve((GoalA,GoalB)) :-!,
   solve(GoalA),
   solve(GoalB).
solve(Head) :-
   clause(Head, Body),
   solve(Body).
```

Figure 5.1: Interpreter for Pure Prolog

What remains now is bringing this technology to common use. Towards this end this paper describes the architecture of ProMiX a partial evaluation system for "full" Prolog. It also describes the systematic development of its important components. To convert a concept into a general purpose tool requires some engineering. The engineering issues involved in developing a practical partial evaluation system are also introduced in this paper. Since ProMiX was developed by the authors to aid in specializing meta-interpreters, the solutions presented are engineered for that purpose. A complete copy of the code is available from the authors both in machine readable form and as a technical report [Lak89].

It is assumed that the reader is familiar with the basic concepts of partial evaluation and its potential use in reducing meta-level overhead. These issues are covered very well in the literature, hence the effort is not duplicated here.

5.2   The Principle of Partial Evaluation

The notion of partial evaluation is very simple. In the context of functional programming languages it is formulated as follows: Suppose there is a function F with parameters $x_1, x_2, \ldots, x_n$. If the values of some of its parameters are known, say $x_1 = a_1, \ldots, x_k = a_k$, where $a_1, \ldots, a_k$ are constants, then a specialized version F' of F may be generated such that

$$F(a_1, \ldots, a_k, x_{k+1}, \ldots, x_n) = F'(x_{k+1}, \ldots, x_n)$$

for all values of x_j, $j = k+1, \ldots, n$. In recursive function theory this is known as Kleene's S-m-n theorem.

In the context of a logic programming language with pure Horn clauses partial evaluation may be stated as follows. Given a program P and a goal G, the result of partially evaluating P with respect to the goal G is the program P' such that for any substitution θ $G.\theta$ has the same (correct and computed) answers with respect to P and P'. The intention is to produce a P' on which $G.\theta$ runs more efficiently than on P.

Program P', the result of partial evaluation of P with respect to a goal G is called the *residue*. It is generated by constructing the "partial" search trees for P and suitably chosen atoms as goals, and then extracting P' from the definitions associated with the leaves of these trees.

The interesting results in partially evaluating interpreters written in Prolog are summarized as follows.

Let I be an interpreter for some language L in Prolog and P be a program in language L. Let $I(P)(D)$ denote the interpretation of P by I with some data D. The result of specializing the interpreter I with respect to P is a Prolog program P' such that $P'(D)$ has the same (correct and computed) answers as $I(P)(D)$.

The generation of P' from $I(P)$ is called "*specialization* of the interpreter I" since P' is a Prolog program specialized to perform some aspects of the interpreter I. It is also called "*compiling* the program P" because P, a program in language L, is translated to an 'equivalent' Prolog program. In the example that follows, the interpreter and the program are both written in Prolog, hence the compilation effect is not very obvious.

5.3   Example

Consider the Prolog program *count* in Figure 5.2. It performs a depth-first left-to-right execution of pure Prolog programs. The relation count(Goal, Count) gives Count the number of reductions made to resolve a Prolog goal Goal. It is a variant of the four clause meta-interpreter commonly found in the literature. Modifications have been made to keep it simple, self-applicable, and executable on contemporary Prolog systems without errors.

Now consider the program *should_take* of Figure 5.3. It is a fragment of a simple medical expert system taken from [TF86]. Patient information is provided to this expert system as a set of facts *complains_of/2*.

The following is a sample session with this expert system and the count interpreter.

```
count(true,0).
count((GoalA,GoalB), Count) :-
   count(GoalA, CountA),
   count(GoalB, CountB),
   Count is CountA + CountB.
count(Goal,0) :-
   sys(Goal),
   call(Goal).
count(Head, Count) :-
   unfold_clause(Head, Body),
   count(Body, CountBody),
   Count is CountBody+1.
```

Figure 5.2: *count* - a Prolog Interpreter to Count Reductions

```
should_take(Person, Medicine) :-
   complains_of(Person, Symptom),
   suppresses(Medicine, Symptom).

suppresses(aspirin, pain).        suppresses(lomotil, diarrhea).
complains_of(john, pain).         complains_of(sue, diarrhea).
```

Figure 5.3: *should_take* - A Rudimentary Medical Expert System

```
| ?- should_take(sue, Y).
Y = lomotil ? ;
no

| ?- count(should_take(sue, Y), C).
C = 3,   Y = lomotil ? ;
no

| ?- count(count(should_take(sue, Y), C1), C2).
C1 = 3,  C2 = 6,    Y = lomotil ? ;
no
```

The expert system makes 3 reductions to solve the goal should_take(sue, Y).
The interpreter itself requires 6 reductions to count these reductions. This is twice
the number of reductions made by the expert system. If queries for counting reductions of *should_take* are made routinely, but with varying parameters, it may
be worthwhile partially evaluating the execution of count(should_take(X,Y), C)
and evaluating only the residue during actual operation.

The residue obtained from partial evaluation varies depending upon when the
unfolding is stopped. When partially evaluating count(should_take(X,Y), C)
the goal may be exhaustively evaluated giving the residue:

```
count(should_take(sue,lomotil), 6).
count(should_take(john,aspirin), 6).
```

or the unfolding may be terminated using the strategy discussed later in Section 5.10
giving the residue in Figure 5.4.
This program may be transformed further to the one in Figure 5.5 by replacing all
count(Goal, Count) goals using the following rewrite rules:

```
count(suppresses(A,B), C)      → suppresses(A, B, C).
count(complains_of(A,B), C)    → complains_of(A, B, C).
count(should_take(A,B), C)     → should_take(A, B, C).
```

The programs in Figure 5.4 and 5.5 are equivalent in the sense that if
Goal → NewGoal holds and Goal succeeds for the program in Figure 5.4 then

```
count(should_take(Person,Medicine), Count) :-
   count(complains_of(Person,Symptom), Count0),
   count(suppresses(Medicine,Symptom), Count1),
   ICount is Count0 + Count1,
   Count is ICount + 1.

count(suppresses(aspirin,pain),1).
count(suppresses(lomotil,diarrhea),1).
count(complains_of(john,pain),1).
count(complains_of(sue,diarrhea),1).
```

Figure 5.4: Result of Compiling *count* with respect to *should_take*

NewGoal succeeds for the one in Figure 5.5 and returns the same answers, and *vice versa*. The answers returned by:

```
| ?- should_take(sue, Y, C).
C = 3,      Y = lomotil ? ;
no
```

are equivalent to the answers for count(should_take(sue, Y), C), as shown before.

The program of Figure 5.5 is however more efficient than the one it is transformed from. The reasons are discussed in the next section.

5.4   Issues in Partial Evaluation

It is our intent to develop a system that is specifically suitable for partially evaluating interpeters written in Prolog with respect to a given object program. The process effectively compiles object programs interpreted by the interpreter into Prolog. This is also called specializing interpreters. The example above demonstrates the various stages in a typical specialization application.

The problem of developing such a system may be decomposed into the following subproblems.

```
should_take(Person, Medicine, Count) :-
   complains_of(Person, Symptom, CountA),
   suppresses(Medicine, Symptom, CountB),
   ICount is CountA + CountB,
   Count is ICount + 1.

suppresses(aspirin, pain, 1).   suppresses(lomotil, diarrhea, 1).
complains_of(john, pain, 1).    complains_of(sue, diarrhea, 1).
```

Figure 5.5: Result of Transforming residue

- How to generate residues for a goal?
- How to control unfolding?
- How to collect residues to get a correct and compiled program?
- How to rewrite the residues to achieve greater efficiency?

These subproblems provide the basis for decomposing a partial evaluation system. Though the questions are suitable for any general purpose partial evaluation system, the corresponding software components in ProMiX are engineered for the purpose of specializing interpreters. The following text discusses these issues.

5.4.1 Generating Residues

The clause in Figure 5.4

```
count(should_take(Person,Symptom), Count) :-
   count(complains_of(Person,Symptom), Count0),
   count(suppresses(Medicine,Symptom), Count1),
   ICount is Count0 + Count1,
   Count is ICount + 1.
```

is a residue for the goal count(should_take(Person,Symptom), Count).
   Creation of residues is an issue central to the partial evaluation problem. The complete program in Figure 5.4 is a collection of residue clauses.

5.4.2 Controlling Unfolding

As was illustrated in the example above, the result of partial evaluation is not unique. On one extreme a goal may be completely evaluated, on the other it may be left as it is. The latter case is redundant as it doesn't achieve anything. Whereas complete evaluation of any goal for a pure logic program returns a set of all the true relations for that goal, assuming the evaluation terminates successfully.

Due to the functional and extra-logical predicates in practical Prolog programs it may not always be possible to exhaustively evaluate a goal with incomplete inputs. Besides, partial input may also lead to infinite computation for recursive programs or a combinatorial explosion of residues.

The termination of partial evaluation may be guaranteed by terminating the unfolding process before entering an infinite loop or on detection of one. A general criterion that detects whether any computation would terminate can never be correct. Such a criterion would solve the halting problem for Prolog programs, and hence for Turing machines. It is however possible to develop a specialized set of criteria specific to an interpreter.

Control of unfolding is also important in the presence of predicates with side-effects, for example *write/1*, and *assert/1*. Such predicates should be detected and suspended during partial evaluation. They can only be evaluated at runtime.

5.4.3   Collecting Residues

The residue from partial evaluation of the goal

```
count(should_take(Person,Symptom), Count)
```

given the program in Figure 5.2 and 5.3 consists only of the first clause of Figure 5.4. The goals such as `count(complains_of(Person,Symptom), Count0)` retained in the residue still require the interpreter and the object program for further evaluation. To remove the need for interpretation completely these goals may be partially evaluated too. The program consisting of the collection of such residues can potentially be executed without the interpreter or the object program.

We say 'potentially' because there are several situations where an interpreter goal cannot be partially evaluated and would need the interpreter for evaluation at runtime. Besides the residue, definition of support procedures used by the interpreter but not evaluated during specialization may also be needed by the compiled program.

5.4.4   Rewriting Goals

The program in Figure 5.4 is a result of partially evaluating the interpreter goal `count(Goal, Count)` with `Goal` instantiated to different procedures of the object program. As it is the result of partial evaluation of *count/2* goals, all the clauses of the resultant program have *count/2* as their head goal. Such programs where all clauses of the residue belong to just one procedure is common while specializing interpreters.

The program in Figure 5.5 is a translation of the above program. The translation defines a mapping between the goals of the two programs such that the computed answers of two mapped goals is the same. Rewriting splits the second program into small procedures. This buys an extra level of indexing in the transformed program. The translated program is therefore more efficient than the original program.

The issue of translating programs as from Figure 5.4 to Figure 5.5 is not necessary for partial evaluation. But the additional efficiency achieved is important when specializing interpreters. It also makes the residue more readable which may be helpful if the residue is to be processed by a human being.

5.5   System Architecture

The ProMiX system consists of three major subcomponents. They are decomposed around the subproblems stated in the previous section and have the following responsibilities.

Kernel : generate and rewrite residues for individual goals.

Driver : provide the user interface, drive the kernel, and collect residues.

Knowledge Base : maintain unfolding and rewrite rules.

The kernel is responsible for generating the residue for one interpreter goal. It is driven by the driver for partially evaluating different goals the collection of whose residues form the final program. The task of generating a residual clause requires collecting the subgoals whose evaluation may be suspended and translating the residue goals into more efficient forms. These two activities may be further separated to be performed by separate program components: *mix* and *rewrite*. *Mix* generates the residue in terms of the interpreter goal, *rewrite* translates these interpreter goals to a more efficient form.

5.6   Mix

Most research in partial evaluation of Prolog has focussed on developing *mix*. This component forms the core of any partial evaluator as the correctness of the transformation rests largely on the functional equivalence of the residue generated with

```
% mix(Goal, Residue)
mix(true, true) :-!.
mix((GoalA,GoalB), (MixA,MixB)) :-!,
   mix(GoalA, MixA),
   mix(GoalB, MixB).
mix(Head, Mix) :-
   should_unfold(Head),!,
   unfold_clause(Head, Body),
   mix(Body, Mix).
mix(Goal, Goal).
```

Figure 5.6: Mix Kernel for Pure Prolog

respect to the original goal. The task involved in doing so is not specific to specialization of interpreters. Thus *mix* is a generic component suitable for any partial evaluator.

When the input consists of "pure" Prolog *mix* can be derived from a meta-interpreter for "pure" Prolog. Figure 5.1 contains the interpreter from which the partial evaluator of Figure 5.6 is derived. The derivation from *solve/1* to *mix/2* is obvious.

In the relation mix(Goal, Residue), Residue is a sequence of goals suspended during the evaluation of Goal. A goal X is unfolded if the rule should_unfold(X) succeeds, otherwise it is suspended. The criteria for unfolding rules are developed in Section 5.10.

This would be sufficient if Prolog were truly logical, but it has side-effect predicates, extra-logical predicates, and the cut. These lead to several interesting problems that should be tackled by the partial evaluator.

The relation between an interpreter and *mix* of "pure" Prolog may be extrapolated to that for "full" Prolog. The extrapolation is not intuitive and needs explanation. As mentioned, complete versions of the code are available from the authors in machine-readable form or as a technical report [Lak89].

The extensions from "pure" to "full" Prolog involves adding 1) control constructs, 2) extra-logical predicates, and 3) side-effecting predicates. The problems associated with partially evaluating programs in the presence of side-effecting and extra-

logical predicates have been studied by Venken [Ven84, VD88]. He classifies the
problems as

- *backward unification*, and
- *multiple clauses* problems.

The problems are described here along with their solutions.

The control constructs and predicates added to "full" Prolog may be classified
as

- *cut*
- *all solutions predicates*
- *additional control constructs*.

Partial evaluation of these is discussed in reverse order. The discussion is deferred
until after *backward unification* and *multiple clauses* since the code developed to
solve these two problems is also useful in processing the additional constructs and
all solutions predicates. Other than the control constructs there are several system
primitives in Prolog. These primitives may be specialized by explictly providing
their definition in Prolog. This is discussed under the heading:

- *reifying system primitives*

Backward Unification   A goal is unfolded by replacing it with the body of a
clause whose head unifies with it. The bindings due to this unification propagate
backward and forward through a program. Forward propagation is useful during
partial evaluation as it helps narrow the options for predicates evaluated later.
Backward propagation is not helpful at compile time. It instead leads to problems
if the bindings are propagated to variables of the preceding extra-logical or side-
effects predicates.

For instance, unfolding only `ilike(X)` in the query

```
?- fruit(X), write('Hello World'), ilike(X), ...
```

with respect to the program

```
fruit(orange).    fruit(apple).    ilike(apple).
```

would result in

```
?- fruit(apple), write('Hello World'), ...
```

The run-time behavior of the two queries are not equivalent. The first one writes "Hello World" twice, whereas the second does so only once.

The problem arises because backward unification propagates the value of X to the goal fruit(X). In the original query the predicate fruit(X) works as a 'generator'; it generates multiple solutions on backtracking. It is converted to a 'tester' due to backward unification; it succeeds only once. This change in behavior affects the number of times *write/1* is performed since it appears after *fruit/1*.

A correct transformation for the above query would be:

```
?- fruit(X), write('Hello World'), X = apple, ...
```

where unifications due to unfolding ilike(X) have been converted into runtime unifications. It may be noted however that occurences of X after the goal ilike(X) may still be unified to apple without affecting the query.

A similar problem arises with extra-logical predicates, such as *var/1*. A goal var(X) whose argument X is not bound during partial evaluation may not be unfolded because when the complete data is given X may actually be bound. Such a goal should thus be left in the residue. The variable X should also be guarded against possible binding due to backward propagation of values.

For example, the unfolding of ilike(X) from the previous example in the clause

```
p(X):- var(X), ilike(X), ...
```

would give:

```
p(apple) :- var(apple), ...
```

This clause would always fail. A correct result would be

```
p(X) :- var(X), X = apple, ...
```

The above behavior may be reflected in the *mix* code of Figure 5.6 by including the following as its second clause.

```
mix((X,Y), (MixX, MixY)) :-
   (side_effect(X); extra_logical(X)),!,
   mix(X, MixX),
   mix_copy(Y, MixY).
```

where *mix_copy/2* generates the residue for a copy of Y. The residue is preceded
by a sequence of unification goals for binding the variables in Y to its copy. The
unifications are performed at runtime.

```
mix_copy(X, (Unifs,MixX)) :-
   copy(X, CopyX),
   variables_in(X, XVars),
   variables_in(CopyX, CopyVars),
   mix(CopyX, MixX),
   generate_unifications(XVars, CopyVars, Unifs).
```

The predicate CopyX is a term identical to X but for variable renaming; it does
not use variables that have already appeared in the program. XVars and CopyVars
are the lists of variables in X and CopyX, respectively, such that the ith element in
XVars is a variable that is replaced by the variable at the ith position in CopyVars.
The binding of variables due to partial evaluation of CopyX is reflected in the list
CopyVars. The bindings in this list along with XVars are used to generate a sequence of unifications between variables in XVars with their corresponding element
in CopyVars. This sequence becomes part of the residue and precedes the residue
from CopyX. The code for *variables_in/2* and *copy/2* is straightforward. The code
for *generate_unifications/2* is as follows:

```
generate_unifications([ ], [ ], true).
generate_unifications([Var|XVars], [CopyVar|CVars], TUnifs) :-
   var(CopyVar), !,
   Var = CopyVar,
   generate_unifications(XVars, CVars, TUnifs).
generate_unifications([Var|XVars], [CopyVar|CVars], Unifs) :-
   generate_unifications(XVars, CVars, TUnifs),
   merge_unifications((Var = CopyVar), TUnifs).
```

```
merge_unifications(Unif, true, Unifs) :-!.
merge_unifications(Unif, Unifs, (Unif, Unifs)).
```

The relations **side_effect(X)** and **extra_logical(X)** guide the partial evaluation. They are provided as a set of declarations, like:

```
side_effect(write(_)).
side_effect(assert(_)).
side_effect(X) :- var(X).
extra_logical(var(X)) :- var(X).
extra_logical(nonvar(X)) :- var(X).
```

A variable goal **X** that is not instantiated at compile time is classified as a *side-effect* since it could potentially be bound to a side-effecting predicate at runtime.

The above properties are not limited to system primitives. They may be propagated to user-defined procedures that use these system predicates. It is for this reason that in the *mix/2* clause above a goal is partially evaluated even though it is extra-logical or generates a side-effect.

The declaration of system primitives with side-effects or extra-logical behavior and the rules to propagate these properties to user-defined predicates are maintained by the *knowledge base* module of the system. It is described in Section 5.9.

Multiple Clauses   Another interesting problem arises when unfolding goals that have multiple residues. Normally separate residue clauses (or goals) may be generated for every residue of the predicate. For instance, consider the program

```
vegetable(X) :- P, fruit(X).

fruit(orange).    fruit(apple).
```

where P is some sequence of predicates. Unfolding **fruit(X)** in **vegetable/1** we get:

```
vegetable(orange) :- P'.
vegetable(apple) :- P''.
```

where P' and P" are derived by applying the corresponding substitutions for X to
P.

Now if P causes a side-effect, the query

```
?- vegetable(X).
```

would perform the side-effect twice in the residual program, and only once in the
original program. On the other hand the extra-logical predicates contained in P
may use the variable X. The unfolding of fruit(X) propagates the bindings to X
backwards thereby splitting the original clause in two. In the presence of extra-
logical or side-effecting predicates in P this raises the question of correctness of the
transformation. In the absence of such predicates in P correctness is not a problem;
there is however another problem. Splitting of the original clause may sometimes
degrade the performance even though it preserves the behavior. This happens when
P has predicates that perform some expensive operation. The residual program
generated due to splitting the clause would perform such an operation multiple
times thereby becoming less efficient.

A solution to all these problems is to expand the multiple residue as a sequence
of disjunctions in the same clause, such as:

```
vegetable(X) :- P, (X = orange; X = apple).
```

Here (X = orange; X = apple) represents the 'bag of all residues' from partially
evaluating the goal fruit(X). This behavior can be accomplished by adding to the
kernel of Figure 5.6 the clause:

```
mix((X,Y), (MixX,MixY)) :-
    (side_effect(X); extra_logical(X)),!,
    mix(X, MixX),
    mix_bag(Y, MixY).
```

in place of the clause added to solve the backward unification problem. The procedure mix_bag(Y, MixY) computes MixY a 'bag of all the residues' of Y. The 'bag'
is represented as a sequence of disjunctions with the elements of this sequence
corresponding to the residues for the goal Y

A first attempt at defining *mix_bag/2* is:

```
mix_bag(Goals, Residue) :-
   findall(R, mix(Goals, R), AllR),
   bag_from_list(AllR, Residue).
```

The *findall/3* returns a 'list' of all residues for Goal. This list is then converted to a 'bag'. An empty list translates to a bag with just *fail*.

The above clause demonstrates the important idea behind *mix_bag/2*; it is however incorrect. The all solution predicate *findall/3* works on a copy of the goal. It returns the solution in terms of a fresh set of variables. Hence, the solutions returned by *findall/3* do not use the variables in Goals. This makes it impossible to relate the solutions in the residue with the variables used in the original program.

With this definition of *mix_bag/2* partially evaluating the previous example would give:

```
vegetable(X) :- P, (_142 = orange; _342 = apple).
```

where _142 and _342 are arbitrary variables. In a correct residue these variables should be replaced by X. This may be done by unifying these variables with X. Note only the variables generated corresponding to the variable X from the original goal should be unified with X. This should be done for each solution returned by *findall/3*. The unifications generated in the bag, such as _142=orange, are not performed at compile time. Doing that would propagate values across different branches of the disjunction which is undesirable.

This logic is incorporated by the following definition of *mix_bag/2*.

```
mix_bag(Goals, Residue) :-
   variables_in(Goals, Vars),
   findall((R,Vars), (nonvar(Vars), mix(Goals, R)), AllR),
   generate_unifications_for_bag(AllR, Vars, ResidueList),
   bag_from_list(Residue, ResidueList).
```

The *findall/3* goal returns a list of pairs. The first element of each pair is a residue from partially evaluating Goals. The residue uses a fresh set of variables in place of variables used in the goal. The second element returns the bindings made in the residue to these fresh variables. The bindings are generated by passing **Vars** the list of variables in the **Goals** along with the *mix/2* goal. When variables in

Goals are renamed the renaming is reflected in this list. The predicate *nonvar/2* is used only to carry the list of variables; it always succeeds.

The predicate *generate_unifications_for_bag/3* uses Vars and the list of bindings for variables in the residue to generate a sequence of unifications for all the solutions returned by *findall/3*.

Control Constructs "Full" Prolog consists of several control predicates besides conjunction. Some of those are *not/1*, *';'/2* (disjunction), and *'→'/2* (if-then-else). The kernel of Figure 5.6 partially evaluates only goals connected by conjunctions. For a practical system the other predicates need to be taken care of as well.

The problems in partially evaluating these control predicates are similar to that in partially evaluating conjunctive goals containing side-effect predicates and that in generating multiple residues. Their residue cannot be split in clauses. Also the bindings due to computing the residues should not be propagated to the rest of the clause unless it is commited to be on the path of evaluation. The latter is possible when there is only one such path and only one residue. Should such an opportunity arise, it should be availed in the spirit of partial evaluation.

When a goal is completely evaluable the result of its evaluation may be used for making control decisions. For instance, in A→B;C if A is completely evaluable the success or failure of its evaluation may be used for committing to B or C, respectively, during partial evaluation. Otherwise B and C may be partially evaluated but not committed to.

The bag of residues is completely evaluable if it contains only one residue and that, besides the sequence of unifications generated internally, is either *true* or *fail*. Such a residue may be completely evaluated. If the bag contains only one residue but it is neither *true* nor *fail* then it is not fully evaluable. However, because there is only one residue the unifications generated in the bag may be performed at compile time. When a bag has multiple residues this cannot be done.

The predicate *mix_bag_eval/2* encodes this logic to evaluate the residue as much as possible.

```
mix_bag_eval(Goal, Residue) :-
    mix_bag(Goal, MixGoal),
    determinate_bag(MixGoal, Residue).

determinate_bag(fail, _Residue) :- !, fail.
determinate_bag((Unifs,Residue), Residue) :- !, call(Unifs).
determinate_bag(Residue, Residue).
```

All Solutions Predicates The *findall/3* predicate used in *mix_bag/3* provides
another interesting case for partial evaluation. The residue for partially evaluating

        ?- findall(X, fruit(X), Y).

with respect to the program

fruit(orange).   fruit(apple).

should be:

        ?- Y = [orange, apple].

Here the *findall/3* goal has been completely evaluated. However, partially evaluating

        ?- findall((X,Y), (fruit(X), p(Y)), Z).

when *p/2* cannot be evaluated at compile time, the residue should be:

        ?- findall((X,Y), (X = orange, p(Y); X = apple, p(Y)), Z).

Such a result can be obtained by performing

mix_bag(Y, MixY), Residue = findall(X, MixY, Z).

for mix(findall(X,Y,Z), Residue) and evaluating the Residue if all the disjunctions in the bag MixY are evaluable at compile time.

Generally speaking a set predicate cannot be fully evaluated at compile time. This is because the set of solutions returned at compile time may be further constrained if the variables of the partially evaluated goal are bound at runtime.

The treatment for *setof/3* and *bagof/3* follows similarly by replacing *findall/3* for the respective predicate. There is a subtle problem. The unfolding of Y introduces new variables in the residue MixY. These variables do not change the set of solutions returned by findall(X, Y, Z) as it is existentially quantified over all variables in Y. For *setof/3* and *bagof/3* the solution should be explicitly quantified over the new variables.

The correct behavior of `mix(bagof(X,Y,Z), Residue)` would be performed by the goals

```
mix_bag(Y, MixY),
extra_variables(MixY, Y, Vars),
Residue = bagof(X, Vars↑MixY, Z).
```

where *extra_variables/3* gives the variables `Vars` that are in `MixY` but not in `Y`.

Cut   The cut in Prolog is perhaps the most widely misused control construct. In most cases it may be done away in favor of the if-then-else construct [O'K85]. But there are cases, such as a cut in disjunction, when it can not be replaced. To partially evaluate "full" Prolog it is necessary for the partial evaluator to handle cut.

The problem in handling cut arises due to its non-local behavior. A clause containing a cut cannot be simply unfolded in the body of a procedure calling it. For instance, unfolding `p(X)` in

```
f(X)  :- ..., p(X).
f(X)  :- q(X).

p(1)  :-!.
p(X)  :- write(X).
```

leaves the residue

```
f(X)  :- ..., (X=1,!; write(X)).
f(X)  :- q(X).
```

The programs are obviously not identical in behavior.

Venken [Ven84] introduced the predicates `mark(_)` and `!(_)` for handling cut. Using the method he proposes the result of unfolding p/1 in the above program would be:

```
f(X)  :- ..., mark(1), (X=1,!(1); write(X)).
f(X)  :- q(X).
```

where **mark(1)** delimits the scope of **!(1)**. Execution of **!(1)** cuts only the choice-point upto **mark(1)** therefore preserving the program's behavior.

As *mark/1* and *!/1* (or their equivalent predicates) are not supported by most Prolog systems this is not a practical solution.

When partially evaluating a program we need to bother only about '!' for which the goals preceding it are not fully evaluable at compile time. In an interpreter cuts are used for committing decisions made on the structure or property of the goal being interpreted. In our experience such usage could be attributed to almost all the cuts in most interpreters. The evaluation of these cuts depends only on the object program and not its data. Since during specialization of an interpreter the object program is specified, these cuts could be compiled away.

For the cuts that remain we collect the goals in the scope of the cut and create a single clause procedure out of it. Variables that are common to the scope and the rest of the clause are chosen as arguments. For the above example this strategy returns the original program as residue.

The code for handling cut is not presented here due to its complexity, but is in the program available from the authors.

Reifying System Primitives   Consider partially evaluating the query

```
?- f(X) = f(Y).
```

A naive but incorrect partial evaluation would simply succeed after unifying variables **X** and **Y**. A correct but non-optimal result would be achieved by leaving the query as it is. The correct and optimal result from partially evaluating the above query would be:

```
?- X = Y.
```

The above result cannot be derived if the partial evaluator depends on the system supported definition of *=/2*. This is because the builtin definition of *=/2* is a unit operation and cannot be decomposed by the partial evaluator. The result can instead be achieved by simulating the behavior of the primitive *=/2* by a Prolog predicate say *unify/2*, and partially evaluating the query as a call to this predicate.

Making implicit behavior of a system explicit is called *reification*. System primitives are treated as unit operations by a naive partial evaluator because they cannot be decomposed. Using the built-in support, system goals arising in the residue may either be evaluated during partial evaluation or left in the residue. To generate efficient residues these primitive may be reified so that they may be evaluated as far as possible.

This can of course be done for only those primitives that can be written in Prolog by using some 'lesser' features of Prolog. Built-in predicates of Prolog that have side-effects cannot be decomposed in this way. There are times when a predicate written using side-effecting predicates can be rewritten using extra-logical features of Prolog. A case in point is the predicate *copy/2*. This predicate is usually defined using *assert/1* and *retract/1* to make copies of variables [SS86].

```
copy(X, Y) :- asserta('$copy'(X)), retract('$copy'(Y)).
```

Now partially evaluating the query

```
?- copy(f(X), Y), p(Y).
```

with the above definition of *copy/2* one gets:

```
?- asserta('$copy'(f(X))), retract('$copy'(Y)), p(Y).
```

This is no more efficient than the initial query. Knowing the behavior of *copy/2* the preferred residue would be:

```
?- copy(X, Z), p(f(Z)).
```

This can generate a more efficient residue because the partially instantiation of the arguments of predicate *p/1* can be used to partially evaluate it further. This result is not achievable using the definition of *copy/2* just presented, but can be achieved with the alternate definition of *copy/2* given in [Lak89].

5.7   Rewrite

The *rewrite* module provides support to translate residue clauses by replacing the 'left over' interpeter goals with new goals as shown in the example in Section 5.3. This activity may not be necessary for general partial evaluation applications. The translations performed by *rewrite* are purely syntactic in nature. The salient features are

   a) translation of "full" Prolog,

   b) use of memoing techniques to remember rewrite relations, and

   c) ease of modification of rewrite rules to suit different applications.

Most of *rewrite*'s code is general enough to be used for syntactic translation of Prolog programs elsewhere. A discussion of its overall logic follows.

Rewrite One Predicate   The procedure *rewrite_rule/2* translates an interpreter goal. Given an interpreter goal `IGoal` with meta-argument `Obj`, `rewrite_rule(IGoal, Pred)` translates it to the term `Pred`. This term's principal functor is the same as the principal functor of `Obj`. Its arguments are generated by concatenating the arguments of `Obj` with the arguments, except the meta-argument, of `IGoal`.

In the interpreter of Figure 5.2 the first argument of *count/2* is its meta-argument. The following query shows the translation of a *count/2* goal taken from the residue in Figure 5.4.

```
?- rewrite_rule(count(should_take(X,Y),C),Z).
Z = should_take(X, Y, C)  ?
```

Only variables relevant to the discussion are shown in the result.

An interpreter goal can be rewritten only if its meta-argument is instantiated. When the meta-argument is a variable the interpreter goal is returned without modification. Example:

```
?- rewrite_rule(count(X,Y), Z).
Z = count(X, Y) ?
```

An interpreter goal is also retained in the residue if there is no residue procedure corresponding to it. This happens when the definition for its meta-argument is inaccessible during partial evaluation.

The definition of a system primitive or a compiled predicate is not accessible. It is also not accessible if the predicate gets defined at runtime. This happens when an object program defines and alters predicates dynamically using *assert* and *retract*. Object program procedures which are provided only during execution are also not accessible.

In all these cases the interpreter goal is retained in the translated program; the interpreter is not compiled away completely. The translated program requires the interpreter during execution to execute the retained interpreter goals.

All decisions made by the procedure *rewrite_rule/2* are easily alterable as they are implemented using separate procedures. The choice of name for a translated procedure, or the order of its arguments, or the decision on when to retain an interpreter goal can be affected by performing changes local to these procedures. This flexibility is acheived at the cost of repeating certain operations across these procedures.

Memoing Rewrite Relations   Interpreter goals are rewritten by making extensive use of system primitives to split and create structures. These primitive operations are rather expensive in time. The *rewrite* module uses memoing technique to remember the translations performed by *rewrite_rule/2*.

The procedure *expand_predicate/2* provides the memoing support. The predicate *rewrite_rule/2* is called through this procedure. When a translation is requested *expand_predicate/2* first checks if the requested goal has been translated before. It calls *rewrite_rule/2* only if the check fails. The operand and result of *rewrite_rule/2* are *asserted* as *'#$$rewrite'/2* relations for later use.

```
expand_predicate(Goal, RGoal) :-
   check_rewrite_relation(Goal, RGoal), !.
expand_predicate(Goal, RGoal) :-
   is_interpreter_goal(Goal),
   rewrite_rule(Goal, RGoal),
   store_rewrite_relation(Goal, RGoal).
```

The procedures *check_rewrite_relation/2* and *store_rewrite_relation/2* implement the memoing capability. The test `is_interpreter(Goal)` is performed inside *expand_predicate/2*, rather than in its caller. This keeps its calling procedure general purpose and usable for translations elsewhere.

In addition to memoing another trick is used to reduce the number of calls to *rewrite_rule/2* and the number of relations *asserted*.

Before applying *rewrite_rule/2* the interpreter goal is translated to a template. The template is a term with the same functor and arity as the initial goal but has all the arguments, except the meta-argument, uninstantiated. The meta-argument is replaced by a term with the functor and arity of its counter-part in the original goal but with variable subterms. All the variables used in the template are new and different.

The conversion of an interpreter goal to its template is done by the procedure *create_goal_template/2*. The following query demonstrates its use:

```
?- create_goal_template(count(should_take(sue,lomotil),3), Z).
Z = count(should_take(_101, _102), _103) ?
```

Using this predicate *expand_predicate/2* is modified to translate the template of an interpreter goal instead of the interpreter goal itself.

```
expand_predicate(Goal, RGoal) :-
   check_rewrite_relation(Goal, RGoal),!.
expand_predicate(Goal, RGoal) :-
   is_interpreter_goal(Goal),
   create_goal_template(Goal, GMetaGoal),
   rewrite_rule(GMetaGoal, RGoal),
   store_rewrite_relation(GMetaGoal, RGoal),
   GMetaGoal = Goal.
```

When there are more than one interpreter goals with the same template the new definition is more efficient. The overheads introduced in creating a template is paid off by reducing calls to *rewrite_rule/2*.

"Full" Prolog The *expand_predicate/2* and *rewrite_rule/2* procedures translate only one predicate at a time. A whole clause or a seqeuence of goals is translated by the procedure *rewrite/2*. This procedure does with *expand_predicate/2* what Prolog does with *expand_term/2*, but with a difference. Only terms treated in the program as Prolog goals are translated using *expand_predicate/2*.

Terms appearing in a conjunctive sequence, in the head and body of a clause, and as arguments of meta-predicates have the potential to become Prolog goals. A conjunctive sequence and a clause are explicitly decomposed by the procedure *rewrite/2* to access their subterms. However, the traversal of a meta-predicate is not coded explicitly in *rewrite/2*. Instead it is guided by meta-knowledge about the usage of the meta-predicate's arguments provided by the relation meta_property(Type, Predicate, Property):

```
meta_property(meta,  →(_,_),  →(+,+)).
meta_property(set, bagof(_,_,_), bagof(-,+,-)).
```

The relation gives the `Property` of the arguments of a `Predicate`. The term
`Property` is of the same functor and arity as the term `Predicate`. There is either
a '+' or a '-' at the argument positions of `Property`. A '+' indicates position for a
Prolog goal or a *meta-argument*, a '-' otherwise.

The relation also associates a `Type` to a meta-predicate `Predicate`. This is a
provision to classify the meta-predicates into different groups, for example `set` and
`meta`. This classification is not useful for the sake of translating predicate names.
It may be used by other procedures that test the property of a predicate and choose
different courses of actions for predicates of different types. The partial evaluator
kernel itself is an example of such a procedure.

A *meta_property/3* fact is written for every meta-predicate. The *rewrite/2* procedure uses the *meta_property/3* declarations to selectively translate meta-arguments.

The 'meta' property of a predicate propagates to procedures using it. Predicates
whose arguments are passed to a meta-predicate as meta-arguments are also meta-
predicates. This is similar to the propagation of the *side-effect* property discussed
in Section 5.6 and may be treated in a similar fashion.

5.8   Driver

The *mix/2* predicate, as one may recall, is a general purpose partial evaluator. It
has no restriction on the nature or the intended usage of its data except that they
be Prolog programs. The input to *mix* is a goal and its output a sequence of goals
suspended while partially evaluating the goal. The evaluation is performed with
respect to program definitions stored in the Prolog database. The suspension of
goals is controlled by rules provided separately.

The important issues for using *mix* as a practical tool for specializing interpreters
are related to:

- creating goals to partially evaluate,
- creating clauses from residues,
- driving *mix* to compile a program, and
- providing an easy and flexible user interface.

These issues are not at the heart of the partial evaluation problem; but are
important for the utility and generality of the tool. They are discussed in the
following text.

Create Goals for Partial Evaluation   The clauses in Figure 5.5 are the result of partially evaluating the following three interpreter goals:

```
count(should_take(X,Y), Z),
count(complains(X,Y), Z), and
count(suppresses(X,Y), Z).
```

These goals specialize the interpreter *count/2* of Figure 5.2 with respect to the program in Figure 5.3. The meta-argument of each goal corresponds to a procedure of the Prolog program in Figure 5.3.

Given `IntGoal` - the skeleton for an interpreter goal, `IntArg` – the variable at its meta-argument position, and `Rhead` – a "rule head", the following clause creates an interpreter goal for partial evaluation.

```
create_goal_to_peval(IntGoal, IntArg, Rhead, PevalGoal) :-
    copy((IntArg,IntGoal), (Rhead,PevalGoal)).
```

This plugs the term `Rhead` into the meta-argument position of the copy of the interpreter goal. The interpreter goal is copied to protect the skeleton goal from being instantiated because the same skeleton term may be used for creating other interpreter goals.

A "rule head" is a term used by an interpreter for unfolding "rules" of the language it interprets. For Prolog interpreters "rules" correspond to clauses and "rule head" to the head of a clause. Generally, the syntactic positioning of such an atom in a rule would depend on the definition of the language being interpreted. This information is provided as a set of declarations, example:

```
% Declarations for Prolog
rule_head((X:-Y), T) :- !, generalize_term(X, T).
rule_head(X, T) :- generalize_term(X, T).

% Declarations for DCG
rule_head((X → Y), X) :- generalize_term(X, T).
```

The predicate `generalize_term(X, T)` creates a term T with the same functor and arity as `X` but with uninstantiated arguments:

```
generalize_term(Term, GeneralTerm) :-
    functor(Term, Functor, Arity),
    functor(GeneralTerm, Functor, Arity).
```

The arguments of the meta-argument carry inputs and outputs of the object program. Since the intent is to specialize an interpreter, the arguments of the meta-argument may not be instantiated.

The interpreter goals required to specialize a given interpreter can be generated from the object program using the predicates defined above.

Create Clause from Residue   The unfolding rules of Section 5.10 are designed to stop unfolding interpreter goals that have rule head terms as meta-arguments. This is done to achieve a correspondence between object program statements and residual clauses. With this strategy *mix/2* returns the interpreter goals created above without unfolding.

To compile a rule the interpreter should be executed so that it unfolds the rule head once. This unfolding is performed by *drive_mix/2* before calling *mix/2*.

```
drive_mix(MetaGoal, (MetaGoal :- MixedBody)) :-
    unfold_clause(MetaGoal, Body),
    mix(Body, MixedBody).
```

The goal *clause/2* does not directly unfold an object program rule. Instead it unfolds an interpreter clause, since **MetaGoal** is an interpreter goal. The object program rule is unfolded due to unfolding the interpreter clause that unfolds a rule. This procedure *drive_mix/2* creates a residue clause with the goal at the head and its residue as the body.

The body of the residual clause requires some further processing. Interpreter goals left as residue in the clause should be rewritten using *rewrite/2* discussed in Section 5.7. Some processing is also required to remove extraneous *true* goals generated as residues during various stages in the partial evaluation. Besides the body also contains a sequence of nested conjunctions. The conjunctions are "flattened".

This postprocessing of residue and 'rewriting' of its residual interpreter goals is performed by *peval/2*.

```
peval(MetaGoal, ResidueClause) :-
   drive_mix(MetaGoal, MixedClause),
   flatten_conjunction(MixedClause, FlattenedClause),
   rewrite(FlattenedClause, ResidueClause).
```

The code for *flatten_conjunction/2* is straightforward.

Drive *mix* to Compile Program Compiling a whole program is a routine exercise with the components developed in the previous sections. The procedure *peval_program/4* takes the interpreter goal, position of the meta-argument, and the list of rule heads as input. It creates an interpreter goal for every rule head in the list and collects all the residual clauses in a list.

The clauses collected are the compiled result. It is likely however that this program is not complete, that is it does not have all the procedures required to execute. The residue from partial evaluation may inherit goals from the interpreter that perform semantic actions. Unlike the residue in Figure 5.5 these goals may not always be system primitives. To execute the compiled program the definitions of these goals would be required. These may be provided by including the complete interpreter with the compiled program. The interpreter is also required for executing interpreter goals that were not 'rewritten' but were retained in the residue as is.

The residue may also inherit Prolog goals from the object program. This happens when a language allows Prolog goals in its rule. DCG is one such language. Its interpreter uses a *call/1* to pass the Prolog goals to the Prolog engine. If these goals are not all system primitives it means that the object program actually has two distinct parts. One written in the language being interpreted (*language part*) and the other in Prolog (*Prolog part*). The Prolog part should be included in the compiled result for completeness.

The matter becomes complex when the interpreter being specialized itself interprets a subset of Prolog. A Prolog interpreter like *count* interprets only conjunction and user-defined goals. It uses the Prolog engine to evaluate *meta-logical* predicates like disjunction, if-then-else, and all solution predicates. These predicates may have user-defined goals as meta-arguments. Thus a user-defined goal may be evaluated by the interpreter as well as the Prolog engine. For instance, the object program used for specializing *count* belongs to both the language part and Prolog part. Thus it should be included with the compiled result.

The possibility of retaining interpreter goals creates a similar complexity for any language. The goal retained may have a variable meta-argument. At runtime this may get instantiated to a rule head that belongs to the language part of the object program compiled.

Should the object part then be included with the compiled result? No, instead the rewrite relations collected by *rewrite* can be used to translate interpreter goals at runtime. A new clause may be added at the beginning of the interpreter which traps calls to rule heads that have already been compiled and maps these calls to the corresponding compiled procedure. For the *count/2* interpreter this clause would be:

```
count(Goal, C) :-
    '#$$rewrite'(count(Goal,C), CompiledGoal), !,
    call(CompiledGoal).
```

Now the rewrite relations should be included with the compiled result.

The final result of compilation is the collection of the following components:

- residues,
- Prolog part of the object program,
- interpreter modified with the extra clause, and
- the rewrite relations.

The components other than the residues may not always be required. The decision to include a component in whole or part requires further processing of the residue. The task involved is equivalent to finding dead code in a program. This is an independent problem in itself and may be handled separately.

Care is also required to avoid conflict between the names of predicates generated in the residues with the predicates of the other components composing the compiled program.

User Interface   The user interface provides the support for handling the input and output of a system. The capabilities of a system may be demonstrated without a good interface, but to translate those capabilities to a useful tool the user interface becomes an important issue in itself. Its design depends on the conditions the tool would be used in and the support provided from the environment. Unlike the other modules there can be no general purpose user interface suitable for all conditions.

The inputs required by the partial evaluator are:

- the interpreter,
- the object program split in language and Prolog parts, and
- meta-knowledge about the interpreter and the language.

The meta-knowledge guides the unfolding, rewrite rules, and extraction of rule head from the object programs.

The output consists of the components of compiled results discussed above. The input interface of ProMiX has three features:

- input is given in files

- a collection of files may be classified as *system*

- "similar" interpreters can share meta-knowledge

Providing inputs through files makes the task of specifying the individual input programs easier. Only the file(s) containing the interpreter, its meta-knowledge, and the object program have to be specified.

The meta-knowledge provides the information to guide the compilation. The information is related to the interpreter, the language it interprets, and the interpretation technique. Interpreters that interpret the same language in the same way may share this information. This is done by classifying similar interpreters in the same *class*. The meta-knowledge is associated to the class.

When a program is distributed over several files it would be easier to group these files as *system*. The name of the system identifies the collection of files. This is useful for real-life programs. Such a system definition can be used by other program manipulation or analysis tools. In our environment it is used by a cross referencer, static analyzer, and a profiler. It is also used by utilities that extend Prolog's capability of *consult*ing files to consulting systems.

The sequence of events for compiling a program are:
- load all the input files in the database
- extract all the rule heads in the object program
- get the interpreter goal and position of meta-argument
- call *peval_program/2* with the appropriate parameters

The interpreter files should be loaded such that its information can be accessed by *clause/2*. The object program should be loaded such that it can be accessed by the predicates used for unfolding the rule heads. In the case of *count/2* it is also *clause/2*.

To port this system to Prolog implementations that do not support *clause/2* or limits the use of *clause/2* some changes are required. This problem may be solved by loading the interpreter as a set of facts instead of a Prolog program. Example:

```
program(count(true,0), true).
program(count(A,B),C),
   (count(A,CA),
```

```
    count(B,CB),
    C is CA + CB).
program(count(X,0),
    (not processed_above(X),
    sys(X),
    call(X))).
program(count(H,C),
    (predicate_property(H, interpreted),
    program(H,B),
    count(B,CB),
    C is CB+1).
```

The Prolog part in the object program should be treated similarly. Now by redefining the **unfold_clause(X,Y)** procedure as:

```
unfold_clause(X, Y) :- program(X, Y).
```

the system would be ready to specialize interpreters given in the above form.

The modified system described above is portable across various Prolog systems. We prefer to use the version with *clause/2* because it enables partial evaluation of programs while they are actually being used. Programs in the above form are not directly evaluable by the Prolog engine.

The output interface of ProMiX provides three options, the compiled result may be:

- displayed on the screen,
- written to a file, or
- bound to a variable.

The first option is good for testing and demonstrating the result of partial evaluation. For compiling file(s) the second option suits better. The compiled result is put in a file and may be used again later. The third option enables postprocessing of the compiled result. The capabilities of the system may be extended by writing 'filters' that take this result and process it further. Removal of dead code or *assert*ing the compiled program into the Prolog database are examples of such processing.

5.9   Knowledge Base

The mix and rewrite modules of ProMiX are general purpose in that the knowledge about properties of predicates whether system defined or user-defined is not hard coded. They use predicates external to these modules to associate a property to a predicate. The criteria for controlling unfolding is also maintained externally as a set of rules. Similarly, knowledge about any specific interpreter is not built into the driver; it is provided to it by separate declarations and annotations.

The collection of such predicates, rules, and declarations, constitute the knowledge base module. This module customizes ProMiX to a particular application. In a way it is the variant component of the system. Its content varies upon the interpreter, the language it interprets, and to some extent the Prolog implementation. The other modules remain unchanged across applications.

The knowledge provided by this module may be classified in the following categories: *property of predicates, declarations for unfolding, rewrite rules* and *declarations for the driver*. Most of the issues underlying the knowledge have been discussed previously The following text only compiles the pieces spread across the previous sections.

5.9.1   Property of Predicates

Naive partial evaluation of predicates with *side-effecting* or *extra-logical* behavior leads to the 'backward propagation' and 'multiple clauses' problems discussed in Section 5.6. The *mix* module is guided by predicates in the knowledge base that declare the system defined and user defined predicates that exhibit such properties. For example:

```
side_effect(write(X)).
extra_logical(var(X)).
```

It is easy to write an exhaustive set of declarations for system defined primitives for a particular Prolog implementation. A user defined predicate can cause a side-effect either if it uses a side-effecting system predicate or another user defined predicate displaying side-effect. This property can therefore be extracted by statically analysing the program before partial evaluation. At present these predicates have to be declared too.

The extra-logical property, just like side-effect behavior, propagates too. A user-defined predicate using an extra-logical system primitive also displays extra-logical behavior. Given a set of system defined primitives that are extra-logical the user-defined extra-logical predicates may be determined by static analysis.

The *rewrite* module too depends on external knowledge. It needs to know which arguments of a meta-logical predicate, like *bagof/3*, can eventually be used as a predicate. This knowledge is provided by the *meta_property/3* relations discussed in Section 5.7.

5.9.2   Declarations for Unfolding

To unfold or not to unfold a goal is an important question for partial evaluation. As observed before there is no automatic way to detect whether unfolding a goal would lead to termination of partial evaluation. Some additional information specific to the program being partially evaluated is required to make this decision. Besides, more than one residue for the same goal may be generated due to different unfolding decisions.

The decision to unfold or not is made by the *mix* module via the predicate *should_unfold/1*. It passes the *Goal* to this predicate to test if it may be unfolded. A set of rules, like:

```
should_unfold(Goal)  :- True if Goal may be unfolded
```

are provided by the user that perform the required test. These rules may be application specific and can use knowledge about the program that is otherwise hard to extract automatically.

Guidelines for developing unfolding criteria for specializing interpreters are given in Section 5.10.

5.9.3   Rewrite Rules

The *rewrite* module is responsible for translating the interpreter goals in the residue. To do that it should generate names for new predicates. If the residue is to be used by a programmer it would help if the names given to the new predicate make sense and are also unique. While the latter condition is easy to satisfy by a machine, it is impossible to mechanically generate names that makes sense too.

Most researchers have implicitly used the principal functor of the object goal in the residual goal as the name of the translated predicate. This is the default scheme used by ProMiX. Considering the fact that the initial object program may at times be included with the compiled result, this scheme may violate the uniqueness

requirement. Besides one may just wish to use a different name since the old functor
name may not be suitable for the compiled predicate.

This can be done by providing new rules to rewrite predicates to overwrite the
default definition. The predicate `expand_predicate(PredIn, PredOut)` provides
this information. It says that a predicate `PredIn` in the residue may be translated
to `PredOut`.

5.9.4 Declarations for Driver

The *driver* module drives the predicate *mix/2* to specialize interpreters. It creates
interpreter goals for *mix/2* to partially evaluate such that the collection of their
residues is the compiled result. To construct an interpreter goal one needs three
things: which goals are interpreter goals, which argument is its meta-argument,
and which object program atoms are used to compile the program. The first two
questions are answered by a declaration with the following signature:

`meta_goal(Goal, MetaArg).`

Here `Goal` is an interpreter goal. `MetaArg` is a variable which also occurs in the
meta-argument position of `Goal`.

Since an interpreter may be used to compile several programs, for ease of reference one may prefer to associate a name with an interpreter rather than referring
to it by a goal. The mapping between interpreter name and the interpreter goal
is declared by: `flavor(Flavor, IntGoal)`. The argument `Flavor` is a name associated to an interpreter and `IntGoal` is its interpreter goal. Such declarations are
also useful when specializing layered interpreters [SY89]. In these interpreters the
task of interpretation is divided between several predicates arranged as a cascade.
The processing of a predicate at the lower level is controlled by that at a higher
level. A predicate processes the input string and invokes a predicate at a lower
level with appropriate substring. This predicate chooses its future course of action
depending on the results returned by the lower level predicate. An object program
goal may therefore be interpreted by more than one interpreter predicate. In order
to specialize layered interpreters all the interpreter predicates should be specialized
with respect to the object program goals. In such a case the same flavor name
may be associated to all the interpreter goals by appropriate *flavor/2* declarations.
Corresponding *meta_goal/2* declarations for each of the interpreter goals would also
be required.

The information about an interpreter provided above remains static with respect
to the interpreter; it does not change for every object program. What changes
with every object program are atomic symbols used to create interpreter goals for

compiling a program. Instead of having the user state all the object program goals, in ProMiX the object program is input via a set of files. It is assumed that the object program consists of a set of Prolog terms, called rules. A definite clause characteristic is also assumed. That is one goal of a rule is used to select that rule. Beyond that the driver does not assume the syntax of the rule and relies on a *rule_head/1* declaration to extract the head atom from the rule. This declaration has the following signature:

`rule_head(R, H).`

where H is the goal used to select the rule R. ProMiX uses this rule to extract all the head atoms in the program files. These goals, it assumes, can potentially become meta-arguments of an interpreter goal.

5.10   How to Control Unfolding

This section gives tips on how to control unfolding when specializing interpreters. An interpreter can be viewed as performing two tasks: parsing and execution. Interpreters are specialized by partially evaluating the parsing activity while leaving the execution component as residue. We give a procedure for identifying goals that participate in the parsing process and present rules for unfolding these goals. This procedure may potentially be mechanized, thereby leading to automated compilation of the object program by specializing interpreters.

5.10.1   Working of an Interpreter

An interpreter performs two functions. First, it parses the incoming term to verify that it belongs to the language it interprets. Second, it simulates the operational behaviour associated to any well-formed string of the language being interpreted. It does so by mapping the meaning associated to these strings to operations in the language in which the interpreter is written. We call these operations *semantic actions*.

The interpreters that we study interpret strings that are valid Prolog terms. We call these strings *rules*. They parse a rule by unifying it with a skeleton of structures acceptable by the language, extracting its subterms, and parsing them recursively. Parsing terminates when an atomic symbol of the language is reached, though the interpretation may still continue. The semantic actions corresponding to an atomic symbol may *chain* the interpretation of other strings. We call such symbols *non-terminal*.

Not all atomic symbols trigger chaining. Symbols that do not chain interpretation we call *terminal*. The interpreters use *checking-predicate* to test if the incoming symbols is terminal. In meta-interpreters cited in [SB89], system defined Prolog goals are terminal symbols. The test is performed by the checking predicate *sys/1*.

As these interpreters are written in Prolog the semantic actions are Prolog goals. These goals may be classified in two categories: system defined goals and user defined goals. Goals that are primitive builtins of the Prolog environment we call system defined goals. Predicates whose definition is given by the user are user defined goals.

5.10.2   An Observation

From experience with specializing interpreters it may be observed that:

- The input to the partial evaluator is the interpeter. When the predicate **mix(Goal, Residue)** of Figure 5.6 is invoked, **Goal** would be instantiated to some goal in the body of the interpreter being specialized. Therefore, goals unfolded by a partial evaluator come from the body of the interpreter.

  Object program rules are unfolded as a result of semantic actions that chain interpretation.

- The result of specializing interpreters is a rule-by-rule translation of the object program into Prolog. In [PS87, TF86] every grammar rule is translated into an equivalent Prolog clause. Similarly in [FF88, SB89, TF86] every clause of a program is translated into another clause (or clauses) with enhanced features inherited from the meta-interpreter used for translation.

  This is akin to compiling the object program into Prolog, where compilation of one rule of the object program is independent of other rules.

From these observations we derive the following guidelines for our unfolding criteria:

- The 'unfolding knowledge' required to do a source-to-source translation of an object program depends only on the interpreter being specialized, it is independent of the object program itself.

- Interpreter goals that lead to unfolding of other object program rules should not be unfolded.

5.10.3   Unfold Criteria

The overhead of interpretation lies mainly in parsing the object program at run-time. Assume that an interpreter is partially evaluated such that all actions related to parsing a program are completely executed. The residue after parsing a rule of the object program would consist of semantic actions associated with parsing it and processing its atomic goals. Hence the residue for a rule would have the same execution behaviour as that associated to interpreting the rule, but would be free of the parsing overhead.

Goals in the residue that are sufficiently instantiated for execution may be further (partially) executed during specialization. As these goals do not incur any interpretation overhead we consider their pre-execution analogous to compile-time optimizations in traditional compilation approaches.

When specializing interpreters our primary interest is to remove the parsing overhead. Optimizations by pre-executing semantic actions, though important, are secondary. We classify our unfolding criteria on the basis of the effects they produce.

Removing Parsing Overhead   Parsing is performed by matching the input structures to constructors of the language interpreted, then decomposing this structure to parse its components recursively. In practice we can extract the set of structures decomposed by an interpreter by scanning the interpreter. We can also mark a set of procedures that participate in parsing. Goals corresponding to this set of procedures we call *meta-goals* and arguments that carry the input term *meta-arguments*. Our first criterion for unfolding is that a meta-goal may be unfolded only if its meta-argument is bound to a structure that is decomposed by the interpreter.

The criterion when translated to Prolog takes the form:

```
should_unfold(Goal) :-
   meta_goal(Goal, MetaArg),
   structure_decomposed(MetaArg).
```

The predicates *meta_goal/2* and *structure_decomposed/1* provide information about the interpreter. The goal **meta_goal(Goal, MetaArg)** says **Goal** is a meta-goal with meta-argument **MetaArg**, and **structure_decomposed(MetaArg)** checks if **MetaArg** belongs to the set of structures decomposed by the interpreter being specialized. By unfolding only those instances of a meta-goal that carry a structure that is decomposed by the interpreter, we implicitly avoid the unfolding of clauses that process atomic goals.

For the vanilla meta-interpreter this knowledge would be:

```
meta_goal(solve(Goal, _Cf), Goal).

structure_decomposed(true).
structure_decomposed((_GoalA,_GoalB)).
```

In an environment where there are several meta-interpreters, as that envisioned by [SB89], one may classify interpreters on the language they process. All interpreters processing the same language decompose the same set of structures. The *structure_decomposed* information can therefore be associated to a class of interpreters rather than an individual interpreter.

The next step after recognizing the meta-goals, meta-arguments, and the structures decomposed is to identify the *imperative goals*. These are goals that are mutually recursive with the meta-goals but are not meta-goals themselves, that is, goals that appear in the recursion path from a meta-goal to a meta-goal. An imperative goal carries the meta-arguments for the recursive calls but does not itself process these arguments. These goals should be unfolded so as to lead the execution to the meta-goals. Hence our second rule of unfolding.

```
should_unfold(Goal) :- imperative(Goal).
```

The interpreters cited in partial evaluation experiences of other researchers [FF88, SB89, TF86] do not have imperative goals. Example of such interpreters may be found in the Prolog text book [SS86].

Pre-execution of Atomic Symbols The above rules refrain from unfolding clauses that process atomic symbols that may chain interpretation to other rules. But as noted before not all atomic symbols chain interpretation. It may thus be worthwhile to unfold the processing of those atomic symbols that terminate interpretation. Thus our third rule that unfolds such goals.

```
should_unfold(Goal) :-
    meta_goal(Goal, MetaArg), terminal_atom(MetaArg).
```

The goal terminal_atom(MetaArg) tests if MetaArg is a terminal atom. The test may be performed by the same predicates as that used by the interpreter for identifying the terminal symbols. This knowledge about the interpreter can be extracted easily by scanning it and can be customized for a class of interpreters. For example:

```
terminal_atom(Term) :- system(Term).
```

is an extract from a Prolog meta-interpreter that uses *system/1* to check if a goal is a system defined primitive.

Compile-time Optimizations   To pre-execute semantic actions that are sufficiently instantiated we fall back to an annotation scheme similar to that of [TF86]. We classify these goals as *export, immediately evaluable*, and *partially evaluable*. An export goal becomes a residue, whereas an immediately evaluable goal is evaluated completely using the underlying Prolog engine. Partially evaluable goals, as the name suggests, continue to be unfolded.

Annotating goals needs partial evaluation expertise or some trial-and-error experimentation. We have some useful hints that may make this task less tedious.

• A goal must fall in one of the three categories: export, immediately evaluable or partially evaluable. Thus goals for only two categories may be annotated, the third category being treated as default. Like Takeuchi & Furukawa [TF86], we assume a goal to be partially evaluable unless otherwise annotated. The fourth unfold rule thus is:

```
should_unfold(Goal) :-
  not export(Goal), not immediate(Goal).
```

• The goals in question now do not participate in parsing. So as a first try one may mark all such goals as *export* and perform the compilation. Then later looking at the goals in the residue one may perform suitable annotations to get the most efficient form of compiled result.

• System defined goals, such as the arithmetic predicates, may either be completely evaluated or exported. The definition of these predicates is inaccessible, so they can not be unfolded.

Being builtins, these predicates are independent of the program being partially evaluated. We suggest these goals be treated separately by the partial evaluator. A database of *executable/1* rules may be maintained as a global information about the system. These rules test if a system goal is sufficiently instantiated for execution. For instance:

```
executable(X is Y + Z) :- nonvar(Y), nonvar(Z).
executable(append(X, Y, Z)) :- complete_list(X).
```

The predicate `complete_list(X)` verifies if X is a complete list, as defined in [SS86].
 • The partial evaluator of Figure 5.6 may be augmented by adding the following clauses.

```
mix(Goal, true) :-
   immediate(Goal), !,
   call(Goal).
mix(Goal, true) :-
   executable(Goal), !,
   call(Goal).
```

These clauses provide the support necessary for the classification of goals given above.

5.11   Background

The theory of partial evaluation originated from mathematics. It is based on Kleene's S-m-n Theorem [Kle52] for recursive functions presented in 1952. The concept was introduced to computer science by Futamura [Fut71] in 1971. In this paper Futamura recognized the relation between interpretation and compilation by the means of partial evaluation. He projected the use of partial evaluation as a compiler, to develop compilers, and compiler-compilers. These projections are now called *Futamura projections*.

Other researchers who actively pursued partial evaluation in the 70's were A. Haraldsson from Sweden and A.P. Ershov from Russia. Haraldsson studied the problem in the context of Lisp while Ershov studied an Algol-like language. The sparks from their work triggered a fire of research activity on partial evaluation in the 80's. The concept has now been studied by researchers around the world. It is beyond the scope of this paper to survey all the efforts. Sestoft and Zamulin [SZ88] have compiled a rather extensive bibliography of over 250 papers related to this subject. A less elaborate bibliography is published in [SS88]. The Workshop on Partial Evaluation and Mixed Computation held in Denmark in August 1987 and organized by D. Bjørner, A.P. Ershov, and N. Jones constitutes a landmark event for this subject. Papers presented during this workshop with relevance to logic programming appear in [BEJ88b], other papers appear in [BEJ88a]. The proceedings of Meta88: a workshop on meta-programming and logic programming [AR89] contains some more recent papers on partial evaluation.

Partial evaluation was introduced to logic programming by Komorowski [Kom81]. Venken [Ven84] was probably the first to report a partial evaluator for Prolog. In this and a later paper [VD88] he raised the various problems that arise due to 'impurities' in Prolog. Several researchers have since reported partial evaluators for "full" Prolog [BEJ88b]. It has been explored as a tool to generate efficient Prolog programs (in terms of logical inferences) by transforming semantically equivalent Prolog programs. Recently Lloyd and Sheperdson [LS87] have attempted at developing the formal foundation for partial evaluation.

The first Futamura projection [Fut71] states how partial evaluation of an interpreter with respect to an object program effectively compiles the object program. This has been the guiding principle for a large segment of the logic programming community interested in partial evaluation. Gallagher, in 1983, observed that this property of partial evaluation can be used to reduce run-time overhead of meta-interpreters. His observations appeared later in 1986. Meanwhile Takeuchi & Furukawa independently came to the same conclusion in a 1985 ICOT technical report published later as [TF86]. Both the papers observe that partial evaluation of an interpreter with respect to an object program has the effect of compiling the object program into a new object program. The new program inherits the functionality of the meta-interpreter but not its overhead. Sterling & Beer [SB89] particularized this technique for expert systems. Pereira & Shieber [PS87] used this method to compile DCG programs to Prolog.

The use of partial evaluation as a compiler provides a very good optimization tool for Prolog meta-programs. Takeuchi & Furukawa [TF86] and Sterling & Beer [SB89] reported up to a factor of 40 improvement in execution time of compiled program over its interpreted counterpart. It is felt, therefore, that partial evaluation can bridge the dilemma between writing programs for machine or writing programs for humans. It promises to make meta-programming a feasible technique for developing production quality expert systems.

The euphoria generated by these initial results raised the expectations of the

Prolog community. Several researchers are now disillusioned since partial evaluation does not deliver the wonders that they thought it would [Owe89, vH89]. In our belief the conflict arises because the term "meta-programming overhead" has never been defined informally or formally. In our experience partial evaluation of interpreters removes only the "parsing activity" associated with executing the specific object program. The "semantic actions" are left for evaluation at run-time (see Section 5.10). If an interpreter spends most of its time in performing these semantic actions, the specialized program would not do any better.

Partial evaluation is just a sequence of carefully guided *unfold* transformations. To do any better transformations other than *unfold* are necessary. Owen [Owe89] has proposed the use of *fold* transformations in the partial evaluator. The proposal has merit since it is known that the *fold* transformation is necessary to change the algorithmic complexity of any program. However, we do not advocate its inclusion in the partial evaluator. If required it should be performed on the residue by a separate 'filter'. In fact a generalized scheme of 'filtering' programs through transformers needs be worked out. This would ensure simplicity of code of individual transformers and also provide flexibility of juxtaposing more transformers at will.

Alternate transformation methods that generate results similar to those from partial evaluation of interpreters have been reported too. Neumann [Neu88] derives a translator from an interpreter. The translator is then used to transform an object program. Louis & Vauclair [LV88] write a translator directly instead of writing a meta-interpreter. It is our hypothesis that one should be able to generate the translators used by Louis & Vauclair [LV88] by partially evaluating the partial evaluator with respect to an interpreter. Similarly the translator-generator used by Neumann [Neu88] should be derivable by partially evaluating the partial evaluator with itself. This hypothesis follows directly from Futamura's second and third projection.

Self-applicability is the most glamorous part of the Futamura projections. So far only a self-applicable partial evaluator for "pure" Prolog has been reported by Fujita & Furukawa [FF88]. A self-applicable partial evaluator for "full" Prolog is required to test the hypothesis above. ProMiX provides a sound foundation for such an experiment. On the same note, a self-applicable partial evaluator for functional programming language was reported by Jones et. al. [JSS85]

Curiously, the word *mix* is a name commonly used for partial evaluators. Its root can be traced to Ershov [Ers77]. Ershov calls partial evaluation *mixed computation*. Presumeably Jones et. al. [JSS85] derived the name *mix* for their partial evaluator from it.

Acknowledgements

We thank members of the Composers Group in the Department of Computer Engineering and Science at CWRU for providing the environment for creative work. Ümit Yalçinalp in particular contributed to the paper through her use of ProMiX to partially evaluate an explanation system [YS89]. She uncovered several important issues related to handling Prolog's extra-logical predicates. This work was funded by NSF grant 1R187-03911, and an NSF equipment grant.

Chapter 6

Generating Natural Language Explanations from Plans

Chris Mellish

Department of Artificial Intelligence,
University of Edinburgh,
80 South Bridge,
Edinburgh EH1 1HN
Scotland, UK
E-mail: c.mellish@ed.ac.uk

6.1 Introduction

A *plan* can be thought of as an arrangement of actions whose aim is to achieve some goal, an arrangement that is *justified* to the extent that the plan is guaranteed to succeed as long as the situation in which it is executed satisfies a set of specified assumptions. The notion of a plan is crucial to problem-solving in a number of areas of AI, for instance game playing and natural language understanding. This chapter presents a simple system that produces natural language 'explanations' of plans. That is, given a plan to achieve some goal, the program produces a natural language text that explains the actions to be performed and why things can be done this way. Plans provide a rich, yet formally delimited, input for a natural language generator, and to a certain extent there are domain-independent strategies for explaining plans. Therefore the program presented here, though lacking some of the sophistication of a system tailored to a particular application, can be applied to different planning domains with relatively little trouble.

A program that can explain plans in natural language could be used in various types of practical systems. First of all, it could be used together with an intelligent program to provide explanations of that program's planned actions. Secondly, it could be used, in conjunction with a planning program, to help another agent (probably a human being) to make plans in a complex domain.

6.2   Plans

This section briefly outlines a representation of plans that can be used as a basis for
generating natural language explanations. One problem that immediately arises is
that, although they are agreed on the general nature of what a 'plan' is, researchers
disagree a lot on the details, and a universally accepted formalism for plans is
therefore not available. If different planners may produce plans in different formats
and by different methods, then a general natural language explainer of plans must
make as few assumptions as possible about its input. We have therefore assumed
that our program will be provided with simply a desired sequence of actions and
the goal of the plan (what it sets out to achieve). This is not a complete plan
in the sense used above, and in order to explain it, the generator must work out
why the sequence of actions is a good way of achieving the goal. To do this, it
must have available general information about actions and their preconditions and
effects. We have chosen to model the program's knowledge of actions on that used
by an early planning program called STRIPS, as this is the basis of a great deal of
planning work done since. For example, the following might be the Prolog clause
representing the action of 'an agent going to a place':

```
operator(go(Agent,PlaceNow,Place),
      [at(Agent,PlaceNow), route(PlaceNow,Place)],
      [at(Agent,PlaceNow)],
      [at(Agent,Place)]).
```

The first line of this clause provides the name of the action. The second gives the
list of preconditions (the agent must be at some place 'PlaceNow' and there must
be a route from there to the desired goal 'Place'). The third gives the propositions
to be "deleted" from the world when the action is performed, and the fourth gives
the propositions to be added.

We will assume here that a plan is always constructed within a particular *planning
domain* which makes available a set of operators for acting in this domain. Here are
some operators for doing various things with a particular type of electrical plug:

```
operator(remove_cover,               % remove the main cover of the plug
    [cover_on],
    [cover_on],
```

```
    [cover_off]).

operator(install_cover,              % attach the main cover of the plug
    [cover_off,flex_bedded],
    [cover_off],
    [cover_on]).

operator(remove_fuse(F),             % remove the given fuse from the plug
    [cover_off,fuse_installed(F)],
    [fuse_installed(F)],
    [spare_fuse(F),fuse_holder_empty]).

operator(install_fuse(F),            % fit the given fuse into the plug
    [cover_off,spare_fuse(F),fuse_holder_empty],
    [spare_fuse(F)],
    [fuse_installed(F)]).

operator(plug_in,                    % plug it into the electricity supply
    [fuse_installed(F),works(F),cover_on, flex_gripped,
    good_wire(red), good_wire(blue), good_wire(green),
    terminal_closed(l), terminal_closed(n), terminal_closed(e),
    wire_in(red,l), wire_in(blue,n), wire_in(green,e)],
    [ ],
    [working_system]).

operator(unscrew_terminal(N),        % unscrew the given terminal
    [cover_off,terminal_closed(N)],
    [terminal_closed(N)],
    [terminal_open(N)]).

operator(screw_terminal(N),          % tighten the screw on the given terminal
    [cover_off,terminal_open(N),wire_in(W,N)],
    [terminal_open(N),wire_free(W)],
    [terminal_closed(N)]).

operator(tighten_grip,               % tighten the screws on the gripper
    [flex_bedded,flex_loose],
    [flex_loose],
```

```
   [flex_gripped]).

operator(loosen_grip,            % loosen the screws on the gripper
   [flex_bedded,flex_gripped],
   [flex_gripped],
   [flex_loose]).

operator(strip_wire(C),          % make a given wire serviceable
   [cover_off,flex_loose,wire_free(C)],
   [flex_bedded],
   [good_wire(C)]).

operator(insert_to_terminal(W,T),   % insert a wire into a terminal
   [wire_free(W),terminal_open(T),terminal_empty(T),cover_off],
   [terminal_empty(T)],
   [wire_in(W,T)]).

operator(remove_from_terminal(W,T), % remove a wire from a terminal
   [terminal_open(T),wire_in(W,T),cover_off],
   [wire_in(W,T)],
   [terminal_empty(T)]).

operator(loop_cover,             % put the flex through the cover loop
   [cover_off,wire_free(red),wire_free(blue),wire_free(green),
    flex_loose],
   [ ],
   [flex_bedded]).
```

The plug has a main cover that can be removed. Inside there are three terminals, labelled 'L', 'N' and 'E', into which wires can be fitted. There is also a place where a single fuse can be fitted. The screws on the terminals can be individually tightened and loosened, and there are three wires (green, red and blue) which can be fitted into them (at most one per terminal). The three wires come from a single flex, which can be fixed firmly to the plug base by means of screws on a simple gripping pad. For the cover to be installed, the flex must pass through a loop in the cover. Since the other end of the flex is assumed to be buried deep in some electrical appliance, this means that the cover has to be looped over the flex before any wires are fixed to the plug. The physical organization of such a plug is detailed in Figure 6.1.

It will be useful to distinguish between two kinds of effects that an action can produce, the *primary* and *secondary* effects. With the 'go' operator, the usual reason for going somewhere is to get to that place, not to get away from the place one is currently at. Hence it is the *added* fact that is of primary importance. In an explanation, one is likely to mention secondary effects only when they are relevant to the plan; primary effects, on the other hand, are likely to be mentioned anyway. Primary effects (or "objects") are represented by the program by clauses such as the following: `object(go(Agent,From,To),at(Agent,To))`.

This general representation of operators (actions) allows one, given a description of an initial state of the world, a sequence of desired actions and a goal, to verify whether the sequence of actions is a successful plan to achieve the goal, starting from the initial situation described. For instance, the sequence of actions:

```
remove_cover,
remove_fuse(fold),
install_fuse(fnew),
install_cover,
plug_in
```

is a valid plan to achieve the goal *working_system* from a world described by the following list of assertions:

```
[cover_on, fuse_installed(fold), spare_fuse(fnew), works(fnew),
good_wire(red), good_wire(green), good_wire(blue), terminal_closed(n),
terminal_closed(l), terminal_closed(e), flex_bedded, flex_gripped,
wire_in(red, l), wire_in(blue,n), wire_in(green,e)]
```

that is, a world in which everything is all right except that the fuse fitted (`fold`) does not work (as with Prolog, we assume that any fact, for instance `works(fold)`, that is missing from such a list is false in the relevant world). We can verify that the sequence of actions is possible by computing the intermediate states of the world that would arise during their execution:

```
remove_cover:
    [cover_off, fuse_installed(fold), spare_fuse(fnew),
    works(fnew), good_wire(red), good_wire(green), good_wire(blue),
    terminal_closed(n), terminal_closed(l), terminal_closed(e),
    flex_bedded, flex_gripped, wire_in(red,l),
```

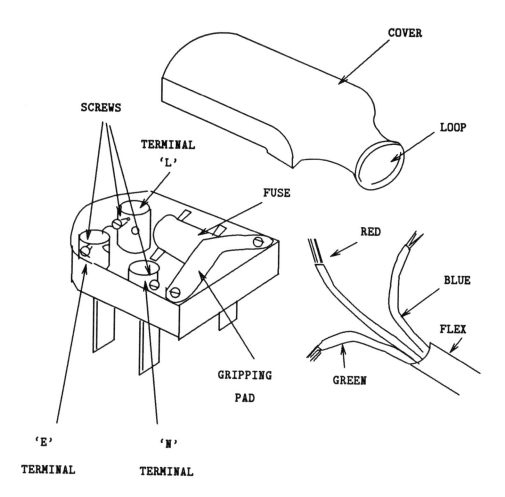

Figure 6.1: An Electrical Plug

```
wire_in(blue,n), wire_in(green,e)]
```

remove_fuse(fold):
```
[spare_fuse(fold), fuse_holder_empty, cover_off, spare_fuse(fnew),
works(fnew), good_wire(red), good_wire(green), good_wire(blue),
terminal_closed(n), terminal_closed(l), terminal_closed(e),
flex_bedded, flex_gripped,
wire_in(red,l), wire_in(blue,n), wire_in(green,e)]
```

install_fuse(fnew):
```
[fuse_installed(fnew), spare_fuse(fold), fuse_holder_empty, cover_off,
works(fnew), good_wire(red), good_wire(green), good_wire(blue),
terminal_closed(n), terminal_closed(l), terminal_closed(e),
flex_bedded, flex_gripped,
wire_in(red,l), wire_in(blue,n), wire_in(green,e)]
```

install_cover:
```
[cover_on, fuse_installed(fnew), spare_fuse(fold), fuse_holder_empty,
works(fnew), good_wire(red), good_wire(green), good_wire(blue),
terminal_closed(n), terminal_closed(l), terminal_closed(e),
flex_bedded, flex_gripped,
wire_in(red,l), wire_in(blue,n), wire_in(green,e)]
```

plug_in:
```
[working_system, cover_on, fuse_installed(fnew), spare_fuse(fold),
fuse_holder_empty, works(fnew), good_wire(red),
good_wire(green), good_wire(blue),
terminal_closed(n), terminal_closed(l), terminal_closed(e),
flex_bedded, flex_gripped,
wire_in(red,l), wire_in(blue,n), wire_in(green,e)]
```

It is easy to verify that:

1. the preconditions of each action are true when that action is to be executed

2. the world following each action reflects correctly the changes brought about by that action

3. the first action is planned to take place in the initial world described

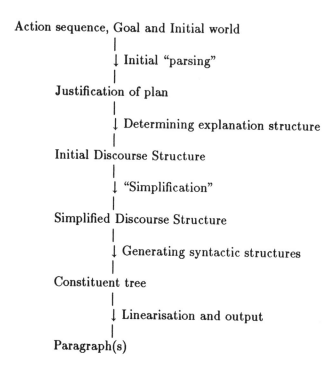

Action sequence, Goal and Initial world
|
↓ Initial "parsing"
|
Justification of plan
|
↓ Determining explanation structure
|
Initial Discourse Structure
|
↓ "Simplification"
|
Simplified Discourse Structure
|
↓ Generating syntactic structures
|
Constituent tree
|
↓ Linearisation and output
|
Paragraph(s)

Figure 6.2: Stages in Explaining a Plan

4. as a result of the final action, the goal is made true.

Hence the sequence of actions is a valid way of achieving the goal.

6.3   Stages in Explaining a Plan

We will now present a simple program that generates natural language text to explain a plan (represented as a sequence of actions, a goal and a description of the initial world) within a given planning domain. The stages through which the program works are shown by Figure 6.2.

In Prolog, this looks as follows:

```
explain_plan(Goal,World,Action_sequence) :-
  parse(Goal,World,Action_sequence,Justification),
  % initial "parsing"
  transform_just(Justification,Discourse_structure),
  % determining explanation structure
  simplify(Discourse_structure,Simplified_discourse_structure),
  % "simplification"
  fill_syntax(Simplified_discourse_structure,Constituent_tree),
  % generating syntactic structures
  % generate(Constituent_tree).
  % linearisation and output
```

Initially, the action sequence must be "parsed" into a representation where the program can see the rationale for each particular action. This is a form of constrained "plan recognition": constrained because the overall goal is given. The idea here is that the hypothetical planner may work in unknown ways, but that only certain kinds of rationalisations for actions can be explained by the generator. It does not matter particularly whether the rationalisation that arises is like the one used by the original planner—it suffices that it provide a complete justification of the actions.

The second stage involves looking at the complexity of the parts of the justification structure and making decisions about strategies for explaining them. For instance, an action that has many complex justifications or preconditions to be achieved may need to be explained by a whole paragraph, with other explanations nested within it; in simpler cases, whole strings of actions can be described by a single sentence. The result of this stage is an outline of the structure of the whole discourse to be produced. This structure is then simplified by a stage of *simplification*.

The discourse structure is now mapped onto a detailed syntactic representation of the text to be generated. This involves recursively working though the levels of structure, generating constituent trees for the paragraphs and sentences involved. At the lowest levels, actual sentence forms and lexical items are selected. However, at this point the constituent trees contain no ordering information—they are solely a representation of constituent structure.

The final stage involves producing a linear output from this constituent tree. This involves introducing ordering and morphology.

Here is what the program described here will produce for the example plan given above:

in order for you to get the plug to be working you must have installed the new fuse.

in order for you to install the new fuse the cover must be off and the fuse holder must be empty. remove the cover and remove the old fuse. then the fuse holder will be empty. install the new fuse.

however now the cover is not on. install the cover. then plug the plug in and the plug will be working.

Here is a more extensive example which describes the actions to be performed if initially the cover is on, there is no fuse in the plug, the 'L' terminal is open (the others are closed), the flex is loose, only the red and green wires are OK, all the wires are free and all the terminals are empty:

in order for you to get the plug to be working you must have installed the fuse, the blue wire must be ok, you must have gripped the flex, you must have closed the L terminal and the blue wire must be in the N terminal. remove the cover and install the fuse. then strip the blue wire and the blue wire will be ok. then insert the flex in the cover and you will have bedded the flex. then tighten the gripper screws and you will have gripped the flex. insert the red wire into the L terminal. then screw up the L terminal and you will have closed the L terminal. then unscrew the N terminal and the N terminal will be open. insert the blue wire into the N terminal.

however now you have not closed the N terminal. in order for you to get the plug to be working you must have closed the N terminal and the green wire must be in the E terminal. screw up the N terminal and you will have closed the N terminal. then unscrew the E terminal and the E terminal will be open. then insert the green wire into the E terminal.

however now you have not closed the E terminal. in order for you to get the plug to be working you must have closed the E terminal. screw up the E terminal and you will have closed the E terminal.

however now the cover is not on. install the cover. then plug the plug in and the plug will be working.

This chapter will present simple Prolog programs for performing the steps described above. It is important to note, however, that the basic task of each step is fairly well-defined and that other programs could easily be substituted for the ones given. Looking at the above examples, it is easy to see where improvements could be made in the output text, though it may not be obvious what the appropriate general principles are. Working out how to perform any one of the subtasks really well would, unfortunately, be a major research effort and would deserve a presentation many times as long as this chapter. So all we can hope to do here is present a helpful framework and encourage the reader to experiment and further develop the parts that are most interesting to him/her.

6.3.1 Justifying the Steps

In order to explain a plan, our program has to understand the purpose of the individual steps in the plan. Thus it starts by constructing a *justification* for the sequence of actions. Here is a sequence of actions:

```
remove_cover,
remove_fuse(fold),
install_fuse(fnew)
```

and here is an example justification of that sequence, in its Prolog representation:

```
j(fuse_installed(fnew), install_fuse(fnew),
   [
     j(cover_off, remove_cover, [ ]),
     j(fuse_holder_empty, remove_fuse(fold), [ ])
   ])
```

A justification is constructed using the functor j with three arguments. The first and second arguments provide (in the opposite order) the name of an action and a goal that the action achieves. The third argument provides (in a list) justifications for actions that achieve preconditions of the main action. These justifications may contain justifications for actions that achieve preconditions of *their* actions, and so on. So, in English, the above justification says the following about the action sequence:

> The main goal is to have the new fuse installed, which is achieved by installing the new fuse. Before this can be done, the cover has to be

off and the fuse holder empty. Removing the cover achieves the first of
these and removing the old fuse achieves the second.

Thus every action in the sequence is motivated in terms of how it contributes to
the main goal.

We will actually make use of two extra types of entry in justifications. Firstly,
if the reason for performing an action is not one of its primary effects, we will
represent the justification in two stages. First of all the action achieves a primary
effect, and then the empty action [ ] achieves the desired goal. So if the primary
effect of removing a fuse was to make that fuse spare, the use of this action to make
the fuse holder empty would be justified as follows:

```
j(fuse_holder_empty, [ ],
  [
  j(spare_fuse(fold), remove_fuse(fold), [ ])
  ])
```

The point of this is that we may want explicitly to highlight non-obvious uses of
actions in our explanations.

The second extra type of element that we will introduce into justifications is to
do with times when doing one action messes something up and necessitates other
actions that did not seem originally to be required. Instead of a simple list of sub-
justifications, a justification can be a term of the form patch(X,Y), where each of
X and Y is a list of sub-justifications (or possibly, in the case of Y, another *patch*).
This has the same basic meaning as the result of concatenating the lists X and Y,
but conveys the extra information that the subgoal achieved by the first element of
Y was originally true, but that some of the actions mentioned in X caused it to be
made false. Here is a complete justification of the sequence of actions for changing
the fuse of the plug:

```
j(working_system, plug_in,
   patch(
        [
        j(fuse_installed(fnew), install_fuse(fnew),
           [
           j(cover_off, remove_cover, [ ]),
           j(fuse_holder_empty, [ ],
              [
              j([ ],remove_fuse(fold), [ ])
```

```
                ])
            ])
        ],
        [
         j(cover_on, install_cover, [ ])
        ])
    )
```

Notice that the action **plug_in** requires the cover to be on and this is initially the case. However, installing the fuse ends us up in the situation where the cover has been taken off, and so another action is required to patch up this new problem that has been introduced. This justification has been constructed on the assumption that **remove_fuse(...)** has no primary effects. Hence the extra level of justification between this action and the intended effect **fuse_holder_empty**.

Constructing a justification from a sequence of actions is a kind of parsing problem, and we will use Prolog grammar rules to handle the sequences of actions that are manipulated. The basic idea of the program is illustrated by the following fragment, but this program *will not work* in its current form:

```
achieve_goal(Goal,j(Goal,Action,Justs)) -->
   achieve_goals(Preconds,Justs),
   [Action],
   {operator(Action,Preconds,_,Adds)},
   {member(Goal,Adds)}.

achieve_goals(Goals,[ ]) --> [ ].
achieve_goals(Goals,[J|Js]) -->
   {member(G,Goals)},
   achieve_goal(G,J),
   achieve_goals(Goals,Js).
```

That is, we recognise a sequence of actions as achieving a goal if they culminate in an action that achieves that goal and if we can see the actions before this as achieving the preconditions of this main action.

What is wrong with this program? First of all it does not check whether it is actually *necessary* to achieve a given precondition or that all the preconditions are satisfied before the action is performed. For these, the program would have to know

the state of the world when an attempt to achieve a goal or to perform an action
might be made. We get over this problem by introducing extra arguments to the
predicates so that the relevant world descriptions are available. In addition, because
we sometimes want to look ahead to see what the state of the world will be at a
given point in the future, we embellish the list of actions so that the intermediate
states can easily be read off. That is, instead of processing raw actions we process
elements of the form act(Action,DB), where DB is the list of assertions describing
the world that results after the execution of the action Action. Here are the revised
predicates that we will use:

achieve_goal(Goal,DB,Just,LA,NewDB) −

>   Recognises a sequence of actions/world states which achieve a given goal
>   Goal starting in a world described by DB and ending up in a world described
>   by NewDB. The justification for the sequence is Just. LA is the list of ac-
>   tions/world states available for *looking ahead*. (see below).

achieve_goals(Goals,ODB,DB,JSofar,LA,Justs) −

>   Recognises a sequence of actions/world states resulting in all the goals Goals
>   being true, starting in a world described by DB. These actions may have been
>   preceded by other actions to achieve some of the goals, with justifications
>   JSofar. ODB holds the description of the world as it was before any of the
>   goals were attempted. Justs is the justifications for the whole sequence (in-
>   cluding the previous actions).

The LA arguments will be described later. Of course, there are also two extra
arguments (unmentioned in the grammar rules) which hold the relevant lists of
actions/world states. The revised definitions have the same basic shape as before,
but with some of the details changed:

```
achieve_goal(Goal,DB,Just,LA,NewDB) -->
    {operator(Act,Pres,_,Adds), member(Goal,Adds)},
    {look_ahead(Act,DB,Pres,LA,LA1)},
    achieve_goals(Pres,DB,DB,[ ],LA1,Justs),
    [act(Act,NewDB)],
    {justify_act(Goal,Act,Justs,Just)}.

achieve_goals(Goals,ODB,DB,Sofar,LA,Sofar) -->
    {not((member(G,Goals),not(member(G,DB))))}.
```

```
achieve_goals(Goals,ODB,DB,Sofar,LA,Justs) -->
   {member(G,Goals),not(member(G,ODB)),not(member(G,DB))},
   achieve_goal(G,DB,Just,LA,DB1),
   {append(Sofar,[Just],NewSofar)},
   achieve_goals(Goals,ODB,DB1,NewSofar,LA,Justs).
achieve_goals(Goals,ODB,DB,Sofar,LA,patch(Sofar,After)) -->
   {member(G,Goals),member(G,ODB),not(member(G,DB))},
   achieve_goal(G,DB,Just,LA,DB1),
   achieve_goals(Goals,ODB,DB1,[Just],LA,After).
```

We now have three clauses for *achieve_goals/6*. The first checks for the situation where all the goals are already true, and the second looks for actions achieving some unachieved member, followed by actions to achieve some of the given goals. The third clause, which is new, recognises the *patch* case. Whereas the second clause will deal with goals that are not true and which also were not originally true, the third clause handles the situation where the goal is not true now but was originally true. In this case, the justification built is of the form patch(Sofar,After), where Sofar is the list of previous justifications for previous actions and After is the justifications for the rest of the actions, including the current one.

The program as described so far is quite inefficient. In achieve_goals, one of the goals is selected and achieve_goal called on it. For this, a possible action that would achieve the goal is found and achieve_goals is called on that action's preconditions. This will call achieve_goal again, and so on. Quite apart from the fact that we could easily encounter infinite loops this way, this approach means that we can do a great deal of work on the basis of selecting an arbitrary precondition at each stage. There will be no confirmation that this was the right one to select until after all the recursive calls have successfully finished. We can improve on this by having the program *look ahead*, i.e. only hypothesise a given goal if there actually is an action somewhere later on which achieves that goal. Thus we provide extra arguments to the predicates which provide the lists of actions/states of the world that are available for looking ahead into. The predicate look_ahead is responsible for checking that the hypothesised action does indeed occur in the lookahead list and if so returning the sequence of actions/world states that occur before that found action. This is then the lookahead list to be used when looking for actions that achieve preconditions of this found action.

In fact, for ease of implementation, the lookahead lists are kept in reverse order, i.e. with later actions occurring before earlier ones. In addition, look_ahead is entrusted with instantiating the list of preconditions to the instance actually required by the found action. Thus its definition is as follows:

```
look_ahead(Act,DB,Pres,LA,LA1) :-
   append(_,[act(Act,_)|LA1],LA),
   prev_db(LA1,DB,PrevDB),
   subset(Pres,PrevDB).

prev_db([ ],DB,DB).
prev_db([act(_,PrevDB)|_],DB,PrevDB).
```

(where **subset** checks that each element of one list occurs in another). The predicate **justify_act** is used to construct a justification from a goal, an action achieving it and a list of sub-justifications. It caters for the fact that we deal specially with the achievement of secondary effects of actions:

```
justify_act(Goal,Act,SubJusts,j(Goal,Act,SubJusts)) :-
   object(Act,Goal), !.
justify_act(Goal,Act,SubJusts,j(Goal,[ ],[j(Obj,Act,SubJusts)])) :-
   object(Act,Obj), !.
justify_act(Goal,Act,SubJusts,j(Goal,[ ],[j([ ],Act,SubJusts)])).
```

Finally, the top-level predicate **parse** embellishes a list of actions with world states, produces the reverse of the sequence as the initial lookahead list and calls **achieve_goal** to produce a final justification.

```
parse(Goal,DB,Actions,Just) :-
   embellish_with_DBs(Actions,DB,Sequence),
   rev(Sequence,LA),
   achieve_goal(Goal,DB,Just,LA,_,Sequence,[ ]).

embellish_with_DBs([ ],_,[ ]).
embellish_with_DBs([Act|Actions],DB,[act(Act,NextDB)|Seq]) :-
   operator(Act,Pres,Dels,Adds),
   subset(Pres,DB),
   alladd(Adds,DB,DB1),
   alldel(Dels,DB1,NextDB),
   embellish_with_DBs(Actions,NextDB,Seq).
```

(**alladd** and **alldel** are used to produce new databases (lists of assertions representing world states) obtained by adding or deleting a given list of assertions).

What we have presented in this section is, essentially, a simple *grammar* for plans. Our generator will simply not be able to explain a plan that it cannot understand according to this grammar. Although the grammar does capture some straightforward ways of stringing actions together, there are many things that it doesn't account for. For instance, it doesn't account for situations where the actions to achieve two goals are interleaved or where an action is performed because a failure to do it would cause a disaster. The reader is encouraged to investigate other ways that plans can be put together and consider how phenomena like these might be recognised.

6.4   Determining Explanation Structure

From the justification, the program now plans the overall "shape" of the discourse to be generated. For this it makes use of a simple "grammar" for discourses, expressed as Prolog terms as follows:

```
DISCOURSE ::=
            [ ]
            do(ACTION)
            result(ACTION,STATE)
            prereqs(ACTION,STATE)
            now(STATE)
            embed(DISCOURSE1,DISCOURSE2,DISCOURSE3)
            seq(DISCOURSE1,DISCOURSE2)
            contra_seq(DISCOURSE1,DISCOURSE2)
            comb(DISCOURSE1,DISCOURSE2)
```

The first five of these forms represent the basic kinds of statements that the program will be able to make (there is no reason, of course, why this set could not be extended). [ ] is the empty statement, do(ACTION) involves commanding that some ACTION must simply be performed, result(ACTION,STATE) involves a statement that doing a particular ACTION causes STATE to result, and prereqs(ACTION,STATE) involves stating the prerequisites (STATE) for some given ACTION. Finally, now(STATE) is used to indicate that at some point the given STATE holds in the world. The other four forms are ways to construct larger discourses out of smaller ones. At this stage, the program must look at patterns in the plan representation and decide whether they are best expressed as single sentences, sequences of sentences or per-haps as complex paragraphs, with sub-explanations embedded within explanations. A state-action pair that has more than one precondition to be established will gen-erally give rise to an **embed** structure, which has an introduction (DISCOURSE1), a main body (DISCOURSE2) and a conclusion (DISCOURSE3). A sequence (*chain*) of actions, each feeding the next in a simple way, will generally give rise to a **seq** structure, where the first action and its result are described (DISCOURSE1), followed by the others in sequence (DISCOURSE2); if there is a **patch** annotation, this might be changed to a **contra_seq**, where some kind of contrastive conjunction is needed between the sentences. Finally, **comb** provides a way of gluing two subdiscourses together without indicating any temporal order or other relationship between the parts. Here is an example discourse structure and a possible rendering in (human-generated) English:

```
embed(
    prereqs(install_fuse(fnew),
            and(cover_off, fuse_holder_empty)),
    seq(do(remove_cover),
        embed(
            prereqs(achieve(fuse_holder_empty),
                    done(remove_fuse(fold))),
            do(remove_fuse(fold)),
            result([ ], fuse_holder_empty))),
    do(install_fuse(fnew)))
```

> In order to install the new fuse you have to have the cover off and the fuse holder empty. Remove the cover. To get the fuse holder empty you need to remove the old fuse. Remove the old fuse and now the fuse holder will be empty. Finally install the new fuse.

This example illustrates that we may need to make use of complex states and ac-tions in formulating desired discourse structures. Thus **achieve(fuse_holder_empty)** is an example of an action and **done(remove_fuse(fold))** is an example of a state. Here is the simple grammar for states and actions that is used for this purpose:

```
STATE ::=
        [ ]                     % the state which is always true
        not(STATE)              % STATE is not the case
        and(STATE1,STATE2)      % STATE1 and STATE2 are both true
```

```
        enabled(ACTION)         % the preconditions of ACTION are true
        done(ACTION)            % ACTION has just been performed
        doing(ACTION)           % ACTION is currently being performed
        PRIMITIVE_STATE

ACTION ::=
        [ ]                     % the empty action
        then(ACTION1,ACTION2)   % doing ACTION1, ACTION2 sequentially
        achieve(STATE)          % making STATE true
        PRIMITIVE_ACTION
```

where PRIMITIVE_STATEs and PRIMITIVE_ACTIONs are states and actions provided by the planning domain.

Generating an initial version of the discourse structure involves a recursive traversal of the justification, looking for local patterns that can be mapped sensibly onto portions of discourse. There are potentially a large number of possible patterns that one might have specific explanation strategies for, and here we just look at three of the more obvious ones. These correspond to the three clauses of the predicate *transform_just/2*:

```
transform_just(Just,Discourse) :-
   transform_chain([Just],Discourse), !.
transform_just(j(Concl,Act,Justs),
            embed(prereqs(achieve(Goal),Preconds), Disc,Do)) :-
   Justs \= patch(_,_), !,
   goals_achieved(Justs,Preconds),
   transform_justs(Justs,Disc),
   goal_tran(Concl,Act,Goal),
   Do = result(Act,Concl).
transform_just(j(Concl,Act,patch(Bef,Aft)),contra_seq(First,Second)):-
   First = embed(prereqs(achieve(Goal),Preconds),Do1,[ ]),
   Second = comb(now(not(Lost)),Patch),
   goals_achieved(Bef,Preconds),
   first_goal(Aft,Lost),
   transform_justs(Bef,Do1),
   goal_tran(Concl,Act,Goal),
   transform_just(j(Concl,Act,Aft),Patch).
```

The first clause applies if the justification is a *chain*, that is, a sequence of actions, each of which achieves a precondition of the next one. In this case, the relevant discourse is simply a sequence of statements describing the actions and their results:

```
transform_chain([j(C,A,Rest)],seq(Prev,result(A,C))) :- !,
    transform_chain(Rest,Prev).
transform_chain([ ],[ ]).
```

The second clause is the other normal case, where there is no **patch** annotation. In this case, the discourse has an **embed** structure. The introduction is a statement describing the relevant preconditions of the main action. Then comes a discourse **Disc** describing how these are achieved, produced by **transform_justs** predicate:

```
transform_justs([ ],[ ]) :- !.
transform_justs([X|Y],seq(X1,Y1)) :-
    transform_just(X,X1),
    transform_justs(Y,Y1).
```

Finally comes a statement **Do** describing the main action and its result.

The final clause of **transform_just** covers justifications in a 'patch' structure. The main discourse structure is now a **contra_seq**. Its first part is an **embed** structure describing the actions **Bef** taking place before the problem point. The second part of the **contra_seq** mentions the goal **Lost** which has now become false, followed by the actions taking place afterwards (**Aft**).

The above definitions make use of a number of subsidiary predicates. **first_goal** is used to find the initial topmost goal in a sequence of justifications. **goal_tran** is used to extract something that can be used as a goal from the first two components of a justification, bearing in mind that the goal provided may be [ ]. Finally, **goals_achieved** goes through a list of justifications and collects their top-level goals into a single description:

```
first_goal(patch(B,_),G) :- !, first_goal(B,G).
first_goal([j(Goal,_,_) | _],Goal).

goal_tran([ ],Act,enabled(Act)) :- !.
goal_tran(Concl,Act,Concl).

goals_achieved([j([ ],Act,_)|Rest],and(done(Act),Cs)) :- !,
```

```
    goals_achieved(Rest,Cs).
goals_achieved([j(Concl,_,_)|Rest],and(Concl,Cs)) :- !,
    goals_achieved(Rest,Cs).
goals_achieved([ ],[ ]).
```

6.5   Simplifying the Explanation

The first-pass discourse structure that results from transform_just has been put
together in a rather simplistic way, and so the next stage of the program serves to
look for ways of altering this structure to make it simpler. In the process, we have
the possibility of making use of simple models of the person that the explanation
will be addressed to. Here is a collection of simplification rules that we can apply to
structures built by the previous stage (the predicate ---> indicates that its second
argument is a simplified version of its first argument):

```
:- op(23,xfx,--->).
```

```
and(X,[ ]) ---> X.
result(Act,[ ]) ---> do(Act).
result(X,done(X)) ---> do(X).
result(Act,Concl) ---> do(Act) :- obvious_result(Act,Concl).
result(Act,Concl) ---> do(achieve(Concl)) :- obvious_act(Concl,Act).
achieve(and(S1,S2)) ---> then(achieve(S1),achieve(S2)).
seq(X,[ ]) ---> X.
seq([ ],X) ---> X.
seq(seq(X,Y),Z) ---> seq(X,seq(Y,Z)).
seq(do(X),do(Y)) ---> do(then(X,Y)).
achieve(done(A)) ---> A.
seq(do(X),seq(do(Y),Z)) ---> seq(do(then(X,Y)),Z).
seq(X,seq(Y,seq(Z,W))) ---> comb(seq(X,seq(Y,Z)),W).
```

Some of these rules are simply a matter of clearing up after the rather rough-
and-ready construction of discourse structures. For instance, occurrences of the
empty action or state [ ] are removed by appropriately changing the context.
Others are to ensure that expressions appear in a *normal form*. For instance,

nested **seqs** are made to branch to the right, rather than to the left, as this will enable better use to be made of conjunctions in English. The last rule ensures that nested **seqs** of length more than 3 are appropriately broken up into smaller chunks combined by **combs**. This is simply to restrict the amount of structure that is repeated and hopefully to introduce more variety into the text. Other rules perform a more obvious simplification by reducing the number of components in the representation. For instance, the penultimate rule performs a kind of factoring where, instead of issuing two commands the system can issue a single complex command. For instance, instead of:

> Remover the cover. Then unscrew the 'L' terminal.

the system might be able to say the simpler:

> Remove the cover and unscrew the 'L' terminal.

The rule before that would enable something like:

`do(achieve(done(remove_fuse(fold))))`

to be simplified to:

`do(remove_fuse(fold))`

> This would be reflected in English by a phrase like:

> Remove the old fuse

rather than

> Get to have removed the old fuse

Finally, two of these rules are conditional - that is, the simplifications will only be applied if certain conditions are satisfied. If the result of an action is obvious to the intended reader, then there is no point in mentioning the result of the action as well as the action itself. Similarly there is no point in mentioning both a goal and the action achieving it if the action is the obvious way of achieving the goal. The predicates **obvious_result** and **obvious_act** test for these possibilities and need to be defined appropriately for the given reader.

The actual simplification code is a traditional Prolog algebraic simplification program, and similar examples can be found in Prolog textbooks, e.g. [CM87].

```
simplify(X,Y) :-
   functor(X,F,N),
   functor(Y1,F,N),
   simp_args(N,X,Y1),
   simp1(Y1,Y).

simp_args(0,_,_) :- !.
simp_args(N,X,Y) :-
   N1 is N-1,
   arg(N,X,X1),
   arg(N,Y,Y1),
   simplify(X1,Y1), !,
   simp_args(N1,X,Y).

simp1(X,Y1) :- lex_rewrite(X,Y), !, simplify(Y,Y1).
simp1(X,Y1) :- X ---> Y, !, simplify(Y,Y1).
simp1(X,X).
```

The only slight change from a conventional algebraic simplifier is the use of the predicate lex_rewrite as an alternative to --->. The idea is that, whilst ---> expresses simplifications that apply independent of the domain, lex_rewrite is intended as a way of introducing *domain dependent* simplifications. In principle, this could be used for all sorts of unstructured programming, but there are places where such a hook could be generally useful to patch over representational inadequacies in the planning domain. For instance, in our plug domain representation we have an action install_fuse(F) and a state fuse_installed(F). In practice, since we are only dealing with a single agent, fuse_installed(F) means exactly the same as done(install_fuse(F)). The advantage of the second representation, however, is that the correspondence between the action and the state is explicit and the extra complexity of the state description (it needs the use of a past tense verb and an explicit agent, whereas the action can be said with a simple verb and omitted agent) is syntactically visible. Thus by including the rule:

```
lex_rewrite(fuse_installed(F),done(install_fuse(F))).
```

we can enable the system to further simplify do(achieve(fuse_installed(fold))) to do(install_fuse(fold)) and so the simplification phase can find a simpler way of phrasing this command.

6.6   Manipulating Syntactic Structures

Instead of generating text directly from the outline discourse structure produced
by the last phase, we first of all produce a representation of the syntactic structure
of the text. Proceeding via an explicit syntactic representation ensures that the
text we are generating will be grammatical. As we shall see, it also facilitates
the propagation of information (for instance, about tense and number) between
different syntactic constituents. For our syntactic representations, we will make
use of a simple kind of *unification grammar*.

In unification grammar, one represents information about a particular phrase
by a *functional description*, which is basically a statement about attributes of the
phrase and their values (the information about a value will in general itself be a
functional description). For instance, here is a possible functional description for a
sentence:

```
[s,
 subj=[person_number=(3+sing),text=[root=it]],
 pred=[
       first=[
              mainverb=[root=hit],
              compls=[
                      first=[np]
                      ]
              ]
       ]
]
```

This says, amongst other things, that the sentence described has a `subj` and a
`pred`. The `subj` has a `text` attribute, whose value has a `root` attribute, whose
value is the atom `it`. Basically, we represent a functional description by a Prolog
list of items. An element of the form `X=Y` states that the value of the `X` attribute is
described by the (functional description or atom) `Y`. On the other hand, an element
that is a simple atom (e.g. `s`) expresses an additional *property* that the thing
described has (as we will see, in general, it serves simply as an abbreviation for a
whole list of `X=Y` type statements).

What functional descriptions actually make sense depends on the natural language that is being used and the way that strings of that language are analysed
syntactically. Thus a separate set of statements, a *grammar*, specifies which such

functional descriptions are legal descriptions of sentences in the given language. There are many different ways used for expressing unification grammars. Given a partial functional description for a sentence, it is generally possible to *match* it against the grammar in such a way as to validate the *grammaticality* of the sentence and fill in any attributes whose values follow from those already given. It is important to note that attributes in a unification grammar may be of a semantic, as well as a syntactic nature.

The way in which we specify a grammar for this program is in several parts. First of all, we specify a fixed set of categories of phrases and describe which attributes a phrase can have depending on which category it has. Secondly we specify rules about how the values of attributes may be *shared* between different phrases. Finally we specify linearisation rules which determine which attributes of a phrase name subphrases and in what order these subphrases appear (this will be discussed in a later section). Here is how we specify the allowed attributes, for a small subset of English.

```
para ↔ aux:word ** morph ** person_number **
   (empty ++
       (epara: para) ++
       (subj:np ** pred:vp ** adv:word) ++
       (conjn:word ** first:para ** rest:para)).


np ↔ person_number ** absent ** referent ** text:word.


word ↔ person_number ** root ** morph.


vp ↔ person_number ** morph ** subj **
   ((aux:word ** evp:vp) ++
       (mainverb:word ** compls:compls) ++
       (first:vp ** conjn:word ** rest:vp)).


compls ↔ empty ++ (first ** rest:compls).


pp ↔ prep:word ** head:np.
```

Each syntactic category (e.g. **para, np**) is introduced by a single rule which states what attributes a phrase of that category can have and what types of values the attributes have. **++** indicates alternatives (*or*) and ****** the presence of several attributes simultaneously (*and*). So, for instance, every paragraph (para) has attributes aux, morph and person_number. Apart from this, it can have the attribute empty (if it is empty), the attribute epara (if it consists of a single *embedded* paragraph), attributes subj, pred and adv (if it is a normal sentence) or attributes conjn, first and rest (if it is two paragraphs joined together by a conjunction). This is the exhaustive set of possibilities (which are also disjoint). It can be seen that we are using the category para to describe any number of sentences that conceptually belong together for some reason. The aux (which must be a word) and morph of a para specify an auxilliary verb that must appear in all the sentences and the morphological form of the verbs that are to follow it. So, for instance, if we decided to produce a paragraph that was entirely in the future tense then we would set the aux to be the word *will* and the morph to inf (indicating that verbs must be in the infinitive form). At the outermost layer for the whole text, we will set the aux to be the dummy verb *do* - this will not actually appear in the output unless we need simple present or past tense negative sentences.

Apart from para, the main categories in our grammar are np and vp. An np (noun phrase) will be a phrase referring to an object, such as *the E terminal*, whereas a vp (verb phrase) will express a command or a proposition about an object, such as *will be closed*. vps can also be conjoined and can include auxilliary verbs and nested vps.

Next we are allowed to specify when a phrase and one of its attributes must share one of their attributes:

```
para/first share aux.
para/rest share aux.
para/pred share morph.
para/first share morph.
para/rest share morph.
para/subj share person_number.
para/pred share person_number.
vp/first share person_number.
vp/rest share person_number.
vp/first share morph.
vp/rest share morph.
vp/mainverb share person_number.
vp/aux share person_number.
vp/mainverb share morph.
vp/aux share morph.
```

```
vp/evp share person_number.
para/pred share subj.
vp/evp share subj.
vp/first share subj.
vp/rest share subj.
```

Here we state, for instance, that a paragraph has the same value for its **aux** and **morph** features as that paragraph's **first** and **rest** do. This allows us to state once and for all that a paragraph should be in the future tense, say, and have it automatically follow that if the paragraph turns out to be a conjunction of sentences then each one will be in future tense. Notice that if a paragraph consists of an **epara**, then that embedded paragraph is not constrained to have the **aux** and **morph** of the paragraph it makes up; the introduction of **eparas** therefore provides a way of locally overriding global specifications of tense, etc.

The statements about **person_number** are there to ensure that the person and number morphology of the first verb of a sentence match up with the characteristics of the sentence's subject. Within a paragraph which is a simple sentence, the **subj** and **pred** must have the same value for **person_number**, because the statements here say that each must have the same value as the **person_number** of the paragraph. Other statements here ensure, for instance, that in a conjoined verb phrase the two conjuncts have the same **person_number** value.

Finally we are allowed to define new properties as abbreviations for combinations of attributes and values already defined:

```
no_subj iff [s, subj=[absent=yes,referent=user]].
```

Thus a sentence will be a **no_subj** if its subject noun phrase has the value **yes** for the attribute **absent** (the phrase will not actually appear in the output) and the value **user** for the attribute **referent** (the phrase will refer to the person to whom the text is addressed). This property will be used in the specification of how a command will be realised as a sentence.

Given this description of valid phrase types in the natural language, we need to provide a way of constructing descriptions of phrases that are guaranteed to be grammatical, that is, consistent with what the grammar says phrases should be like. For instance, we do not want to be able to construct a noun phrase that has a **mainverb** or a sentence in which the subject noun phrase does not agree with the first verb. For efficiency, we will actually represent a phrase by a Prolog term, where

the functor of the term is the name of the syntactic category and the arguments
are used to hold the attributes of the phrase, each attribute being allocated a fixed
position within the term. If the value of a given attribute is itself a phrase of some
category, then that argument position will be filled with another complex Prolog
term, which itself will have slots for attributes, and so on. For instance, here is
the Prolog representation for the structure of the paragraph that will be realised in
English as "you must have installed the new fuse":

```
para([ ], [ ], [ ], _1,
   vp([ ], [ ], [ ], [ ], [ ],
      vp([ ], [ ], [ ], compls(_2,
         np(word(_3, 'the new fuse', _4), fnew, _5, 3 + sing), [ ]),
         word(en, install, 2 + sing),
         [ ], [ ],
         np(word(_6, you, _7), user, _8, 2 + sing),
         en, 2 + sing
         ),
      word(inf, have, 2 + sing),
      np(word(_6, you, _7), user, _8, 2 + sing),
      inf, 2 + sing
      ),
   np(word(_6, you, _7), user, _8, 2 + sing),
   [ ], [ ], 2 + sing, inf,
   word(_9, must, _10)
   )
```

The predicate *matches/2* (defined as an infix operator) is used to construct a
representation X of a phrase which satisfies a given functional description. What it
does is instantiate X just enough so that it has the relevant attributes and values. If
X cannot be instantiated in such a way as to give rise to a legal phrase description,
then **matches** fails. Here are some example uses of matches in use:

```
?- X matches [word, root=fantasy],
   X matches [person_number = (3+sing)].
X = word(_1, fantasy, 3 + sing) ?

?- X matches [compls, first=[pp, prep=[root=to]]].
X = compls(_1, pp(_2, word(_3, to, _4)), [ ]) ?
```

```
?- X matches [np, text=[person_number=(2+sing)]].
X = np(word(_1, _2, 2 + sing), _3, _4, _5) ?

?- X matches [np, aux=[root=foo]].
no
```

The operation of **matches** is based on a set of low-level clauses which tell it how to access given attributes for given types of objects. The predicate **ident_patt** describes how each syntactic category is represented:

```
ident_patt(word, word(_1, _2, _3)).
ident_patt(pp, pp(_1, _2)).
ident_patt(np, np(_1, _2, _3, _4)).
...
```

Thus, for instance, a phrase with category **word** is represented by a functor with three arguments. These are used for the **morph**, **root** and **person_number** attributes in this order. The predicate **attr_patt** is used for accessing a given attribute from a given type of phrase:

```
attr_patt(person_number, word(_1, _2, _3), _3).
attr_patt(root, word(_1, _2, _3), _2).
attr_patt(morph, word(_1, _2, _3), _1).
attr_patt(prep, pp(_1, _2), _2) :-
    ident_patt(word, _2).
attr_patt(text, np(_1, _2, _3, _4), _1) :-
    ident_patt(word, _1).
attr_patt(rest, vp(_1, _2, _3, [ ], [ ], [ ], [ ], _4, _5, _6), _1) :-
    attr_patt(subj, _1, _4),
    attr_patt(morph, _1, _5),
    attr_patt(person_number, _1, _6),
    ident_patt(vp, _1).
attr_patt(evp, vp([ ], [ ], [ ], [ ], [ ], _1, _2, _3, _4, _5), _1) :-
    attr_patt(subj, _1, _3),
    attr_patt(person_number, _1, _5),
    ident_patt(vp, _1).
...
```

Thus, for instance, to get the **root** of a **word** one extracts the second argument. The **attr_patt** clauses build in the constraints described in the grammar in three ways. First of all, sometimes the existence of one attribute precludes the existence of another. The non-existence of a given attribute value is represented by the value [ ] - here, for instance, the **rest** of a verb phrase is represented by the first component, but if we are required to build a verb phrase structure with an **evp** value then we wish to exclude the possibility of ever finding a **rest** value. Secondly, when an attribute is extracted and the type of that attribute is known, then this extra information is filled in (e.g. by the call of **ident_patt** when the **prep** is extracted from a **pp**). Finally, when an attribute is extracted, one of whose attributes shares a value with the original phrase, then that sharing is forced to occur (e.g. for the sharing of the **morph** value when the **rest** is extracted from a **vp**). Because **attr_patt** embodies the sharing constraints, when we specify a phrase by a functional description we don't have to specify every value for every attribute. Instead we need only specify the bare bones and **matches** will fill out the rest (everything that follows from what we do specify according to the grammar).

Setting up all the **ident_patt** and **attr_patt** clauses by hand to reflect a given grammar would be extremely hard work, but this can be done automatically (although we will not show it here).

Given this raw material, we can present the definition of **matches** and its subsidiary predicates:

```
:- op(40,xfx,matches).

X matches Y :- var(Y), !, X=Y.
X matches [ ] :- !.
X matches [Descrip|Descrips] :- !,
   matchspec(X,Descrip),
   X matches Descrips.
X matches X.


:- op(40,xfx,=+).

matchspec(X,Attr = Descrip) :-
   attr_patt(Attr,X,Val), !,
   Val \== [ ],
   Val matches Descrip.
```

```
matchspec(X,Attr =+ Descrip) :-
    attr_patt(Attr,X,Val), !,
    Val \== [ ],
    addspec(Descrip,Val).
matchspec(X,Prop) :-
    atom(Prop),
    ident_patt(Prop,X), !.

addspec(Descrip,Val) :-
    attr_patt(first,Val,Val1),
    Val1 \== [ ],
    Val1 matches Descrip, !.
addspec(Descrip,Val) :-
    attr_patt(rest,Val,Val1), !,
    Val1 \== [ ],
    addspec(Descrip,Val1).
```

The predicate *matchspec/2* is used to ensure that the object satisfies a single *description*. Such a description can be of the form Attr = Descrip or of the form Attr =+ Descrip, or it can be a simple atom. The first case involves extracting the value of the attribute Attr and ensuring that it matches Descrip. Note the test that the value is not [ ] - i.e. that the value has not been prohibited from existing by some previous constraint. The last case handles the case of *properties* - an object can be instantiated so as to satisfy a property if it unifies with that property's ident_patt. The intermediate case is for when we wish to have values that are lists. We encode lists using the attributes first and rest; thus the pattern:

```
[first = [root=by],
 rest = [first = [root=your],
         rest = [first = [root=leave]
                 rest = [empty]]]]
```

can be used to construct a representation of a list of three words "by your leave". The description Attr =+ Descrip is used when we want to specify that the value of the attribute Attr should be a list that contains the object described by Descrip but where we don't wish to state where in the list it should occur. In practice our implementation finds the first possible place in the list Attr where Descrip can be put.

Notice that, for efficiency, most of these clauses contain *cuts*. One major function of these is to suppress the trying of alternative `attr_patt` clauses, once a first solution has been found. However, `attr_patt` is only deterministic if both of its first two arguments are instantiated. If we call it in any other way, then in general the *cuts* will cause us to lose solutions. Thus, in particular, with `matches` we can only expect to extract attributes from an object whose syntactic category is already known.

6.7   Generating Syntactic Structures

To generate syntactic structures from a discourse structure, we simply need a rule for every type of **DISCOURSE** saying what syntactic structure corresponds to it. We can then recursively traverse the structure, producing syntactic output as we go. The top level of this program is the predicate *fill_syntax/2*, which ensures that the syntactic form is of category **para** and then calls the predicate `fill`:

```
fill_syntax(Discourse,Syntax) :-
    Syntax matches [para, aux=[morph=pres,root=do]],
    fill(Discourse,Syntax).
```

The first part of *fill/2* is devoted simply to determining how the paragraph is to be broken up and what conjunctions are to be used to link the parts:

```
fill(seq(Thing1,Thing2),Para) :- !,
    Para matches
        [conjn = [root = '.then'],
         first = First,
         rest = Rest],
    fill(Thing1,First),
    fill(Thing2,Rest).
fill(comb(Thing1,Thing2),Para) :- !,
    Para matches
        [conjn = [root = '.'],
         first = First,
         rest = Rest],
    fill(Thing1,First),
    fill(Thing2,Rest).
fill(contra_seq(Thing1,Thing2),Para) :- !,
```

```
    Para matches
        [conjn = [root = '.@however'],
         first = First,
         rest = Rest],
    fill(Thing1,First),
    fill(Thing2,Rest).
fill(embed(First,Inside,[ ]),Para) :- !,
    Para matches
        [conjn = [root = '.'],
         first = Intro,
         rest = Body
        ],
    fill(First,Intro),
    fill(Inside,Body).
fill(embed(First,Inside,After),Para) :- !,
    Para matches
        [conjn = [root = '.'],
         first = [conjn = [root = '.'],
                           first = Intro,
                           rest = Body],
         rest = Concl
        ],
fill(First,Intro),
fill(Inside,Body),
fill(After,Concl).
```

For instance, a **seq** discourse is realised as a conjunction of two paragraphs, the word "then" being used to separate them. For simplicity, we have often combined several layout specifications into a single "conjunction". Thus .**@however** is to be generated as a period (to terminate the previous sentence), followed by a blank line (indicated by **@**), followed by the word **however**.

So far, we have dealt with discourse structures which contain sub-discourses. As we look inside these we eventually reach those types of discourse which are the primitive types of statements we can make about plans:

```
fill(do(Act),Para) :- !,
    Para matches [no_subj, pred=VP],
    fill(Act,VP).
```

```
fill(result([ ],State),Para) :- !,
   Para matches [epara=EPara],
   EPara matches [aux=[root=will],morph=inf],
   fill(State,EPara).
fill(result(Act,State),Para) :- !,
   Para matches
   [conjn = [root = and],
   first = DoAct,
   rest = Result],
   DoAct matches [no_subj, pred=VP],
   fill(Act,VP),
   Result matches [epara=R],
   R matches [aux=[root=will],morph=inf],
   fill(State,R).
fill(now(State),Para) :- !,
   Para matches
   [conjn = [root = now], rest = [empty=[ ]], first = Para1],
   fill(State,Para1).
fill(prereqs(Act,States),Para) :- !,
   Para matches
   [conjn = [root = 'in order for'],
   first = Goal,
   rest = Subgoals],
   Goal matches [epara=G],
   G matches [para,aux=[root=to],morph=inf,pred=VP],
   Subgoals matches [epara=S],
   S matches [aux=[root=must],morph=inf],
   fill(Act,VP),
   fill(States,S).
```

At this point we are beginning to have expectations about what internal structure the sentences will have. For instance, for a do construction we mark the sentence as having no subject and then recursively call fill to generate the verb phrase from the action to be performed. With a result construction we construct a conjunction where the first half is a sentence missing a subject and the second half is in the future tense. This will give rise to text like "close the window and the room will be warm". Once again the internal details of the paragraph are obtained by calling fill recursively on the action and the state mentioned in the result construction.

Finally we get to the point where we are trying to fill a state or action and produce a representation of a sequence of sentences which would realise that intended
discourse. Once more we look at the more complex cases first - where we will need a
conjunction of sentences or a complex verb phrase involving extra auxilliary verbs:

```
fill(and(S1,and(S2,S3)),Para) :- !,
    Para matches [para, first = F, conjn = [root = ','], rest = R],
    fill(S1,F),
    fill(and(S2,S3),R).
fill(and(S1,S2),Para) :- !,
    Para matches [para, first = F, conjn = [root = and], rest = R],
    fill(S1,F),
    fill(S2,R).
fill(not(S),Para) :- !,
    Para matches [adv=[root=not]],
    fill(S,Para).
fill(enabled(Act),Para) :- !,
    Para matches [pred = [aux=[root=can],evp=VP]],
    VP matches [morph=inf],
    fill(Act,VP).
fill(done(Act),Para) :- !,
    Para matches [pred = [aux=[root=have],evp=VP]],
    VP matches [morph=en],
    fill(Act,VP).
fill(doing(Act),Para) :- !,
    Para matches [pred = [aux=[root=be],evp=VP]],
    VP matches [morph=ing],
    fill(Act,VP).
fill(then(Act1,Act2),VP) :- !,
    VP matches [first=F, conjn=[root=and], rest=R],
    fill(Act1,F),
    fill(Act2,R).
fill(achieve(State),VP) :- !,
    interp_constit(user,NP),
    VP matches [mainverb = [root=get], subj=NP],
    Para1 matches [para, aux=[root=to],morph=inf],
    fill(State,Para1),
    VP matches [compls =+ Para1].
```

Here we have decided to realise a complex **and** state by simply putting commas between sentences describing the individual states (and the word "and" before the last one). The first two clauses ensure that this happens. The realisation of an **enabled** construction involves using the extra verb "can", with the embedded action expressed as a sentence in the infinitive form.

The recursive traversal of the discourse structure "bottoms out" when it hits a primitive state or action from the planning domain. Now one of the final two clauses of **fill** applies, according to whether we are trying to construct a **Para** or a **VP**:

```
fill(Prim,Para) :-
   Para matches [para, pred=VP], !,
   lex(Prim,Verb,Slots),
   VP matches [mainverb = [root = Verb]],
   absorb(Slots,VP).
fill(Prim,VP) :-
   lex(Prim,Verb,Slots),
   VP matches [vp, mainverb=[root=Verb]],
   absorb(Slots,VP).
```

The predicate **lex** is used to link a domain state or action with the use of an English verb and an assignment to roles like **subj** and **obj**:

```
?- lex(install_cover,Verb,Slots).
Verb = install
Slots = [subj: user, obj:cover]
```

The objects assigned to the roles are then realised as noun phrases by the use of the predicate **referent** which retrieves a fixed phrase and a **person_number** value:

```
?- referent(cover,X,Y).
X = the cover
Y = (3+sing)
```

The retrieved verb is installed as the **mainverb** and the noun phrases arising from the domain objects are spliced into relevant parts of the sentence, depending on their roles. For an imperative sentence, the subject of the sentence will already have been set to the reader, **user**, and so it will be necessary to retrieve a verb entry that has **user** as the **subj**. The predicate **absorb** is in charge of installing all the non-subj role noun phrases into a verb phrase:

```
:- op(30,xfx,:).

absorb([Role:Constit|Rest],VP) :- !,
   interp_constit(Constit,NP),
   fill_role(Role,VP,NP),
   absorb(Rest,VP).
absorb([ ],_).

interp_constit(Ref,NP) :-
   referent(Ref,String,PN), !,
   NP matches [text=[root=String], referent=Ref, person_number=PN].
interp_constit(Word,NP) :-
   atom(Word), !,
   NP matches [root=Word].
interp_constit(NP,NP).

fill_role(P,VP,NP) :-
   preposition(P), !,
   PP matches [pp, prep=[root=P], head=NP],
   VP matches [compls =+ PP].
fill_role(obj,VP,NP) :- !,
   VP matches [compls =+ NP].
fill_role(complement,VP,NP) :- !,
   VP matches [compls =+ NP].
fill_role(subj,VP,NP) :- !,
   VP matches [subj = NP].
fill_role(Role,_,_) :-
   error('Unknown role type',[Role]).
```

The predicates **lex** and **referent** are used to retrieve information about how to
linguistically realise a domain state or action and a domain object. The clauses for
these predicates make up the system's "lexicon", which we now consider further.

6.8   The Lexicon and Domain-dependence

The building of individual sentences makes use of specific linguistic information
recorded about entities in the planning domain, and it is to this that we now turn.
It is this lexical information that will need to change for each different planning

domain that we use the system for. The most important predicate in the lexicon is
`lex`, which indicates how a particular state or action of the domain can be expressed
in language:

```
lex(bed_flex,bed,[subj:user,obj:flex]).
lex(close_terminal(X),close,[subj:user,obj:X]).
lex(insert_to_terminal(W,T),insert,[subj:user,obj:W,into:T]).
```

The first component of a `lex` fact is the name of the state or action involved. The
second is the verb that can be used to describe it, and the third is an indication
of how surface cases of that verb are to be filled in. This third component can
specify that a case (`subj`, `obj` or a preposition) can be filled by a noun phrase
denoting a particular individual (e.g. `user` - the reader), or a noun phrase denoting
an individual mentioned in the state or action (e.g. X in the `close_terminal` case).
As we saw above, sometimes a particular action or state in the domain cannot be
expressed in English as a simple (present tense, active) use of a verb. In this case,
it can be convenient to consider the action or state as a complex object formed
from a hypothesised primitive object that *can* be expressed as a simple use of a
verb. This is another form of domain-dependent information. Here are some such
"rewrite rules" from the plug domain:

```
lex_rewrite(flex_gripped,done(grip_flex)).
lex_rewrite(fuse_installed(X),done(install_fuse(X))).
```

The problem of how to choose a noun phrase to mention a particular object
is complex, and we have deliberately avoided addressing it here. Thus, instead
of trying to work out whether a given object would be best mentioned as a full
description ("the E terminal"), an abbreviated description ("the terminal") or a
pronoun ("it"), the program simply retrieves a fixed phrase from the lexicon. Thus
the lexicon provides a fact to map every possible referent onto a fixed noun phrase.
Here are some examples:

```
referent(user,you,(2+sing)).
referent(e,'the E terminal',(3+sing)).
referent(cover,'the cover',(3+sing)).
referent(plug,'the plug',(3+sing)).
referent(red,'the red wire',(3+sing)).
referent(gripper_screws,'the gripper screws',(3+plur)).
```

Here the referent • has been mapped onto the fixed phrase "the E terminal", which is 3rd person singular, for instance.

One of the prime advantages of having a general natural language generator, rather than a system relying on fixed templates, should be that an explanation generated can be finely tailored to the needs and abilities of the reader. We can obtain a degree of user-dependence by incorporating in the program fixed knowledge about what things the user finds *obvious* - which actions are suggested obviously by certain goals, and which results obviously follow from certain actions. Here are some *obviousness* clauses used in the plug domain:

```
obvious_result(remove_cover,cover_off).
obvious_result(install_cover,cover_on).
obvious_result(install_fuse,fuse_installed).
obvious_result(insert_to_terminal(X,Y),wire_in(X,Y)).
obvious_act(_,_) :- fail.
```

We saw above the use of *obviousness* clauses in message simplification. Although they are not strictly expressing knowledge of lexical items, nevertheless they form part of the domain-dependent side of the program and it is hence convenient to think of them together with the lexicon.

6.9 Linearisation and Output

The phrase description (constituent tree) generated in the last stage contains no ordering information, and thus we need specific rules for each kind of constituent dictating the order in which the parts should appear. The program therefore recursively walks round the Prolog phrase representation, generating words according to these strict rules. It is at this stage that morphological processing is done.

We could write a set of special-purpose Prolog clauses which would walk around the constituent tree in a fixed order, printing out the actual words it encounters, but such clauses would be lengthy and would have to change whenever the grammar changed. So instead we will define a format for more compact *linearisation rules* and write an interpreter that can apply the rules to a given constituent tree to produce the output. Here are some rules in the approved format:

```
:- op(400,xfy,⟹).
:- op(200,xfy,if).
```

```
[np, absent=no, text=P] ⟹ [P] if true.
[np, absent=yes] ⟹ [ ] if true.
[vp, aux=A, evp=V] ⟹ [A,V] if true.
[vp, mainverb=V, compls=C] ⟹ [V,C] if true.
[vp, first=F, conjn=W, rest=R] ⟹ [F,W,R] if true.
```

Each rule consists of a *pattern*, a ⟹, a list, the word if and a Prolog goal. The idea is that the *pattern* can be compared with an input constituent tree by the **matches** predicate. If it does indeed match, and if the Prolog goal is also true, then the rule is deemed to apply, and the list determines which parts of the input tree are to be output and in what order. For instance, the last rule above specifies that if a verb phrase has features first, conjn and rest (i.e. if it is a conjoined verb phrase) then the order in which its parts are to be output is as follows: the first value (F), the conjn value (W) and then the rest value (R). No other attributes of the verb phrase are to be output.

The interpreter for these rules (predicate generate) needs to do the following, given some input constituent tree. It needs to try the rules in order, for each one determining whether the *pattern* matches the tree and whether the Prolog goal is satisfied. If so, it decides to use this rule only (so the order of the rules matters) and derives the output list specified by the rule. Now the elements of this list may be individual word structures, or they may be structures representing more complex phrases. Thus the interpreter calls itself recursively on each element of the list, bottoming out when it reaches a word or some other Prolog structure that does not represent a complex phrase (this allows us, for instance, to leave Prolog variables standing for optional attributes that do not happen to be filled in a given sentence).

```
generate(X) :-
   var(X), !.
generate(Tree) :-
   (Patt ⟹ Seq if Cond), Tree matches Patt, Cond, !,
   generate_list(Seq).
generate(Tree) :-
   generate_word(Tree), !.
generate(Tree).
generate_list([ ]) :- !.
generate_list([X|Y]) :- !,
   generate(X), generate_list(Y).
```

The last clause for **generate** expresses a default that if no linearisation rule applies to a given structure then that structure will not lead to any words being output. The predicate **generate_word** is in charge of taking a word structure and printing an appropriate character representation. Notice that the Prolog conditions on linearisation rules are tested *after* the pattern has been matched against the input; this allows the rules to specify conditions on the parts of the tree. For instance, the Prolog predicate **infix_conj** tests whether a given English conjunction is *infix*, i.e. should appear between the two phrases it combines. Thus we can have the following rules for **para** conjunction:

```
[para, first=F, conjn=[root=C], conjn=W, rest=R] ⟹
   [F,W,R] if infix_conj(C).
[para, first=F, conjn=W, rest=R] ⟹ [W,F,R] if true.
```

Generating a single **word** structure may simply involve printing out the value of its **root** attribute, but if the word is a verb (in our domain, only verbs need inflectional morphology) we may need to add a suffix to the root. We can detect this by looking to see whether the **morph** attribute of the word has been assigned - if so, then we have a verb and closer examination is needed. This examination is performed by the predicate **verb_morph**, which uses the information in the **word** structure to construct an output word, taking into account both irregular and regular verb forms.

```
generate_word(W) :-
   W matches [root = 'EMPTY'], !.
generate_word(W) :-
   W matches [morph=M, root=R, person_number=PN],
   nonvar(M), !,
   verb_morph(M,PN,R,A),
   write(' '), write(A).
generate_word(W) :-
   W matches [root = Root],
   name(Root,Na),
   output_word(Na).


verb_morph(pres,(3+sing),be,is) :- !.
verb_morph(pres,(2+sing),be,are) :- !.
verb_morph(pres,(_+plur),be,are) :- !.
```

```
verb_morph(pres,(3+sing),do,does) :- !.
verb_morph(pres,(2+sing),X,X) :- !.
verb_morph(pres,(_+plur),X,X) :- !.
verb_morph(pres,(3+sing),X,X1) :- !,
   name(X,Na), append(Na,"s",Na1), name(X1,Na1).
```

The definition of **verb_morph** is obviously something that could be considerably developed. Finally, as can be seen from the above code, the appearance of a verb in the output is always preceded by the appearance of a space. This is a convention that is worth imposing for all words (so that two words are always separated by a space), except special words like '.' and ','. To handle these cases, we send most output through the predicate **output_word**. This looks for special punctuation characters like '.' and ',' at the start of a word and prints them without extra spaces. In this context we have introduced the extra layout character '@' which indicates that a new paragraph is to be begun in the output.

```
output_word([ ]) :- !.
output_word([44|Na]) :- !, write(','), output_word(Na).
output_word([46|Na]) :- !, write('.'), output_word(Na).
output_word([64|Na]) :- !, nl, nl, output_word(Na).   % @
output_word([N|Na]) :- !, write(' '), name(A,[N|Na]), write(A).
output_word(Na) :- write(' '), name(A,Na), write(A).
```

6.10 Background

The original STRIPS planner is described in [FN71]. We have taken from it a coherent, if rather old-fashioned and restrictive, notion of a plan operator and a plan. It is important to note that research in automatic planning nowadays makes use of much richer models of states and actions. The interested reader is referred to sources such as [Sac77, AK83, Tsa87, Tat85]. Plans have been used in game playing by [Wil82], in natural language understanding by [SA77, Wil83] and [All83], and as a way of controlling natural language generation [App85].

We have also presented a very cut-down account of unification grammar. For more formal and sophisticated presentations, the reader should consult [Shi86] or [GM89].

The program described here is a cut-down version of an early version of a program that has been described, though not at such a detailed level, elsewhere [Mel88,

ME89]. For reasons of space, we have had to exclude minor parts of even the cut-down program; the complete code can be obtained from the author at the address given above. We would like to thank the British Science and Engineering Research Council for making this work possible through the provision of research grant GR/D/08876 and an Advanced Fellowship.

Chapter 7

A Simple Learning Program

Richard O'Keefe

Department of Computer Science
Royal Melbourne Institute of Technology,
GPO Box 2476V,
Melbourne,
Victoria 3001,
Australia.
E-Mail: ok@goanna.cs.rmit.oz.AU

Abstract

In this chapter, we develop a very simple machine learning program. The point of this is to see how one might go about developing such a program in Prolog, not to produce a particularly capable program.

7.1   The Task

We start with a very simple task indeed. To make it concrete, suppose we want, as one tiny part of a natural language learning program, to learn when it is appropriate to use which English pronoun. We suppose (and this is a big assumption) that we have obtained a set of examples like

- two things were referred to

- the things referred to included the speaker in the conversation

- the reference is in the subject position of a sentence

- the word used was "we".

The program will be given a set of pairs *ObjectDescription-Class*. This set is called the *training set*. A *Class* is simply the name of a class. An *ObjectDescription* is a tuple of attribute values. The appearance of a particular pair in the training set means that an object whose attributes match the *ObjectDescription* is to be regarded as belonging to the named *Class*.

For the English pronouns application, each example will have the form

```
pronoun(Person, Number, Case) -- Pronoun
```

where the possible values are

Person = [s,h,i,m,f] standing for Speaker, Hearer, Inanimate, Masculine, and Feminine

Number = [s,d,p] standing for Singular, Dual, and Plural

Case = [s,o,p,g] standing for Subject, Object, Possessive, and Genitive

and the possible values for Pronoun are the pronouns themselves.

The program may need to know what the possible classes and values of the attributes are, so we shall also provide it with a *ProblemDescription* which is a pair *AttributeDescriptions–Classes*, where *Classes* is a set of the class names, and *AttributeDescriptions* is a tuple of sets of attribute values.

For the English pronouns application, the *ProblemDescription* will be

```
pronoun([s,h,i,m,f],[s,d,p],[s,o,p,g])
        -- [i,me,mine,my, ..., they,them,their,their]
```

The program is to produce a set of rules, where a rule has the form *Generic-ObjectDescription–Class*. As before, the *Class* is a class name. A *GenericObject-Description* is a tuple of sets of attribute values. A rule means that any object each of whose attributes is an element of the corresponding set in the *GenericObject-Description* is to be regarded as belonging to the named *Class*.

For the English pronouns application, one of the rules we are expecting to see is

```
pronoun([i,m,f],[d,p],[g]) -- their
```

which means that the pronoun "their" is to be used when the Person is inanimate, masculine, or feminine, the Number is dual or plural, and the Case is genitive.

The *RuleSet* produced by the program may contain any number of rules with the same Class.

We shall call the program *learn_rules/3*. It will be called as

```
learn_rules(ProblemDescription, TrainingSet, RuleSet)
```

where **ProblemDescription** and **TrainingSet** are ground, and the program is to compute **RuleSet**. The **RuleSet** produced should correctly classify each example in the **TrainingSet**, and should misclassify no example.

7.2   A Trivial Implementation

When starting out on a task like this, it is often a good idea to play around with
your data structure design for a while to make sure that it is easy to work with. It
is an especially good idea to develop some debugging tools in advance.

The first thing we might do is verify that a given TrainingSet is consistent with
its ProblemDescription. It is easier to define that test in Prolog than in English:

```
valid_inputs(Attributes-Classes, TrainingSet) :-
    valid_problem_description(Attributes, Classes),
    compatible_training_set(TrainingSet, Attributes, Classes),
    consistent_training_set(TrainingSet).

valid_problem_description(Attributes, Classes) :-
    list_of_constants(Classes),
    functor(Attributes, _, N),
    valid_attributes(N, Attributes).

valid_attributes(N, Attributes) :-
    ( N =:= 0 → true
    ; arg(N, Attributes, ValueSet),
      list_of_constants(ValueSet),
      M is N-1,
      valid_attributes(M, Attributes)
    ).

list_of_constants([ ]).
list_of_constants([Constant|Constants]) :-
    atomic(Constant),
    list_of_constants(Constants).

compatible_training_set([ ], _, _).
compatible_training_set([Object-Class|Examples], Attributes, Classes) :-
    atomic(Class),
    memberchk(Class, Classes),
    compatible_object(Object, Attributes),
    compatible_training_set(Examples, Attributes, Classes).
```

```
compatible_object(Object, Attributes) :-
   functor(Attributes, ProblemName, N),
   functor(Object, ProblemName, N),
   compatible_object(N, Object, Attributes).
compatible_object(N, Object, Attributes) :-
   ( N =:= 0 → true
   ; arg(N, Attributes, ValueSet),
     arg(N, Object, Value),
     memberchk(Value, ValueSet),
     M is N-1,
     valid_attributes(M, Attributes)
   ).
```

```
memberchk(X, [X|_]) :- !.        % This should be in your
memberchk(X, [_|L]) :-           % Prolog system, or in its
   memberchk(X, L).              % library.
```

```
consistent_training_set(TrainingSet) :-
   \+ (
     member(ObjectDescription-Class1, TrainingSet),
     member(ObjectDescription-Class2, TrainingSet),
     Class1 \== Class2
   ).
```

```
member(X, [X|_]).                % This should be in your
member(X, [_|L]) :-              % Prolog system, or in its
   member(X, L).                 % library.
```

Now that we can check a problem, it is time for us to type in a sample problem, and check the checker.

```
english_pronouns_application(
   pronoun([s,h,i,m,f], [s,d,p], [s,o,p,g] )
   -- [i,me,mine,my, we,us,ours,our, you,yours,your, it,its,
      he,him,his, she,her,hers, they,them,theirs,their],
   [
      pronoun(s,s,s)-i,            pronoun(s,s,o)-me,
      pronoun(s,s,p)-mine,         pronoun(s,s,g)-my,
      pronoun(s,d,s)-we,           pronoun(s,d,o)-us,
      pronoun(s,d,p)-ours,         pronoun(s,d,g)-our,
      pronoun(s,p,s)-we,           pronoun(s,p,o)-us,
      pronoun(s,d,p)-ours,         pronoun(s,p,g)-our,
      pronoun(h,s,s)-you,          pronoun(h,s,o)-you,
      pronoun(h,s,p)-yours,        pronoun(h,s,g)-your,
      pronoun(h,d,s)-you,          pronoun(h,d,o)-you,
      pronoun(h,d,p)-yours,        pronoun(h,d,g)-your,
      pronoun(h,p,s)-you,          pronoun(h,p,o)-you,
      pronoun(h,p,p)-yours,        pronoun(h,p,g)-your,
      pronoun(i,s,s)-it,           pronoun(i,s,o)-it,
      pronoun(i,s,p)-its,          pronoun(i,s,g)-its,
      pronoun(m,s,s)-he,           pronoun(m,s,o)-him,
      pronoun(m,s,p)-his,          pronoun(m,s,g)-his,
      pronoun(f,s,s)-she,          pronoun(f,s,o)-her,
      pronoun(f,s,p)-hers,         pronoun(f,s,g)-her,
      pronoun(i,d,s)-they,         pronoun(i,d,o)-them,
      pronoun(i,d,p)-theirs,       pronoun(i,d,g)-their,
      pronoun(m,d,s)-they,         pronoun(m,d,o)-them,
      pronoun(m,d,p)-theirs,       pronoun(m,d,g)-their,
      pronoun(f,d,s)-they,         pronoun(f,d,o)-them,
      pronoun(f,d,p)-theirs,       pronoun(f,d,g)-their,
      pronoun(i,p,s)-they,         pronoun(i,p,o)-them,
      pronoun(i,p,p)-theirs,       pronoun(i,p,g)-their,
      pronoun(m,p,s)-they,         pronoun(m,p,o)-them,
      pronoun(m,p,p)-theirs,       pronoun(m,p,g)-their,
      pronoun(f,p,s)-they,         pronoun(f,p,o)-them,
      pronoun(f,p,p)-theirs,       pronoun(f,p,g)-their
   ]).
```

Now we can ask

```
?- english_pronouns_application(P, T), valid_inputs(P, T).
```

To indicate the practical utility of testing code even as early as this, this code
is being developed in much the order that you see it here. I tried this test when
I got to this point in the text. And it didn't work. I had forgotten to define
compatible_training_set/3 and *consistent_training_set/1*. Having fixed that, it still
didn't work. I had changed my mind about passing the `ProblemDescription`
around intact and passing it as separate `Attributes` and `Classes` arguments,
and both approaches remained in the code. Finally, *valid_inputs/2* worked, and
it promptly found a mistake in *english_pronouns_application/2*. (I had originally
used '1' and '2' where now I use 's' and 'h'.) How much easier to find and fix these
mistakes while I have nothing else to worry about! Now we can proceed with the
rest of the problem, knowing that we have a sensible training set correctly entered.

We note that the specification given in the previous section says nothing about the
`RuleSet` being the smallest possible one. In fact, if we simply copy the `Training-
Set`, turning attribute values into singleton sets, we will get a program which meets
the specification! To implement that, we just map down the `TrainingSet` and
`RuleSet` together.

```
learn_rules(ProblemDescription, TrainingSet, RuleSet) :-
    trivial_learn_rules(TrainingSet, RuleSet).

trivial_learn_rules([ ], [ ]).
trivial_learn_rules([Object-Class|Examples], [Generic-Class|Rules]) :-
    object_to_generic(Object, Generic),
    trivial_learn_rules(Examples, Rules).

object_to_generic(Object, Generic) :-
    functor(Object, ProblemName, N),
    functor(Generic, ProblemName, N),
    object_to_generic(N, Object, Generic).

object_to_generic(N, Object, Generic) :-
    ( N =:= 0 → true
    ; arg(N, Object, Value),          % a constant
      arg(N, Generic, [Value]),       % a singleton set
```

```
   M is N-1,
   object_to_generic(M, Object, Generic)
).
```

What's the point of this? Testing. If the learning program was part of a larger program, and the specification we gave above was all that the larger program absolutely required, we could provide this trivial definition to whoever was working on the larger program, and let him or her get on with their code while we finished this. More to the point, we'll want to check that the real *learn_rules/3* produces correct output, and we need some correct output to check the checker!

Recall that the specification said that the rule set should correctly classify each example in the training set, and should misclassify no example. Any number of rules might apply to any given example.

```
training_set_correctly_predicted([ ], _).
training_set_correctly_predicted([Object-Class|Examples], RuleSet) :-
    at_least_one_correct_prediction(RuleSet, Object, Class),
    no_incorrect_prediction(RuleSet, Object, Class),
    training_set_correctly_predicted(Examples, RuleSet).

at_least_one_correct_prediction(RuleSet, Object, Class) :-
    member(Generic-Class, RuleSet),
    covers(Generic, Object),
    !.

no_incorrect_prediction([ ], _, _).
no_incorrect_prediction([Generic-Prediction|Rules], Object, Class) :-
    ( covers(Generic, Object) → Prediction = Class
    ; /* Generic does not cover Object */ true
    ),
    no_incorrect_prediction(Rules, Object, Class).

covers(Generic, Object) :-
    functor(Generic, ProblemName, N),
    functor(Object, ProblemName, N),
    covers(N, Generic, Object).
```

```
covers(N, Generic, Object) :-
  ( N =:= 0 → true
  ; arg(N, Generic, ValueSet),
    arg(N, Object, Value),
    memberchk(Value, ValueSet),
    M is N-1,
    covers(M, Generic, Object)
  ).
```

We can test this by doing

```
?- english_pronouns_application(P, T),
   learn_rules(P, T, R),
   training_set_correctly_predicted(T, R).
```

Once again, testing uncovered a problem: I had forgotten to code the *covers/2* predicate. We are now in a good position to test the rest of the program.

7.3   Simplifying the Problem

Consider a single *Class*, and the *Rules* the program is to learn for it. We can divide the *ObjectDescriptions* in the *TrainingSet* into two groups: a *Positive* group (the ones which are to be classified into that *Class*) and a *Negative* group (the ones which are to be classified into some other class).

The specification tells us that

- each element of the *Positive* set must be covered by at least one of the *Rules*

- no *Rule* may cover any element of the *Negative* set.

These conditions do not make any reference to the rules for the other classes, or to the class assigned to the elements of the *Negative* set (except that it is not the current *Class*). So we can check (and learn) the *Rules* one *Class* at a time.

What we shall do, then, is write a program which reduces the main problem to the following subproblem:

given two disjoint sets of *ObjectDescriptions*, *Positive* and *Negative*, find a set *Generics* of *GenericObjectDescriptions* such that

$\forall p \in Positive \; \exists g \in Generics \; \text{covers}(g, p)$

$\forall n \in Negative \; \forall g \in Generics \; \neg\text{covers}(g, n)$

Note the difference in the quantifiers. We shall see later that this asymmetry between the Positive and Negative examples is a practical problem.

In reducing the main problem to instances of the subproblem, we use the fact that the `ProblemDescription` argument tells us what the classes are. We can use that to control the division.

```
learn_rules(Attributes-Classes, TrainingSet, RuleSet) :-
    learn_rules_for_each_class(Classes, TrainingSet, RuleSet).

learn_rules_for_each_class([ ], _, [ ]).
learn_rules_for_each_class([Class|Classes], TrainingSet, RuleSet0) :-
    partition_training_set(TrainingSet, Class, Positive, Negative),
    find_covering_set(Positive, Negative, Generics),
    found_rules(Generics, Class, RuleSet0, RuleSet1),
    learn_rules_for_each_class(Classes, TrainingSet, RuleSet1).

partition_training_set([ ], _, [ ], [ ]).
partition_training_set([Object-Class|Examples], Class,
                                          [Object|Ps], Ns) :- !,
    partition_training_set(Examples, Class, Ps, Ns).
partition_training_set([Object-_other|Examples], Class,
                                          Ps, [Object|Ns]) :-
    /* _other \== Class */
    partition_training_set(Examples, Class, Ps, Ns).

found_rules([ ], _, Rules, Rules).
found_rules([Generic|Generics], Class, [Generic-Class|Rules1],
                                          Rules) :-
    found_rules(Generics, Class, Rules1, Rules).
```

The important thing to notice about this is that it is independent of how we handle each separate class. As soon as we have found a suitable cover `Generics` for a given `Class`, we can commit to that cover.

In order to test this much of the code, we can provide a trivial implementation of *find_covering_set/3*.

```
find_covering_set(Positive, Negative, Generics) :-
    trivial_find_covering_set(Positive, Generics).

trivial_find_covering_set([ ], [ ]).
trivial_find_covering_set([Object|Objects], [Generic|Generics]) :-
    object_to_generic(Object, Generic),
    trivial_find_covering_set(Objects, Generics).
```

The test call is

```
?- english_pronouns_application(P, T),
   learn_rules(P, T, R),
   training_set_correctly_predicted(T, R).
```

as before.

Before looking at the subproblems, let's reflect on what we have achieved here. Not only have we broken the main task up into subproblems (one for each *Class*), but they are *independent* subproblems. This means that we can solve them in any order, and that if one subproblem fails there isn't any point in looking for more solutions to any of the other subproblems. This is considered further below, in Section 7.7.

7.4 Solving the Subproblem

Let us consider one element g of the set of Generics that we are supposed to find. There will be some subset

$$\pi(g) \equiv \{p \in Positive \mid \text{covers}(g,p)\}$$

of examples which g covers. We know that g covers p if each attribute value of p is an element of the corresponding value set of g. If we "lift" an example p to the smallest generic description $\gamma(p)$ which covers it:

$$\gamma(p) = \langle\{a_1\}, \ldots, \{a_n\}\rangle$$

where

$$p = \langle a_1, \ldots, a_n \rangle$$

we see that covers(g, p) only if

$$\forall_i \ 1 \le i \le n \ \gamma(p)_i \subseteq g_i$$

It follows that the most specific g which covers all of $p_1, \ldots, p_m$ is

$$\forall_i \ 1 \le i \le m \ g_i = \bigcup_{1 \le j \le n} \gamma(p_j)_i$$

If we are given a list `Pos` = $[P_1, \ldots, P_m]$ of *ObjectDescriptions*, this means that we can calculate the most specific *GenericObjectDescription* `Gen` which covers all of them thus:

```
most_specific_cover(Attributes, Pos, Gen) :-
    vacuous_description(Attributes, Gen0),
    most_specific_cover_1(Pos, Gen0, Gen).

vacuous_description(Attributes, Gen0) :-
    functor(Attributes, F, N),
    functor(Gen0, F, N),
    vacuous_description_1(N, Gen0).

vacuous_description_1(N, Gen0) :-
    ( N =:= 0 → true
    ; arg(N, Gen0, /* empty set */ [ ]),
      M is N-1,
      vacuous_description_1(M, Gen0)
    ).

most_specific_cover_1([ ], Gen, Gen).
most_specific_cover_1([Example|Examples], Gen0, Gen) :-
    covering_new_case(Gen0, Example, Gen1),
    most_specific_cover_1(Examples, Gen1, Gen).

covering_new_case(Gen0, Example, Gen1) :-
    functor(Gen0, F, N),
    functor(Example, F, N),
    functor(Gen1, F, N),
```

```
      covering_new_case(N, Gen0, Example, Gen1).

covering_new_case(N, Gen0, Example, Gen1) :-
    ( N =:= 0 → true
    ; arg(N, Gen0, Set0),
      arg(N, Example, V),
      arg(N, Gen1, Set1),
      add_element(V, Set0, Set1),
      M is N-1,
      covering_new_case(M, Gen0, Example, Gen1)
    ).

add_element(Element, Set0, Set) :-
    ( memberchk(Element, Set0) →
      Set = Set0
    ; Set = [Element|Set0]
    ).
```

Of course, since set union is commutative and associative and a lot of other nice things besides, there are many other ways we could compute this answer.

The problem is, we now know how to compute the most specific generalisation of a set of positive examples, so once we have figured out how to group the positive examples into subsets, we know how to calculate the *Generics*. And this calculation is logically determinate. But we don't know how to divide up the positive examples among the *Generics*, nor indeed how many *Generics* there are.

We do know that there must be at least one *Generic*, and we saw before that having one *Generic* for each *Positive* example will suffice. So we can try having one *Generic*, then two, ..., then finally as many as the number of the *Positive* examples, and that many *must* be enough (because the trivial method works). So we can do this:

```
find_covering_set(Positive, Negative, Attributes, Generics) :-
    vacuous_description(Attributes, Vacuous),
    at_most(Positive, Vacuous, Generics0),
    distribute_consistently(Positive, Negative, Generics0, Generics),
    !.
```

```
at_most(_, _, [ ]).
at_most([_|Limit], Element, [Element|List]) :-
    at_most(Limit, Element, List).

distribute_consistently([ ], _, Generics, Generics).
distribute_consistently([Positive|Positives], Negatives, Generics0,
                                                    Generics) :-
    select(Gen0, Generics0, Gen1, Generics1),
    covering_new_case(Gen0, Positive, Gen1),
    \+ ( member(Negative, Negatives), covers(Gen1, Negative) ),
    distribute_consistently(Positives, Negatives, Generics1, Generics).

select(X, [X|Zs], Y, [Y|Zs]).
select(X, [H|Xs], Y, [H|Ys]) :-
    select(X, Xs, Y, Ys).
```

There is no intelligence here at all. We simply guess the number of *Generics* which will be required, and initialise each of them to the empty description. Then for each *Positive*, we try adding it to each current generic description, rejecting a guess only if an incorrect prediction would result.

The cut in *find_covering_set/4* ensures that it reports at most one solution to its caller. In fact, it does more than that. *at_most/3* enumerates solutions in increasing order of length— `at_most([1,2,3], a, X)` reports

```
X = [ ] ; X = [a] ; X = [a,a] ; X = [a,a,a]
```

for example—so *find_covering_set/4* will report the *shortest* solution it can find.

We can improve *distribute_consistently/4* by noting that if a *Positive* example is already covered by an existing *Generic*, there is no need to add it to any generic. For example, if we have combined $\langle a, x \rangle$, $\langle a, y \rangle$, and $\langle b, x \rangle$ into the single *Generic* $\langle \{a, b\}, \{x, y\} \rangle$, the example $\langle b, y \rangle$ need not be placed elsewhere. So this suggests

```
distribute_consistently([ ], _, Generics, Generics).
distribute_consistently([Positive|Positives], Negatives, Generics0,
                                                    Generics) :-
    ( member(Gen0, Generics0), covers(Gen0, Positive) →
```

```
    /* this example is already handled */
    Generics1 = Generics0
; /* we have to guess where it will go */
    select(Gen0, Generics0, Gen1, Generics1),
    covering_new_case(Gen0, Positive, Gen1),
    /* check that that placing is consistent */
    \+Negative ↑(
        member(Negative, Negatives),
        covers(Gen1, Negative)
    )
),
distribute_consistently(Positives, Negatives, Generics1, Generics).
```

Now we have a complete learning program which finds the shortest set of rules it can represent.

7.5   What does it Cost?

How expensive is it to learn a *RuleSet* from a *TrainingSet*? This is a fairly easy program to analyse, because it is mostly determinate, and the costs depend directly on simple features of the input.

learn_rules/3 is called once.

learn_rules_for_each_class/4 is called once at the end of the list of *Classes* (when its first clause is used) and once for each *Class* (when its second clause is used). The second clause calls *partition_training_set/4* each time it is applied. Those calls cost $O(|TrainingSet|)$ each time, and create a similar amount of space. So partitioning costs a total of $O(|Classes| \times |TrainingSet|)$ in time and turns over a similar amount in space.

found_rules/4 costs $O(|Generics|)$ in time. It is called once for each *Class* by *learn_rules_for_each_class/4*, and all the *Generics* together form the *RuleSet*, so the combined cost is $O(|RuleSet|)$. Since the size of the *RuleSet* is bounded above by the size of the *TrainingSet*, the cost of everything except *find_covering_set/4* comes to $O((1 + |Classes|) \times |TrainingSet|)$.

Now consider *find_covering_set/3* for a particular set of *Positive* examples and a particular set of *Negative* examples, where $|Positive| = p$ and $|Negative| = n$, and consider an iteration of *at_most/3* which yields $|Generics0| = g$. We try placing each *Positive* example in each *Generic*. **Bad news:** this means that we might make as many as g^p attempts.

An exponential cost like g^n means that for non-trivial problems the algorithm is quite impractical. Can we do better than that?

One obvious flaw is that each arrangement of the p items into g groups may be considered in up to $g!$ different disguises. (The order of the groups makes no difference to the solution.) This is easy to fix. Suppose that at some iteration of *distribute_consistently/4* *Generics0* has the value

$$[v_1, \ldots, v_k, e, \ldots, e]$$

where the last $g - k$ elements are still vacuous descriptions which have not been augmented by any *Positive* example. *distribute_consistently/4*, as written above, will try adding the next *Positive* example to each of $v_1, \ldots, v_n$, but after that will try adding it to *each* of the $g - k$ copies of e. But it isn't going to make any difference which copy we pick, so we should pick one and stick with it. One might be tempted to stick a cut in somewhere, but it is easy to do this in pure Prolog, by making the distinction between the two parts of *Generics0* explicit. We'll use the representation

$$`.'(v_1, \ldots, `.'(v_k, `!'([e, \ldots, e])), \ldots)$$

```
find_covering_set(Positive, Negative, Attributes, Generics) :-
    ...
    distribute_consistently(Positive, Negative, !(Generics0), Generics),
    !.

...

distribute_consistently([Positive|Positives], Negatives, Generics0,
                                               Generics) :-
    select1(Generics0, Gen0, Generics1, Gen1),
    ...

select1(!([X|Zs], X, [Y|!(Zs)], Y).
select1([X|Zs], X, [Y|Zs], Y).
select1([H|Xs], X, [H|Ys], Y) :-
    select1(Xs, X, Ys, Y).
```

This is a rather pretty technique, and I wish I'd thought of it years ago. But it doesn't really answer the purpose. Since $g! \leq g^g$, taking out the factor $g!$ leaves the cost at g^{p-g} attempts.

As we have seen, it is important to analyse the cost of an algorithm, because code which is easy to understand may be impractical to use. But the next question is whether we just have a bad algorithm, or whether the difficulty lies in the specification. If the task is intrinsically hard, it would be a waste of time looking for a better algorithm. To answer that question, it really helps to know some of the "standard" NP-complete problems (it helps even more to have a copy of Garey and Johnson!). If you can find a known NP-complete problem such that any instance of that problem can be turned into an instance of the current problem, then the current problem must be at least that hard.

Definition 1 Given a graph $G = (V, E)$ and a positive integer k, the **Chromatic Number** problem is to determine whether it is possible to colour the vertices V with k colours so that no two vertices adjacent in E have the same colour.

Definition 2 The **Chromatic Number** $\chi(G)$ of a graph G is the smallest positive integer k such that G can be coloured with k colours but not with $k - 1$.

THEOREM 1 The Chromatic Number problem is NP-complete in the size of G.

We can reduce any instance of the Chromatic Number problem to an instance of *distribute_consistently/4* thus:

$Positives = \{\{x\}|x \in E\}$

$Negatives = \{\{x, y\}|(x, y) \in V\}$

The graph $G = (E, V)$ can be coloured with k colours if the *Positives* can be merged into k *Generics* none of which contains any of the *Negatives*.

It follows that finding the smallest set of *Generics* (and thus the smallest set of *Rules*) is at least as hard as calculating the Chromatic Number of an arbitrary graph. That is a remarkably unpleasant result, because this learning problem is rather seriously restricted. (It's not altogether surprising, though. Finding the best decision tree is also hard.)

Considering the cost first showed us that the algorithm was impractical for large problems, and then showed us that the problem is intrinsically hard. What can we do about it? Only one thing: **solve some other problem instead**. In particular, we can use an incremental method which is not guaranteed to find the best possible answer, but isn't obviously bad.

```
find_covering_set(Positive, Negative, Attributes, Generics) :-
   vacuous_description(Attributes, E),
   distribute_consistently(Positive, Negative, E, [ ], Generics).

distribute_consistently([ ], _, _, Gs, Gs).
distribute_consistently([P|Ps], Ns, E, Gs0, Gs) :-
   member(G0, Gs0),
   covers(G0, P),
   !, % Already handled
   distribute_consistently(Ps, Ns, E, Gs0, Gs).
distribute_consistently([P|Ps], Ns, E, Gs0, Gs) :-
   random_permutation(Gs0, Gs1),
   select(G1, Gs1, G2, Gs2),
   covering_new_case(G1, P, G2),
   \+ N ↑ ( member(N, Ns), covers(G2, N) ),
   !, % Commit to this guess
   distribute_consistently(Ps, Ns, E, Gs2, Gs).
distribute_consistently([P|Ps], Ns, E, Gs0, Gs) :-
   covering_new_case(E, P, G2),
   distribute_consistently(Ps, Ns, [G2|Gs0], Gs).
```

7.6 Basing the Task on Lattices rather than Sets

So far, a *Generic* description has had the form of a tuple of sets, and the only
use made of attribute values is to check whether two values are the same or not.
However, the learning algorithm as such doesn't need such a specific structure. All
we require is that *vacuous_description/2*, *covering_new_case/3*, and *covers/2* should
have certain properties: the *Generic* description we end up with by starting with a
vacuous description and extending it to cover a set of examples P should depend
only on the set P, and not on which vacuous description we start with, nor on the
order in which the elements of P are covered.

It turns out that this is equivalent to demanding that the *Generic* descriptions
form a mathematical structure called a **semi-lattice**. That is, there is a constant
0 and a binary operation $\vee$ such that

$$x \vee y = y \vee x \qquad\qquad \text{$\vee$ is commutative}$$
$$x \vee x = x \qquad\qquad\quad\; \text{$\vee$ is idempotent}$$
$$x \vee (y \vee z) = (x \vee y) \vee z \quad \text{$\vee$ is associative}$$
$$x \vee 0 = x \qquad\qquad\quad\; \text{0 is an identity for $\vee$}$$

Clearly, 0 is the vacuous description, and if we can identify an `Object` description with the `Generic` description obtained by calling `covering_new_case(0, Object, Generic)`. We see that the generic description covering a set $\{P_1, \ldots, P_n\}$ is

$$0 \vee P_1 \vee \cdots \vee P_n$$

which is unique as desired.

Given a semi-lattice, we can define a partial order $\preceq$ thus:

$$x \preceq y \equiv x \vee y = y$$

It is a standard mathematical result that this has all the usual properties of a partial order. We see that for two generic descriptions g_1, g_2,

- $g_1 \vee g_2$ is the most specific description which describes everything that g_1 describes and everything that g_2 describes

- $g_1 \preceq g_2$ if and only if g_2 describes everything that g_1 describes.

That's all very nice and mathematical, but what *use* is it? The answer is that our program generalises to *any* description space having these properties, not just sets.

Some examples:

- the subsets of some given set S form a semi-lattice; take $0 = \emptyset$, $x \vee y = x \cup y$.

- if $L_1, \ldots, L_n$ are semi-lattices (which might be the same but need not be), then the product $L_1 \times \cdots \times L_n$, whose elements are tuples $\langle x_1, \ldots, x_n \rangle$ is a semi-lattice; take $0 = \langle 0, \ldots, 0 \rangle$, $\langle x_1, \ldots, x_n \rangle \vee \langle y_1, \ldots, y_n \rangle = \langle x_1 \vee y_1, \ldots, x_n \vee y_n \rangle$.

- intervals $[L, U]$ of numbers form a semi-lattice; take $0 = [+\infty, -\infty]$ (an empty interval), $[a, b] \vee [c, d] = [\min(a, c), \max(b, d)]$. Note that intervals are sets, and $\preceq$ in this semi-lattice is the same as $\subset$, but the generalisation operator is *not* set union.

- (equivalence classes of) Prolog terms (under renaming of variables) form a semi-lattice, with any variable as 0 and unification as $\vee$. There is also a dual operation called *anti-unification*.

Another example, of interest in AI, is that a type hierarchy is a semi-lattice. I would really like to describe the English Pronouns in terms of trees:

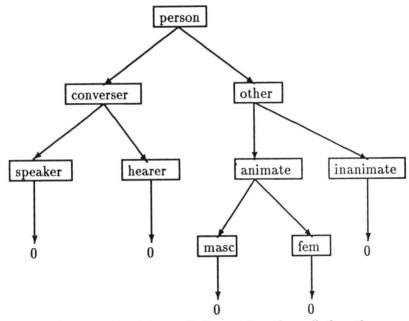

0 in such a case is a "dummy" element less than all the others, and the generalisation $(g1 \vee g2)$ is the nearest common ancestor of the two. For example, ('masc' $\vee$ 'inanimate') = 'other'.

7.7 Explorations

Back in Section 7.3 we noted that by considering each *Class* separately we obtained independent subproblems. What practical difference does this make?

Suppose we have three subproblems $p(A)$, $q(B)$, $r(C)$, and that they are actually independent, having N_a, N_b, and N_c solutions respectively, so that the total number of solutions is $N_a \times N_b \times N_c$. Suppose further that we are interested in all the solutions, and that the cost of finding a solution is T_p, T_q, and T_r time units respectively for *p, q, and r*.

If we code this in Prolog as

```
p(A), q(B), r(C)
```

then what happens is

for each solution of **p(A)**   cost $N_a \times T_a$
  for each solution of **q(B)**   cost $N_a \times N_b \times T_b$
    for each solution of **r(C)**   cost $N_a \times N_b \times N_c \times T_c$
      report **(A,B, C)**

If we use *findall/3* and *member/2*, assuming that each solution enumerated by *member/2* costs 1 unit and that each solution gathered by *findall/3* costs T_f units, we can code this as

```
findall(A, p(A), As),   % cost  N_a × (T_a + T_f)
findall(B, q(B), Bs),   % cost  N_b × (T_b + T_f)
findall(C, r(C), Cs),   % cost  N_c × (T_c + T_f)
member(A, As),          % cost  N_a
member(B, Bs),          % cost  N_a × N_b
member(C, Cs)           % cost  N_a × N_b × N_c*
```

The total cost with the first method is

$$N_a \times T_a + N_a \times N_b \times T_b + N_a \times N_b \times N_c \times T_c$$

The total cost with the second method is

$$N_a \times T_a + N_b \times T_b + N_c \times T_c + (N_a + N_b + N_c) \times T_f + (N_a + N_a \times N_b + N_a \times N_b \times N_c)$$

For even modest values of N_a, N_b, N_c, the dominant factor is soon the $N_a \times N_b \times N_c$ one, and the relative cost of **r(C)** and **member(C,Cs)** is what matters. Even the cost of *findall/3* isn't as important. As an illustration of this, I tried

```
buzz :-                 % time-consumer
   length(L, /*N=*/10)  % N=30;N=90 also tried
   member(X, L),
   nonvar(X).           % will fail

buzz.

p(1) :- buzz.           % 10 time-consuming solutions
⋮
p(10) :- buzz.
```

with similar definitions for *q/1* and *r/1*. In order to estimate the effect of *findall/3*, I also coded

```
all_ps([1,2,3,4,5,6,7,8,9,10]) :-
    buzz, buzz, buzz, buzz, buzz,
    buzz, buzz, buzz, buzz, buzz.
```

which finds all the solutions of *p/1* directly. The figures I obtained on a Sun-3/60 running Quintus Prolog release 2.4 were

N= 10	N= 30	N= 90	
1.150	3.130	9.120	seconds for p(_), q(_), r(_)
0.110	0.170	0.330	seconds for the *findall/3* version
0.075	0.130	0.300	seconds for the "direct" version
0.030	0.085	0.245	seconds just for "buzzing"

This isn't something you'd want to do when the subproblems are trivial (on the other hand, making and searching a 10-element list isn't *that* complex a subproblem), but as you see from this table, the savings can be substantial.

We've seen that it can pay to use *findall/3* or *setof/3* when *all* the solutions of a set of independent subproblems are wanted. But that's not the case in Section 7.3. There we only want *one* solution for the RuleSet as a whole, which means that we need only one solution from each independent subproblem. Is there anything to be gained in that case?

Suppose we have

```
p(A), q(B), r(C)
```

as before, where p, q, r have N_a, N_b, and N_c solutions each, at a cost of T_a, T_b, T_c per solution, plus a cost of F_a, F_b, F_c if and when they fail.

Now suppose that each of the subproblems has at most one solution, so that if we do (p(A), fail) the cost will be T_a to find the first and only solution plus F_a to look for another solution and fail. If we call p(A), q(B), r(C), the sequence of events will be

p($\mathbf{A}$) reports a solution   (cost T_a)
  q($\mathbf{B}$) reports a solution   (cost T_b)
    r($\mathbf{C}$) reports a solution   (cost T_c)
    caller fails
    r($\mathbf{C}$) fails to find another   (cost F_c)
  q($\mathbf{B}$) fails to find another   (cost F_b)
r($\mathbf{A}$) fails to find another   (cost F_a)

for a total cost of $T_a + T_b + T_c + Fa + Fb + Fc$. If we know that we are only interested in a single solution of this conjunctive query, we can wrap the whole thing in a 'once' construct. If your Prolog implementation has 'once' built-in, you would write

```
once(( p(A), q(B), r(C) ))
```

If it hasn't got *once/1*, it most certainly should have if->then;else, and you would write

```
( p(A), q(B), r(C) -> true )
```

This prunes away the search for alternative solutions; which in this case means that the failure cost $F_a + F_b + F_c$ is eliminated.

But that still doesn't apply to the problem we have. Each of the subproblems may have several solutions, or none. Suppose that N_a and N_b are non-zero, but that r(C) has no solutions, so that $N_c = 0$. Now we have

for each solution of p($\mathbf{A}$)   cost $(N_a \times T_a + Fa)$
  for each solution of q($\mathbf{B}$)   cost $(N_b \times T_b + Fb) \times N_a$
    r($\mathbf{C}$) has no solution   cost $(Fc) \times N_a \times N_b$

for a total cost of $F_a + N_a \times (T_a + F_b) + N_a \times N_b \times (T_b + F_c)$, and wrapping the conjunction in a once(−) form saves us nothing.

The answer is that if we are satisfied with one solution from each of the independent) subgoals, the subgoals themselves should be wrapped in once(−) forms:

```
once(p(A)),          % cost Ta if Na > 0, Fa otherwise
once(q(B)),          % cost Tb if Nb > 0, Fb otherwise
once(r(C))           % cost Tc if Nc > 0, Fc otherwise
```

Of course, inserting special wrappers like this into your program is almost always an indication that you have designed it badly in the first place. Whenever you have **once(Goal)**, it is an indication that you *should* have designed the predicate in question so that it has at most one solution.

What this tells us about the program we constructed above is that since the *find_covering_set/3* goals are independent, and since we are only interested in a single solution from *learn_rules/3*, the right thing to do is to make sure that *find_covering_set/3* is coded so that it has at most one solution.

Two (pure) Prolog goals are independent if they do not share any unbound variables. If, instead of using *findall/3*, we use *setof/3*, for example

```
setof(A, p(X,Y,A), As),
setof(B, q(Y,Z,B), Bs),
setof(C, r(Z,X,C), Cs),
member(A, As),
member(B, Bs),
member(C, Cs)
```

where we expect **X**, **Y**, and **Z** to be ground by the time this is called, it will deliver the correct answers even if our expectation is wrong. (Provided, as with most all-solutions predicates, that **p**, **q**, **r** deliver ground results.)

In *distribute_consistently/4*, whenever we try adding a **Positive** example to a generic **Gen0** yielding **Gen1**, we then check *every* Negative example to see if it is covered by **Gen1**. But since the previous value **Gen0** was consistent with all the **Negative** examples, a **Negative** example will be covered by **Gen1** only if the **Positive** example changed it in some *relevant* way. That is, there must be at least one attribute i where

$$Negative_i \notin Gen0_i$$

$$Negative_i \in Gen1_i = Gen0_i \cup Positive_i$$

For this to be true, it must be the case that

$$Negative_i = Positive_i$$

This means that we only need to check the *Negative* examples which have at least one attribute in common with the current *Positive* example.

This makes quite a difference. For the English pronouns training set, the number of checks required is

minimum	average	maximum	
54	56	59	all *Negative* examples
29	32	35	relevant *Negative* examples

While the number of checks was reduced, keeping track of which Negative examples were relevant actually slowed the program down. The heuristic may be useful in other applications: if the description space is a semi-lattice, it is straightforward to show that

Negative $\not\preceq$ *Generic*

Negative $\preceq$ *Generic* $\vee$ *Positive*

together imply that

Negative $\wedge$ *Positive* $\succ$ 0

so the heuristic can be used with semi-lattices.

7.8   Conclusions

We found that writing the learning program was simple. It was easy to test the code as we developed it, and that was important, because even the best of us make typing mistakes. The resulting program turned out to be costly, but while some of that was poor coding (corrected by introducing *select1/4*) the real difficulty turned out to be inherent in the problem. An "approximate" algorithm which is not guaranteed to produce optimal results fixed that.

Writing the program in Prolog kept it small enough so that it was easy to correct and easy to extend.

Chapter 8

Stream Data Analysis in Prolog

D. Stott Parker

Computer Science Department
University of California
Los Angeles, CA 90024-1596
E-Mail: stott@cs.ucla.edu

Abstract

Today many applications routinely generate large quantities of data. The data often takes the form of a time series, or more generally just a *stream* – an ordered sequence of records. Analysis of this data requires stream processing techniques, which differ in significant ways from what current database query languages and statistical analysis tools support today. There is a real need for better stream data analysis systems.

Stream analysis, like most data analysis, is best done in a way that permits interactive exploration. It must support 'ad hoc' queries by a user, and these queries should be easy to formulate and run. It seems then that stream data analysis is best done in some kind of powerful programming environment.

A natural approach here is to analyze data with the stream processing paradigm of transducers (functional transformations) on streams. Data analyzers can be composed from collections of functional operators (transducers) that transform input data streams to output streams. A modular, extensible, easy-to-use library of transducers can be combined in arbitrary ways to answer stream data analysis queries of interest.

Prolog offers an excellent start for an interactive data analysis programming environment. However most Prolog systems have limitations that make development of real stream data analysis applications challenging.

We describe an approach for doing stream data analysis that has been taken in the Tangram project at UCLA. Transducers are implemented not directly in Prolog, but in a functional language called Log(F) that can be translated to Prolog. Many stream processing programs are easy to develop this way. A by-product of our approach is a practical way to interface Prolog and database systems.

---

[0] This work done under the Tangram project, supported by DARPA contract F29601-87-C-0072.

8.1   Stream Data Analysis

Suppose we are trying to make a killing in the stock market, somehow taking advantage of our knowledge of Prolog. It goes without saying that there are many possible strategies. When using computers, however, it is natural to consider 'technical' strategies, which somehow implement the belief that insight about future behavior can be gotten by analyzing historical information (such as past stock quotations). In other words, many strategies involve computer processing of history. Although the effectiveness of technical approaches is controversial, at least some people have made killings with them [Dar86]. Also, *ignoring* history is obviously a bad idea.

There are many ways to go about the analysis of history, but one important field to know about is *time series analysis*, which is concerned with mathematical techniques for investigating sequences of data [Ful76]. Time series analysis provides methods for discerning different components of behavior in sequence data, including:

- real long-term trends

- seasonal variations

- non-seasonal cycles

- random fluctuations.

As stock investors we are basically interested in detecting long-term upward trends in prices. We certainly do not want to be distracted by random (short-term) fluctuations, and do not want to be fooled into mistaking cyclic behavior for long-term trends.

How can we discern trends in a history? One popular technique is to compute *moving averages* of the history. The m-th moving average of a sequence of numbers S is just the sequence whose i-th element is the average of elements i, $i + 1$, ..., $i + m - 1$ in S. Moving averages smooth out fluctuations, and thereby (hopefully) expose real trends. They are simple, and are used very widely. For example, when its weekly closing price is above the 40-week moving average, the stock market is called a *bull* market, and otherwise a *bear* market.

Therefore, to decide if we want to invest in AT&T we might want to ask a query like

show the 5-day moving averages for AT&T stock in 1989

and have the answer displayed quickly in a graphic format. If there seemed to be an upward trend, we could follow up with other queries.

Unfortunately, the stock market does not stay in indefinite upward trends, but follows very pronounced cyclic patterns. Between 1929 and 1977 there were nine major bull markets, and nine major bear markets. Bear markets tend to last about two years, and bull markets about three years, so the probability being in a bull market has been about 60% for the past fifty years [Fis87]. Cyclic components of behavior require more sophisticated techniques than moving averages, and require fairly powerful tools for effective analysis.

The stock investment scenario discussed here is an instance of a more general problem: we have an ordered sequence of data records that we wish to analyze. We call this ordered sequence a *stream* for the moment. At the very least, we want to get more "intuition" about the structure of the data. Generally we want to do much more, however, such as compare it with other streams or check its agreement with a model we have developed. We call this general problem *stream data analysis*.

Amazingly, today there is not nearly enough in the way of software to deal with this problem. Database management systems (DBMS) permit certain kinds of analysis of data. In modern DBMS users can use a query language (typically SQL) to ask specific questions. DBMS cannot yet handle stream data analysis, however.

We do not mean to imply that there is *no* software today that supports stream data analysis. We are now entering a period where powerful data analysis tools are being combined with external data sources. For example, DBMS are being combined with statistical analysis packages. This combination should support 'exploration' of the data in the way that exploratory data analysis systems do, like the *S* statistical analysis system of AT&T [BC84]. Also, time series analysis packages have grown in importance recently, as more applications of event data (historical data, temporal data) have developed [PMC89].

Given all these developments, it is natural to ask about Prolog's potential for addressing this problem. Below, once we are armed with some clever techniques, we will see that it is possible to use Prolog very effectively for stream data analysis.

8.2   Basics of Stream Data Analysis

Stream processing is a popular, well-established AI programming paradigm. It has often been used in languages such as APL and Lisp, although it has certainly been applied in other languages. In this section we review basic stream processing concepts, and how they may be implemented naively in Prolog. This is enough to introduce the stream data analysis paradigm.

To keep the presentation simple, we begin with list processing. Although list processing is not the same as stream processing, it is similar, and a good place to start. Stream processing can be grasped with only a few extensions.

8.2.1 Basic Stream Processing

A *stream* is an ordered sequence of data items. As Prolog users, we can initially conceptualize a stream as a list of terms. For example, the list

```
[
quote( 'F',   '87/10/19', 32,      20,    23+1/8 ),
quote( 'IBM', '87/10/19', 130+1/4, 18,    125+1/4 ),
quote( 'TUA', '87/10/19', 83,      69,    69      ),
quote( 'X',   '87/10/19', 32+1/2,  21,    21+1/2  )
]
```

represents a stream with four items. Sometimes it is important that the stream contain only *ground* terms (terms with no variables), so to keep things simple let us assume from now on that all streams contain only ground terms.

A *stream transducer* is a function from one or more input streams to one or more output streams. For example, a transducer could map the stream above to the stream

```
[ 23+1/8, 125+1/4, 69, 21+1/2 ]
```

by selecting the final value from each quotation.

As transducers are functions, they may be composed in arbitrary ways to form new transducers. For example, the definition

```
portfolio_value => sum(
                  products(
                          lasts(closing_quotes),
                          quantities(holdings)
                          )
                   ).
```

uses an expression involving the composition of several transducers; the sum transducer sums a stream of numbers, and the products transducer produces a stream of pairwise products of two streams. This composition produces results in *pipeline*, as suggested by Figure 8.1. Stream processing is then just the paradigm in which

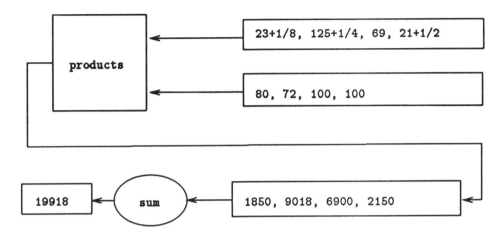

Figure 8.1: The Sum of Pairwise Products of Two Streams

compositions of transducers are used to both define and to manipulate streams.

Although we present them simply as functions, transducers actually relate closely to a number of other important programming paradigms, including automata, objects (as in object-oriented programming), actors, and parsers. Automata, objects, and actors all accept a sequence of inputs which they use to change their internal state, while possibly issuing a sequence of outputs. Parsers take a sequence of symbols as input and produce a summary that describes patterns they have recognized. While transducers have features of each of the paradigms just mentioned, they are really more general. For example, since transducers can take parameters, and need not have only a finite number of states, it is not accurate to think of them as just automata. Perhaps a better way to look at transducers is as a *generalization* of automata, objects, actors, and parsers.

For the moment, then, let us define *stream processing* to be the programming paradigm in which transducers are composed to define or manipulate streams.

8.2.2   Kinds of Transducers

Certain kinds of transducers appear frequently, and are worth taxonomizing. Abelson and Sussman [AS85] point out four kinds of transducer: enumerators, maps, filters, and accumulators.

Enumerators   Enumerators (or generators) produce a stream of values. In Prolog, an enumerator could generally look as follows:

```
enumerate(Stream) :-
                    initial_state(State),
                    enumerate(State,Stream).

enumerate(S,[X|Xs]) :-
                    next_state_and_value(S,NS,X),
                    !,
                    enumerate(NS,Xs).
enumerate(_,[ ]).
```

Here the `State` variable can be viewed as a collection of parameters. For example, the following enumerator generates all the integers in a given range:

```
% intfrom(M,N,Stream) :-
%       Stream is the list of integers [M,...,M+N].
intfrom(_,0,[ ]).
intfrom(M,N,[M|L]) :-
        N > 0,
        M1 is M+1,
        N1 is N-1,
        intfrom(M1,N1,L).
```

The parameters M and N can be thought of as state variables.

Maps Maps transform an input stream to an output stream by applying a specific function to each element. We can write maps in Prolog directly as follows:

```
map_f([X|Xs],[Y|Ys]) :- f(X,Y), map_f(Xs,Ys).
map_f([ ],[ ]).
```

A common generic version, which applies any mapping, is as follows:

```
mapcar([ ],F,[ ]).
mapcar([X|Xs],F,[Y|Ys]) :-
                        apply(F,[X,Y],FXY),
                        call(FXY),
                        mapcar(Xs,F,Ys).
```

```
apply(F,Vs,FVs) :-
                   F =.. FL,
                   append(FL,Vs,FVsL),
                   FVs =.. FVsL.
```

This implementation, however, is expensive since $=../2$, *append/3*, and *call/1* are expensive. Thus Prolog discourages use of *mapcar* or *apply*, and encourages transducers that do explicit tasks:

```
% squares(L,NL) :-
%       NL is the result of squaring each member of L.
squares([X|Xs],[Y|Ys]) :- Y is X*X, squares(Xs,Ys).
squares([ ],[ ]).
```

```
% project(I,L,NL) :-
%       NL is the stream of I-th arguments of terms in L.
project(I,[X|Xs],[Y|Ys]) :- arg(I,X,Y), project(I,Xs,Ys).
project(_,[ ],[ ]).
```

Map transducers arise constantly in practice, since people tend to want to view any given data in many different ways. For example, the result of the Prolog goal

```
?- L = [
   quote( 'F',    '87/10/19',  32,        20,     23+1/8 ),
   quote( 'IBM',  '87/10/19', 130+1/4,    18,    125+1/4 ),
   quote( 'TUA',  '87/10/19',  83,        69,     69     ),
   quote( 'X',    '87/10/19',  32+1/2,    21,     21+1/2 )
   ],
   project(5,L,NL).
```

is the binding

```
NL = [ 23+1/8, 125+1/4, 69, 21+1/2 ]
```

giving the stream that we wanted earlier.

Filters Filters transmit to the output stream only those elements from the input stream that meet some selection criterion. Filters usually look something like the following:

```
filter([X|Xs],Ys) :- inadmissible(X), !, filter(Xs,Ys).
filter([X|Xs],[X|Ys]) :- filter(Xs,Ys).
filter([ ],[ ]).
```

A specific example of a filter is a transducer that, given a fixed integer Q, lets only non-multiples of Q pass to the output stream:

```
% non_multiples(L,Q,NL) :-
%       NL is the sublist of L of non-multiples of Q.
non_multiples([X|Xs],Q,NL) :- multiple(X,Q), !,
                                   non_multiples(Xs,Q,NL).
non_multiples([X|Xs],Q,[X|NL]) :- non_multiples(Xs,Q,NL).
non_multiples([ ],_,[ ]).
```

```
multiple(A,B) :- (A mod B) =:= 0.
```

We can also develop a generic filter called *select/4* that is something like *findall/3* in Prolog, but which works on streams. Its output consists of those elements in the input stream that simultaneously match a given template pattern and satisfy a given condition:

```
% select(L,Template,Condition,NL) :- NL is the sublist of L
%       of terms matching Template and satisfying Condition.
select([X|Xs],T,C,Ys) :- \+ (X=T, call(C)), !, select(Xs,T,C,Ys).
select([X|Xs],T,C,[X|Ys]) :- select(Xs,T,C,Ys).
select([ ],_,_,[ ]).
```

With this transducer, the goal

```
?- L = [
   quote( 'F',    '87/10/19',  32,       20,     23+1/8 ),
   quote( 'IBM',  '87/10/19',  130+1/4,  18,     125+1/4 ),
   quote( 'TUA',  '87/10/19',  83,       69,     69      ),
   quote( 'X',    '87/10/19',  32+1/2,   21,     21+1/2 )
   ],
   select(L,
          quote(Symbol,Date,High,Low,Last),
          ((High-Low) > 100),
          NL).
```

yields the binding

```
NL = [quote('IBM', '87/10/19', 130+1/4, 18, 125+1/4)]
```

of all quotes whose **High** and **Low** values differed by at least one hundred points.
(Someone was truly desperate to sell IBM on Black Monday.)

Accumulators Accumulators compute 'aggregate' functions of the input stream.
That is, they accumulate or aggregate all the elements in the stream into a single
value. Generically, they might be written in Prolog as follows:

```
accumulate(List,Value) :-
                        initial_state(State),
                        accumulate(List,State,Value).

accumulate([X|Xs],S,Value) :-
                        next_state(X,S,NS),
                        accumulate(Xs,NS,Value).
accumulate([ ],S,Value) :-
                        final_state_value(S,Value).
```

Letting the **State** variable be the partial sum, we get the simple sum accumulator:

```
% sum(List,Sum) :-
%        Sum is the result of summing the elements in List
sum(List,Sum) :- sum(List,0,Sum).

sum([ ],V,V) :- !.
sum([X|Xs],OldV,V) :- NewV is X+OldV, sum(Xs,NewV,V).
```

Other Kinds of Transducers The four kinds of transducers above do not ex-
haust all possible transducers. For example, the moving averages transducer below
is not an enumerator, map, filter, or accumulator:

```
% moving_avg(M,L,NL) :- NL is the list of
%      Mth-moving averages of L. That is, item [i] in NL
%      is the average of items [i],...,[i+M-1] in L.
moving_avg(M,[ ],[ ]).
moving_avg(M,[X|Xs],[Y|Ys]) :-
         first(M,[X|Xs],L),
         sum(L,LS),
         Y is LS/M,
```

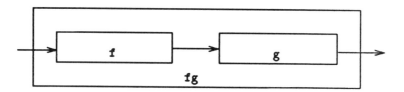

Figure 8.2: Composition of Transducers

```
moving_avg(M,Xs,Ys).
```

```
first(0,_,[ ]) :- !.
first(_,[ ],[ ]) :- !.
first(M,[H|T],[H|L]) :- M1 is M-1, first(M1,T,L).
```

There are many different kinds of transducers, just as there are many different paradigms in programming.

8.2.3 Composing Transducers

Transducers can be combined with logical variables in Prolog. Given two transducers *f/2* and *g/2*, we can easily form their pipeline composition *fg/2* with a single rule:[1]

```
fg(S0,S) :- f(S0,S1), g(S1,S).
```

Pictorial displays of transducers are suggestive. If we use boxes to represent transducers, then *fg* can be displayed as in Figure 8.2.   The arrows in these diagrams represent either streams or single parameters. Sometimes these displays are called dataflow diagrams, or 'Henderson diagrams' [AS85].

Through composition, we can build up large numbers of useful transducers. The library, or 'kit', concept is one of the main advantages of the stream processing paradigm: sophisticated transducers can be built up from simpler existing ones. For example, the transducer below computes standard deviations using the *sum/2* and *squares/2* transducers we developed earlier:

```
% stddev(List,Stddev) :-
%        Stddev is the standard deviation of List.
```

---

[1]Notice that this rule is the result of expanding the Definite Clause Grammar rule **fg** --> **f, g**. This is not a wild coincidence. We mentioned earlier that there is a close relationship between transducers and parsers. Much of the transducer code given in the previous section can be rewritten as DCG rules.

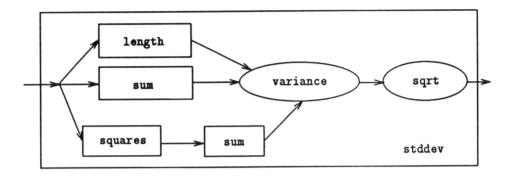

Figure 8.3: A Transducer that Computes Standard Deviations

```
stddev(List,Stddev) :-
        length(List,N),
        sum(List,Sum),
        squares(List,SqList),
        sum(SqList,SumSquares),
        variance(N,Sum,SumSquares,Variance),
        sqrt(Variance,Stddev).

variance(N,_,_,0) :- N =< 1, !.
variance(N,Sum,SumSq,Variance) :-
        Variance is (SumSq - (Sum*Sum/N)) / (N-1).
```

Figure 8.3 shows the composition of transducers in stddev, where rectangles represent transducers on streams, and ovals represent transducers on individual values. This is not the fastest transducer to form the standard deviations. A faster transducer would accumulate the length, sum, and sum of squares of the list simultaneously. The point, however, is that new transducers can be constructed quickly by composing existing transducers. The flexibility of using a library can outweigh the importance of speed.

Transducers can also be combined *recursively*. A classic example of recursive composition is in the computation of primes via Eratosthenes' method of sieves:

```
% primes(M,List) :-
%       List is the list of primes not larger than M.
primes(M,Primes) :-
```

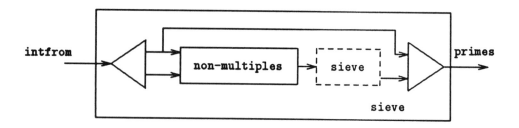

Figure 8.4: Recursive Transducer that Finds Primes

```
            N is M-1,
            intfrom(2,N,Integers),
            sieve(Integers,Primes).
```

```
sieve([X|Xs],[X|R]) :- non_multiples(Xs,X,L), sieve(L,R).
sieve([ ],[ ]).
```

```
non_multiples([Y|Ys],X,NL) :- multiple(Y,X), !,
                                  non_multiples(Ys,X,NL).
non_multiples([Y|Ys],X,[Y|NL]) :- non_multiples(Ys,X,NL).
non_multiples([ ],_,[ ]).
```

```
multiple(A,B) :- (A mod B) =:= 0.
```

This defines the enumerator *primes/2* to be a combination of an enumerator *intfrom/3* and a recursive filter *sieve/2*. Displaying *sieve* diagrammatically requires some innovation. The diagram of Henderson [Hen80] shown in Figure 8.4 represents the recursive use of *sieve* with a dashed box, and the breakdown of the stream into its head and tail (through use of the 'cons' functor [_|_]) with a triangle.

8.2.4 Stream Processing is more than List Processing

We have treated streams like lists above to introduce the ideas of transducers and stream processing. Two important things differentiate stream processing from list processing, however.

1. *Infinite streams.* Streams can represent infinitely long (non-terminating) sequences of values. For example, each of the following sequences is an infinite stream:

   [1,1,1,1,1,...]   the stream of ones

```
[1,2,3,4,5,...]   the stream of positive integers
[2,3,5,7,11,...]  the stream of prime numbers
```

In Prolog, some infinite streams can be constructed as infinite lists, by exploiting features of Prolog's unification. Executing

```
?- Ones = [1|Ones].
```

creates a structure representing an infinite list of ones.[2] However, this is not a general way to create infinite streams, such as the primes.

2. *Lazy evaluation.* Stream processing includes the use of *lazy evaluation*, a 'demand driven' mode of computation in which elements of a stream are produced by a transducer only on demand. Although programs are written as though the stream is completely available, actually the elements of the stream are produced only incrementally. (This permits us to use infinite streams.) Thus we integrate a view of the stream as a single object with a view of it as a sequence of objects. Lazy evaluation is a computation scheme in which goals are evaluated only on demand.

By contrast, *eager evaluation* is a mode of computation in which elements of a stream are produced immediately. Most programming languages, including Prolog, normally act in an eager way. That is, normal behavior is to evaluate a goal to completion when it is given to the Prolog interpreter.

Lazy evaluation permits us to apply some algorithms that are difficult to use otherwise, such as the algorithm above that finds prime numbers. Each time a new prime number is demanded of *sieve*, it produces a new call to itself and a call to the filter *non_multiples*, which eliminates all multiples of the head of the stream that was passed to its *sieve*. All computation can be done on demand.

The list processing programs above cannot handle infinite streams, and do not implement lazy evaluation. For example, if we tried to compute the stream of

---

[2]Using unification to create these 'circular terms' can be dangerous, unfortunately. First, printing the results of executing this goal (its bindings) will not terminate in some Prolog systems. Second, unification without the occur check can lead to unsound inferences. For example, with the rule surprise :- less_than(1+N,N) and the definition less_than(X,1+X) the goal ?- surprise will succeed quietly, giving the impression that there exists a number N such that 1+N is less than N. Third, and most seriously, in goals such as ?- X = [1|X], Y = [1|Y], X = Y the third unification will loop without halting in many Prolog implementations. We need an approach for representing infinite streams that avoids these problems.

all prime numbers with the Prolog program above, we would never get past the *intfrom/3* subgoal! We would spend our lives accumulating integers...

Although list processing can be accomplished easily in Prolog, it is not so obvious how stream processing can be accomplished in Prolog. We will come back to this problem shortly.

8.2.5   The Stream Data Analysis Paradigm

In stream data analysis, we put all of our data in the form of streams, and all of our analysis tools in the form of transducers. Just as in a functional programming environment, these transducers should be viewed as basic building blocks that can be accessed whenever necessary by data analysts.

A sample list of transducers is presented below, using functional syntax. Although they seem insignificant individually, as a group they become quite powerful.

Expression	Result
agg(Op,S)	result of applying infix (binary) operator Op to stream S
	Op can be +, *, ∧, ∨, min, max, avg, sum, count, etc.
append(S1,S2)	concatenation of S1 and S2
avg(S)	average of terms in stream S
comparison(Rel,S1,S2)	stream with ith value 1 if (S1[i] Rel S2[i]), otherwise 0
	Rel can be =, <, >, =<, >=, ==, \=, =\=, \==, etc.
constant_stream(C)	infinite stream of constant C
constant_stream(C,N)	stream of constant C of length N
length(S)	number of terms in stream S
difference(S1,S2)	difference of S1 and S2
distribution(D)	stream of values following distribution description D
first(N,S)	stream of the first N elements of stream S
intersect(S1,S2)	intersection of S1 and S2
intfrom(N)	infinite stream [N, N+1, N+2, ...]
intfrom(N,M)	finite stream [N, N+1, N+2, ..., M]
keysort(S)	result of keysorting stream S
lag(S,N)	stream with constant 0 repeated N times, followed by S
mapcar(F,S)	stream of results F(X) for each term X in stream S
max(S)	maximum value of terms in stream S
merge(S1,S2)	interleaving of S1 and S2
min(S)	minimum value of terms in stream S
moving_avg(M,S)	M-th moving average of stream S
naturaljoin(S1,S2)	join of S1 and S2
project(N,S)	stream of Nth arguments of each term in stream S
repeat(S,N)	stream with every element of S repeated N times
reverse(S)	reversal of stream S
select(T,C,S)	stream of terms in S that match T and satisfy C
sort(S)	result of sorting stream S
stddev(S)	standard deviation of terms in stream S
sum(S)	sum of terms in stream S
sumsq(S)	sum of squares of terms in stream S
union(S1,S2)	union of S1 and S2

This list resembles that of the *S* data analysis system [BC84], which extends it only with a few statistical operators. Collections like this one can be useful in many surprising contexts. Waters [Wat79] pointed out that a large percentage of the loops in the IBM Fortran Scientific Subroutine Package amount to stream transducers like these.

Any ordered sequences of data items can be treated as a stream. For example, arrays of data can be treated like streams, and many matrix algebra operations also fit the stream data analysis paradigm. This is sometimes cited as a basis of the success of the APL programming language. The stream data analysis paradigm has proven itself in both statistical and scientific areas. With an approach like the one we describe below, it should be possible to adapt it for other fields.

8.3 Limitations of Prolog for Stream Data Analysis

Prolog seems to be an excellent starting point for stream data analysis. There are at least two reasons for optimism:

1. Today, Prolog is arguably the best existing candidate for a language combining data processing with 'intelligent' analysis functions. It integrates relational database functionality with complex structures in data, and its logical foundations provide many features (unification and pattern matching, logical derivation and intensional query processing, backtracking and search, and declarativeness) that are useful in high-level analysis and interpretation of data.

2. Prolog is flexible. It is an outstanding vehicle for rapid prototyping, and permits access to systems that perform computationally intensive tasks better than it. Much of data analysis is of a 'rapid prototyping' nature – one wants to 'get a feel' for the data, without spending a great deal of time doing it.

On the other hand, Prolog has real limitations for large-scale applications such as stream data analysis. A number of complaints have been leveled against today's Prolog systems for stream processing (and other applications), including:

- Prolog requires lots of memory

- Prolog lacks a string datatype

- Prolog requires stack maintenance

- Prolog's I/O mechanisms are inadequate

- Prolog's control mechanisms are inadequate

- Prolog has an impedance mismatch with database systems.

We will see how most of these problems can be circumvented. Some of the problems may be only transitory, and will disappear with better Prolog implementations, cheaper memory, and new operating systems. Also, some of these problems are not Prolog-specific at all, but are problems that arise in most high-level languages. In any case, programmers that are interested in stream processing applications should be aware that the problems exist, and are serious problems in some systems today.

8.3.1 Prolog Requires Lots of Memory

Prolog systems today consume a relatively large address space. Prolog process images contain the following areas:

The Control Stack (or Local Stack)
Like most programming languages, Prolog uses a stack to manage calls to predicates. When a predicate call occurs, a frame is pushed on the stack to record the call and the arguments passed. The control stack is also commonly used to hold 'choice point' frames to implement backtracking.

The Heap (or Global Stack)
Prolog goals will create structures as a result of unification against program clauses. These structures are created by allocating cells incrementally from the top of the heap. Since the structures can be freed as soon as the goal that created them fails, the heap can be implemented as a stack whose entries are popped upon failure of the goal that created them.

The Trail
All bindings that are made in the process of executing a goal must be undone if the goal fails. The unification routine uses the trail as a stack to hold information that tells how to undo these bindings when failure occurs.

The Atom Table (or Name Table)
The names (character string representations) of all atoms in Prolog are stored in a large table, which permits fast lookup.

The Database (or Code Space)
All asserted clauses, and associated objects like indices, are stored as data structures in an area called the database.

These areas can each grow to be quite large. As a consequence, moderately large Prolog programs run as processes with a memory image of several megabytes.

Even though Prolog programs do show locality in their memory references [Tic88], machines without substantial amounts of memory may produce poor Prolog performance due to swapping overhead. A related problem is that since most Prolog implementations do not share text among processes, it can be very difficult to run several large Prolog processes on one machine. Parallel Prolog systems may eventually eliminate this problem.

8.3.2 Prolog Lacks a String Datatype

Prolog systems usually have no special string datatype. Instead, two approaches are used for representing strings:

- strings are represented as lists of integers (representing ASCII codes)

- strings are represented as Prolog atoms.

The *name/2* predicate is used to convert between these representations. Unfortunately, both representations present problems.

Using lists of ASCII codes to represent strings is elegant, in that it reduces string processing to list processing. However, the list representation is very space-inefficient, requiring one or more machine words for each cons and each character. (In typical Prolog implementations with 4-byte words and single-word representations of cons and integer structures, for example, an n-character string will require $8n$ bytes.) Furthermore, processing these strings can be time-inefficient, and connection to efficient external string-manipulation routines (which expect a packed-array-of-byte representation) can become very awkward. For these reasons atoms are often used to represent strings instead in data-intensive programs.

An atom is essentially a pointer to a string in the atom table. As new atoms are introduced into the Prolog system, they are *interned*, i.e., entered into the atom table (with a packed-array-of-byte representation) and replaced by a pointer. One main benefit of this implementation is speed: checking whether two atoms unify can be accomplished very quickly with just a comparison of pointers (one machine instruction), while checking whether two strings are equal requires calling a subroutine on most machines.

This implementation of atoms is basic to most Prolog implementations today, and cannot really be changed. Unfortunately, a serious problem with the atom table approach is that only a modest amount of string data can be stored in the atom table. This limitation makes Prolog unable to cope with large-scale data processing. If we connect a stream of data with Prolog, the strings in the stream will not be in the Prolog atom table when they are encountered. The question is: *should strings in the input stream be converted to Prolog atoms as they are encountered?* If the answer is no, we will pay a price in unifying Prolog atoms with these strings, and at the very least will have to extend the internal unification primitives to handle strings. If the answer is yes, we run the risk of overflowing the Prolog atom table. (And: when the stream is large, this risk is not just a risk, but a certainty.)

To appreciate this problem, consider the following very simple program:

```
% print_stream(Filename) :-
%        all terms in file Filename are printed.
print_stream(Filename) :-
        open(Filename,read,Descriptor),
        read(Descriptor,Term),
        print_stream_term(Term,Descriptor).

print_stream_term(end_of_file,D) :-
        !,
        close(D).
print_stream_term(T,D) :-
        print(T),
        nl,
        read(D,NT),
        print_stream_term(NT,D).
```

This innocuous-looking program will not work for most large files. Whenever the files it reads contain enough atoms to overflow the atom table, it will abort in failure.

Many approaches have been proposed to answer the question above. They include adding a string datatype to Prolog, and adding periodic garbage collection of the atom table. These approaches require significant amounts of work, unfortunately, and are not available in most Prolog systems today [Pag89].

8.3.3 Stream Processing Requires Stack Maintenance

Stream processing programs are basically iterative: the program repeatedly accepts a new input from a stream, does something with it, and incorporates the input into its current 'state' and/or produces some output stream element based on the input and its state.

Unfortunately, iteration in Prolog (and Lisp, for that matter) can cause stacks to overflow. Specifically, when iterative programs read streams that are arbitrarily long, it is likely that Prolog stack overflows will occur before the program finishes.

To guarantee a program will work for arbitrarily long streams requires some understanding of stack maintenance.

There are basically two ways to write iterative programs in Prolog:

- recursion

- repeat-fail loops.

Recursion is the natural way to iterate. The following simple program sums a list recursively:

```
% sum(List,Sum) :-
%       Sum is the result of summing the elements in List.
sum([ ],0) :- !.
sum([X|Xs],Sum) :- sum(Xs,XsSum), Sum is X+XsSum.
```

This program has a serious problem, however: when the input is a very long list, the program can overflow the control stack. Each time a list member is inspected by the *sum/2* predicate, its recursive call allocates a new control stack frame. This recursion will lead to control stack overflows when the input list is long.

Happily it turns out that we can avoid control stack overflows by using *tail recursion*. A tail recursive version of the program above looks as follows:

```
% sum(List,Sum) :-
%       Sum is the result of summing the elements in List.
sum(List,Sum) :- sum(List,0,Sum).


sum([ ],V,V) :- !.
sum([X|Xs],OldV,V) :- NewV is X+OldV, sum(Xs,NewV,V).
```

This program is 'tail recursive' in *sum/3*. In other words, the last goal in the last clause of *sum/3* is a recursive call to *sum/3*. The importance of tail recursion is that the control stack frame for a tail recursive predicate is re-used by the recursive subgoal. With the program above, this means that we can sum an arbitrarily long list with only one control stack frame for *sum/2*, one for *sum/3*, and whatever is needed by *is/2*. This reclaiming of control stack frames is called *Tail Recursion Optimization (TRO)*.[3] TRO thus solves some problems of control stack usage.

---

[3] More accurately, it could be called *Last Call Optimization*, since the control stack frame for a goal can be reclaimed when calling the last subgoal in the last clause for the goal. For example, with the program p :- q,r. p :- s,t,u. p :- v,w. and the goal ?- p, if in execution we get to the subgoal w, then the control stack frame allocated for p can be re-used as the frame for w. At that point, execution of p is complete except for executing w, so p's control stack frame can be used by w.

Generally, it is a good idea to write iterative programs as tail recursive programs. However, even tail recursive programs can still cause storage overflows. All programs that create data structures allocate cells on the Prolog heap. The heap can overflow when an output stream being constructed by a program is very long, even if the program is tail recursive. For example, the program

```
squares([X|Xs],[Y|Ys]) :- Y is X*X, squares(Xs,Ys).
squares([ ],[ ]).
```

creates a list of squares of length as long as the first. But both lists remain in their entirety on the heap until the goal that called *squares/2* fails.

To avoid heap overflows, we can use a Prolog system with *Garbage Collection (GC)*. Where TRO permits re-use of control stack frames by iterative programs, GC permits reclamation of storage structures allocated by previous iterations. GC inspects the heap for data structures that are no longer actively pointed to by variables, marks their cells for reclamation, then compresses the heap by reclaiming all marked cells.

Not all Prolog systems provide complete GC and TRO. (In fact, Prolog *interpreters* can defeat TRO and GC even though the underlying system supports them for compiled code.) But without them, stream processing cannot be done with recursive programs.

There is an alternative to recursion that can be used successfully when reading streams from a file: *repeat-fail loops*. The sum program above can be written with a loop that repeatedly reads a number and adds it to the current sum.

```
% sum(Sum) :- Sum is the sum of all numbers read.
sum(Sum) :-
        asserta('%%sum'(0)),
        repeat,
                read(X),
                add(X),
                X == end_of_file,
        retract('%%sum'(Sum)),
        !.

add(X) :-
        number(X),
        retract('%%sum'(OldSum)),
        NewSum is X+OldSum,
```

```
        asserta('%%sum'(NewSum)),
        !.
add(_).
```

Repeat-fail loops are inelegant, to say the least. Worse than this, they are usually awkward to write, and require the programmer to use *assert* and *retract* (or other primitives with side-effects) to save information obtained in the loop. Both *assert* and *retract* are extremely slow, requiring milliseconds to complete in most Prolog systems. Repeat-fail loops do have one important feature, however: they will not overflow the Prolog stacks. The only storage danger is that a program may overflow the database area provided for *assert*ed clauses, or possibly the atom table.

So, for doing iteration on streams we have a choice. If we wish to write our programs as recursive list manipulators, then they must be written tail recursively, and we must use a Prolog system with Tail Recursion Optimization and Garbage Collection. Alternatively we can write programs as repeat-fail loops around either I/O calls, *assert*s and *retract*s, or some other primitives with side effects.

8.3.4   Prolog's I/O Mechanisms are Inadequate

Real data streams often come from files and external devices, sometimes available over computer networks. Therefore, real stream processing requires a comprehensive set of I/O primitives. No Prolog standard currently exists for these, and many Prolog systems have little in the way of I/O support. This means that, first of all, I/O primitives must be added as needed to the Prolog system as 'foreign functions'.

For example, if we wanted to perform database I/O, at minimum we would need to add something like the following primitives:

open_relation(Relation/Arity,Cursor)
> Attempts to open the database relation Relation/Arity for sequential retrieval, and returns the descriptor Cursor for subsequent accesses if successful.

retrieve(Cursor,Term)
> Retrieves a tuple from the database relation indicated by Cursor. The tuple is returned in Term, and takes the value end_of_file if no further tuples remain. This predicate does not backtrack. Although Cursor does not change above the Prolog interface, a subsequent retrieval will obtain the next tuple in the relation.

close_relation(Cursor)
> Terminates retrieval from the relation indicated by Cursor.

This interface accomplishes basically what we need for database I/O, but its use
in Prolog presents a new problem. I/O managers expect client programs to manage
their file descriptors and cursors, while Prolog's control model encourages programs
to forget about them completely. Specifically, a goal's control stack frame can be
popped before all choicepoints of the goal have been exhausted, leaving any cursors
or file descriptors associated with the goal 'dangling'. In other words, Prolog's
stack-orientation makes it easy to pop away a goal that intends to close a cursor or
file descriptor.

For example, consider the following program.

```
my_portfolio_value(Date,Value) :-
      quote('F',Date,_,_,FPrice),
      quote('IBM',Date,_,_,IBMPrice),
      quote('TUA',Date,_,_,TUAPrice),
      quote('X',Date,_,_,XPrice),
      Value is FPrice*80 + IBMPrice*72
               + TUAPrice*100 + XPrice*100,
      !.


%  transparent interface to relational database from Prolog
quote(Symbol,Date,High,Low,Last) :-
      open_relation(quote/5,Cursor),
      repeat,
         retrieve(Cursor,Term),
         (
             Term = quote(Symbol,Date,High,Low,Last)
         ;
             Term = end_of_file,
             close_relation(Cursor),
             !
         ).
```

Although *portfolio_value/2* runs correctly, each time it is called it creates four cursors and leaves them open![4] Computing several portfolio values this way can consume all the cursors provided by the database interface.

---

[4] Leaving cursors open can be serious. In shared database systems, the act of opening a relation
for read access will obtain a *read lock* for the relation. Forgetting to close the cursor is then the
same as forgetting to unlock the relation, which will prevent others from modifying the relation,
and possibly cause deadlocks.

Improved Prolog technology has provided a solution to this problem. When the SICStus Prolog goal undo(G) is executed, G will be executed whenever the goal's control frame is popped off [CW88]. Thus if we change the definition of *quote/5* above to the following program, cursors will be reclaimed as soon as the goal that initially called *quote/5* fails:

```
quote(Symbol,Date,High,Low,Last) :-
        open_relation(quote/5,Cursor),
        undo( close_relation(Cursor) ),
        % this close_relation goal is executed when the
        % control stack frame for this clause is popped.
        repeat,
            retrieve(Cursor,Term),
            (
                Term = quote(Symbol,Date,High,Low,Last)
            ;
                Term = end_of_file,
                !
            ).
```

The *undo/1* primitive is very useful, and will find its way into more Prolog systems in the future.

Another disturbing problem is that I/O primitives like *read* typically cannot be used directly by nondeterministic programs, because they have side effects. Each read from a cursor modifies the meaning of a cursor. There is usually no way to 'unread' what one has read, so backtracking programs such as nondeterministic parsers will not work with primitives like *read*.

The problems just mentioned can be summarized in a more general way: *the concept of cursors has not yet been cleanly integrated into Prolog.* Only recently have *open-read-write-close* primitives been added to the language, supplementing the simple *see-read-seen* and *tell-write-told* primitives that were available. However, this extension is incomplete. For example, in Prolog there is still no cursor-oriented interface to the Prolog database [PPM88]. The only direct interface to the database is through the *clause* primitive. Since this interface works only by backtracking, it is not possible to implement predicates like *bagof* and *findall* without using primitives like *assert* that have side effects. These problems could be avoided if we had an interface like the one above for external database relations that could be used for predicates:

```
open_predicate(Predicate/Arity,Cursor)
```

```
retrieve(Cursor,Clause)
close(Cursor)
```

We are not arguing that the interface should look precisely like this; we are pointing out only that no such interface exists, and that Prolog should be extended with one.

Most Prolog systems lack other important I/O features. Specifically, they have no interrupt handling mechanisms or asynchronous I/O primitives. These features are especially important in stream applications where high performance is critical. Fortunately, Prolog systems may permit these extensions without serious changes.

8.3.5 Prolog's Control Mechanisms are Inadequate

General stream processing programs must selectively read data items from multiple input streams, process these items, and then selectively write multiple output streams. To do this requires the ability to *coroutine* among stream processing goals. That is, the execution of producers of streams must be interleaved with the execution of their consumers.

It is not obvious how to achieve coroutining in Prolog. In ordinary Prolog systems, backtracking is the only control mechanism for clause selection, and this prevents interleaved execution of goals.

An example will make this point clear. Suppose that *stock/3* and *quote/5* are relational database predicates whose clauses are stored in sorted order by their stock symbol, and we wish to find all results of the Prolog goal

```
?- stock(Symbol,Name,Address),
   quote(Symbol,'87/10/19',_,Price,Price).
```

This will give us the stocks whose last price matched its low price on Black Monday. Finding all results with backtracking will require looking through all of the clauses of the *quote* predicate for each clause in the *stock* predicate. This takes time proportional to the *product* of the number of clauses of the predicates.

A much better way to perform this query is by performing what in the database field is called a *merge join*. A merge join of two predicates with clauses in sorted order works by interleaving (i.e., coroutining) a sequential scan through the clauses of the two predicates, in precisely the same way that a merge sort interleaves scans through two sorted files. It takes time proportional to the *sum* of the number of clauses of the predicates. For the goal above, a merge join would work by repeatedly:

1. retrieving the next stock(Symbol,Name,Address) clause from the *stock* predicate;

2. given the `Symbol` value obtained in step 1, retrieving (scanning sequentially for) the next clause that matches the pattern

```
quote(Symbol,'87/10/19',_,Price,Price)
```

and yielding it as a result;

3. on backtracking, resuming the scan for *quote* clauses as long as further results are found;

4. as soon as the *quote* scan fails to match, however, resuming the scan for the next *stock* clause in step 1 above.

The specific problem we are pointing out is that Prolog is currently not capable of performing merge joins for predicates in its database. Fortunately, Prolog can be extended to do so by adding a cursor-like interface to the database [PPM88], like the one described in the preceding section. The more general problem we are concerned with is that coroutining is not an easy thing to do in Prolog. Shortly we will see how coroutining can be implemented by developing a stream processing meta-interpreter with better control mechanisms.

8.3.6 Prolog has an Impedance Mismatch with DBMS

It is difficult to interface Prolog systems with database systems because they seem inherently mismatched. The control model of Prolog is one of finding a single 'proof', selecting one clause at a time and backtracking when necessary to consider alternatives. The DBMS control model, by contrast, is one of batch processing: large queries are run at one time, and all alternatives are considered simultaneously. The fundamental question is how one can interface a 'set-oriented' system like a DBMS with a 'single-clause-oriented' system like Prolog.

The query shown above illustrates some of the issues here. Let us assume, for example, *quote/5* is indexed on its first argument and date together and has 100,000 clauses, but *stock/3* is not indexed and has 1000 clauses. Then the query above

```
?- stock(Symbol,Name,Address),
   quote(Symbol,'87/10/19',_,Price,Price).
```

will take enormously less time than the 'equivalent' query

```
?- quote(Symbol,'87/10/19',_,Price,Price),
   stock(Symbol,Name,Address).
```

If the first query were to take one minute to find all solutions, the second query would take more like 70 days (100,000 minutes).

A DBMS may run this query efficiently. If we issue a query to the DBMS as

```
?- sql_query('select *
            from    stock, quote
            where   stock.symbol = quote.symbol
            and     quote.date = "87/10/19"
            and     quote.low = quote.last').
```

then the DBMS can, and will, optimize the query in the most advantageous way possible, and return the results much more quickly than the Prolog approach. (The results obtained by this goal are understood to be *asserted* in the Prolog database.)

Many attempts have been documented over the past few years in connecting Prolog with Relational DBMS, but for the most part they amount to 'glue jobs' (in the all too accurate words of Mike Stonebraker). These connections are inefficient and not practical for large-scale stream processing applications. Later, we will show how stream processing provides a way to integrate Prolog and DBMS in an elegant way.

8.3.7   Summary: Problems and Solutions

We have shown that, without changes, Prolog has many limitations that make its use in stream processing a challenge. We have also shown that these limitations can be circumvented with modest improvements in Prolog technology or adroit programming techniques:

Prolog lacks a string datatype

> The atom table used in almost all Prolog implementations to implement a string type has the serious flaw that it can overflow. Introduction of a string datatype will mostly eliminate this problem, although overflow will then still be a possibility with poorly-written programs.

> Currently, processing of very large streams can be done by restricting the data analyzed to be numeric, with perhaps a bounded amount of string data (e.g., all stock symbols). This numeric restriction is annoying, but permits a great deal of useful analysis.

Prolog requires stack maintenance

> Restricting stream transducers to be deterministic, tail recursive predicates avoids most problems in processing of large streams in Prolog systems with

Tail Recursion Optimization (TRO) and Garbage Collection (GC). TRO eliminates the danger of stack overflows, and GC also avoids the problem of heap overflows that transducers can encounter in transforming large streams.

Prolog's I/O mechanisms are inadequate

Prolog should be augmented with new primitives, including more comprehensive I/O interfaces, the *undo/1* primitive of SICStus Prolog, and some cursor-like mechanism for accessing the Prolog database [PPM88]. Also, it is desirable to develop (expensive) versions of I/O primitives like *read* that are side-effect-free, i.e., that can back up in their streams, so that nondeterministic programs can be applied to those streams that are accessible only through I/O (streams that will not fit entirely in the Prolog heap, for example).

Prolog's control mechanisms are inadequate

Prolog's poor control seems at first to be the biggest impediment to its use in stream processing. Some problems are avoidable by adding new primitives. For example, the cursor-like mechanism for accessing the Prolog database just mentioned can be used to permit Prolog implementation of merge joins in particular, and coroutining in general.

With a little cleverness, we can overcome most control problems with no change to Prolog. In section 8.4, especially 8.4.4, we will see how Prolog can be extended with a meta-interpreter that permits general stream processing.

Prolog has an impedance mismatch with DBMS

Today Prolog and DBMS work with different models of data processing. Where Prolog operates on single sets of bindings at a time, DBMS work on whole predicates at a time. In section 8.6, we will see that both of these models can be integrated under the model of stream processing.

Thus most problems can be solved without sweeping changes, but some problems cannot. In particular, there is no simple solution to the problem that Prolog requires lots of memory. Fortunately, this does not appear to be a long-term problem, but is a concern today because of current memory prices, and may be a problem that advances in technology will permit us to ignore.

8.4 Log(F): A Rewriting System in Prolog

We pause here to study Log(F), the language we will use shortly to write stream transducers that run in Prolog. Log(F) is a combination of Prolog and a functional language called F*, developed by Sanjai Narain at UCLA [Nar87, Nar88, Nar89, Nar90]. Log(F) is the integration with Prolog of a functional language in which one programs using rewrite rules. This section reviews the major aspects of Log(F), and describes its advantages for stream processing.

8.4.1 Overview of F* and Log(F)

F* is a rewrite rule language. In F*, all statements are rules of the form

```
LHS => RHS
```

where *LHS* and *RHS* are structures (actually Prolog terms) satisfying certain modest restrictions summarized below.

A single example shows the power and flexibility of F*. Consider the following two rules, defining how lists may be appended:

```
append([ ],W) => W.
append([U|V],W) => [U|append(V,W)].
```

Like the Prolog rules for appending lists, this concise description provides all that is necessary. The two F* rules are essentially equivalent to the usual Prolog definition

```
append([ ],W,W).
append([U|V],W,[U|L]) :- append(V,W,L).
```

Log(F) is the integration of F* with Prolog. In Log(F), F* rules are compiled to Prolog clauses. The compilation process is straightforward. For example, the two rules above are translated into something functionally equivalent to the following Prolog code:

```
reduce( append(A,W), Z ) :-
                        reduce( A, [ ] ),
                        reduce( W, Z ).
reduce( append(A,W), Z ) :-
                        reduce( A, [U|V] ),
                        reduce( [U|append(V,W)], Z ).
reduce( [ ], [ ] ).
reduce( [X|Y], [X|Y] ).
```

Unlike the rules in many rewriting systems, the *reduce* rules here can operate non-deterministically, just like their Prolog counterparts. Many ad hoc function- or rewrite rule-based systems have been proposed to incorporate Prolog's backtracking, but the simple implementation of F* in Prolog shown here provides non-determinism as a natural and immediate feature.

An important feature of F* and Log(F) is the capability for *lazy evaluation*. With the rules above, the goal

```
?- reduce( append([1,2,3],[4,5,6]), L ).
```

yields the result

```
L = [ 1 | append([2,3],[4,5,6]) ].
```

That is, in one *reduce* step, only the head of the resulting appended list is computed. (Try it!) The tail, `append([2,3],[4,5,6])`, can then be further reduced if this is necessary.

In order for the *reduce* rules above to work properly, we need the two rules for [ ] and [_|_]:

```
reduce( [ ], [ ] ).
reduce( [X|Y], [X|Y] ).
```

In F*, the function symbols (functors) like [ ] and [_|_] of terms that reduce to themselves are called *constructor symbols*. Below we will call any term whose functor is a constructor symbol a *simplified* term. Simplified terms reduce to themselves. Constructors are the things in F* and Log(F) that implement lazy evaluation, since they terminate reduction.

Where F* computations are naturally lazy because of their implementation with reduction rules, Log(F) permits some *eager computation* as well. Essentially, eager computations are invocations of Prolog predicates. Thus, in the Log(F) rule

```
intfrom(N) => [N|intfrom(N+1)].
```

the subterm N+1 is recognized by the Log(F) system as being eager, and the resulting code produced is equivalent to

```
reduce( intfrom(N), Z ) :-
                    N1 is N+1,
                    reduce( [N|intfrom(N1)], Z ).
```

Programmers may declare their own predicates to be eager. By judicious combination of eager and lazy computation, programmers obtain programming power not available from Prolog or F* alone. For a number of useful examples of this combination, see [Nar88].

8.4.2   F* – A Rewrite Rule Language

In this section we present F* more carefully. F* rules have the form

LHS => RHS

where **LHS** and **RHS** are terms. These terms are made up of variables and function symbols, which may or may not be constructor symbols. Certain restrictions are made on **LHS** and **RHS**. After defining terminology, we list these restrictions below.

    Constructor symbols are special function symbols that are not reducible by F*. Examples of predefined constructor symbols are true, false, [ ], [_|_]. *Rewrite rules* give reduction relationships between terms. Examples of F* rules are as follows:

```
if(true,X,Y) => X.
if(false,X,Y) => Y.

and(X,Y) => if(X,Y,false).
or(X,Y) => if(X,true,Y).
not(X) => if(X,false,true).
```

F* rules **LHS => RHS** satisfy the following restrictions [Nar87]:

(a) **LHS** cannot be a variable.

(b) **LHS** cannot be of the form $c(T_1, \ldots, T_n)$ where c is an n-ary constructor symbol, $n \geq 0$.

(c) If **LHS** is $f(T_1, \ldots, T_n)$, $n \geq 0$, then each T_i is either a variable, or a term of the form $c(X_1, \ldots, X_m)$ where c is an m-ary constructor symbol, $m \geq 0$, and each X_j is a variable.

(d) There is at most one occurrence of any variable in **LHS**.

(e) All variables appearing in **RHS** also appear in **LHS**.

    An *F* program* is a collection of F* rules. Below is an example of an F* program, where it is assumed that *s/1* is a constructor symbol:

```
equal(0,0) => true.
equal(s(X),s(Y)) => equal(X,Y).

lessEq(0,X) => true.
lessEq(s(X),s(Y)) => lessEq(X,Y).
```

```
sum(0,X) => X.
sum(s(X),Y) => s(sum(X,Y)).
```

A *reduction* using an F* program begins with a ground term G, produces a sequence of rewrites – or reductions – of G, and terminates in a term whose function symbol is a constructor. That is, given G, a reduction is a sequence of ground terms G_0, G_1, ..., G_n such that

1. $G = G_0$.

2. For each i, $0 \le i \le n - 1$, there exists a rule $f(T_1, \ldots, T_m) => T$ such that

   a. $G_i = f(S_1, \ldots, S_m)$;

   b. For each j, $1 \le j \le m$, S_j is either a variable or recursively has a reduction to T_j. If S_j is a variable, we construct the binding $\theta_j = \{S_j \leftarrow T_j\}$. Otherwise we let θ_j be the bindings obtained recursively in the reduction of S_j to T_j;

   c. If we let θ be the accumulated bindings $\theta_1 \cdots \theta_m$, then $G_{i+1} = T\theta$, where T is the right hand side of the rule.

3. The function symbol of G_n is a constructor, i.e., G_n is simplified.

For example, with the program

```
equal(0,0) => true.
equal(s(X),s(Y)) => equal(X,Y).

sum(0,X) => X.
sum(s(X),Y) => s(sum(X,Y)).
```

the term `equal(sum(s(s(0)),s(0)),s(s(s(0))))` has the reduction

```
equal( sum(s(s(0)),s(0)), s(s(s(0))) )
equal( s(sum(s(0),s(0))), s(s(s(0))) )
equal( sum(s(0),s(0)), s(s(0)) )
equal( s(sum(0,s(0))), s(s(0)) )
equal( sum(0,s(0)), s(0) )
equal( s(0), s(0) )
equal( 0, 0 )
true.
```

In this reduction we alternated applications of the fourth and second rules in the first 4 steps, and then used the third, second, and first rules in the last 3 steps.

The restrictions above are carefully designed to be sufficient for proving soundness and completeness properties of F* reductions [Nar88]. However, they also have intuitive practical justifications:

1. F* programs are understood to be used only in rewriting *ground terms*, terms that do not contain any variables. That is, if we try to reduce a term T using an F* program, then T should contain no variables. Restriction (e) then guarantees that whatever T is rewritten to will also contain no variables.

2. Restrictions (d) and (e) above mean that F* programs use only *pattern matching* (matching of terms with no duplicated variables against ground terms), and not the full power of unification. Restriction (d) is sometimes called a 'linearity' restriction, and avoids unification. This is actually an advantage! It leads to fast implementations, and in many situations causes no loss in power. Note that the program above defines equality of terms without using unification.

3. Restriction (c) is the main restriction on F* rules. It requires that the head of a rule be of the form

$f(T_1, \ldots, T_n)$

where each T_i is either a variable, or a term whose functor is a constructor symbol. This restriction guarantees efficient implementation. Rather than requiring a general equality theory for pattern matching of arguments, all that is needed is binding to variables, or reduction to simplified terms.

These restrictions are really very natural, and are easily grasped once one has written a few F* programs.

8.4.3   Log(F): Integrating F* with Prolog

Because constructor symbols in F* terminate reduction, we call F* a *lazy rewriting language*. Constructors terminate reduction (evaluation) of a term; for further evaluation the constructors must be removed. Since Prolog has no delayed computation *per se*, we tend to think of Prolog computations as *eager* by contrast with F*.

Log(F) is the integration of F* with Prolog. It therefore combines both lazy F* computations with eager Prolog computations. This combination has many practical applications. For example, in the Log(F) code

```
count([X|S],N) => count(S,N+1).
```

the subterm N+1 is recognized by the Log(F) compiler as being eager, and the resulting code produced is something equivalent to

```
reduce(count(A,N),Z) :-
                  reduce(A,[X|S]),
                  M is N+1,
                  reduce(count(S,M),Z).
```

Arbitrary Prolog predicates can be declared to be eager. Among other predicates, we can introduce a general eager Prolog interface called success that yields the value true if its argument succeeds when called, and the value false otherwise:

```
success(G,true) :- call(G), !.
success(G,false).
```

With this interface to 'eager' Prolog predicates we can develop significant programs with compact sets of rewrite rules. For example, the following is an executable Log(F) program for computing primes:

```
primes => sieve(intfrom(2)).

intfrom(N) => [N|intfrom(N+1)].

sieve([U|V]) => [U|sieve(filter(U,V))].

filter(A,[U|V]) => if(
                  success(U mod A =:= 0),
                       filter(A,V),
                       [U|filter(A,V)]
              ).
```

The *intfrom* rule generates an infinite stream of integers. The rule for filter uses the eager Prolog interface success.

Compilation of Log(F) rules to Prolog is easy to implement in principle. Following the definition of reductions above, the F* rule

```
f(T1,...,Tn) => T
```

can be compiled to the Prolog *reduce* clause

```
reduce( f(A1,...,An), Z ) :-
                  reduce(A1,T1),
```

```
          ...,
          reduce(An,Tn),
          reduce(T,Z).
```

provided that each of *T1*, ..., *Tn* and *T* is a nonvariable term. If any of *T1*, ..., *Tn* or *T* is a variable, the *reduce/2* subgoal for it in the body of this clause is replaced with a unification. The compilation of rules with eager primitives, like + and **success**, is only mildly more complex.

Using this compilation algorithm extended for eager predicate calls, the Log(F) *primes* program above would be compiled to the following Prolog rules:

```
reduce(primes,Z) :-
            reduce(sieve(intfrom(2)),Z).
reduce(intfrom(N),Z) :-
            N1 is N+1,
            reduce([N|intfrom(N1)],Z).
reduce(sieve(A),Z) :-
            reduce(A,[U|V]),
            reduce([U|sieve(filter(U,V))],Z).
reduce(filter(A,B),Z) :-
            reduce(B,[U|V]),
            success((U mod A =:= 0),S),
            reduce(if(S,filter(A,V),[U|filter(A,V)]),Z).
reduce(if(A,X,Y),Z) :-
            reduce(A,true),
            reduce(X,Z).
reduce(if(A,X,Y),Z) :-
            reduce(A,false),
            reduce(Y,Z).
reduce([U|V],[U|V]).
reduce([ ],[ ]).
reduce(true,true).
reduce(false,false).

success(G,true) :- call(G), !.
success(G,false).
```

As an example of execution, if we define the predicate

```
reducePrint(X) :-
        reduce(X,[H|T]), write(H-T), nl, reducePrint(T).
```

then the goal

```
?- reducePrint(primes).
```

produces the following (non-terminating) output:

```
2 - sieve(filter(2,intfrom(3)))
3 - sieve(filter(3,filter(2,intfrom(4))))
5 - sieve(filter(5,filter(3,filter(2,intfrom(6)))))
7 - sieve(filter(7,filter(5,filter(3,filter(2,intfrom(8))))))
   ...
```

The compiled code here is not nearly the best possible, and one can spend a great deal of time improving the compilation of Log(F) into Prolog or other languages. In this presentation, however, we will not discuss compilation further.

8.4.4 Stream Processing Aspects of Log(F)

The example above shows that Log(F) naturally provides *lazy evaluation*. Functional programs on lists can produce terms in an incremental way, and incremental or "call by need" evaluation is an elegant mechanism for controlling query processing.

Furthermore, Log(F) supports stream processing, and thus stream data analysis. From the examples above, it is clear that the rules have a functional flavor. Stream operators are easily expressed using recursive functional programs.

Log(F) also has a formal foundation that captures important aspects of stream processing:

1. Determinate (non-backtracking) code is easily detected through syntactic tests only. A benefit of the F* restrictions is that deterministic computations are easily detected. If the heads of rules for a symbol do not unify, and only ground terms are reduced, then the reduction will be deterministic. For example, with the rules

```
sum(0,X) => X.
sum(s(X),Y) => s(sum(X,Y)).
```

when reducing terms like sum(s(s(0)),s(0)) only one rule can be chosen at any point. Determinate code avoids the overhead of "distributed backtracking" incurred by some parallel logic programming systems.

2. Log(F) takes as a basic assumption that stream values are *ground terms*, i.e., Prolog terms without variables. This avoids problems encountered by parallel Prolog systems which must attempt to provide consistency of bindings to variables used by processes on opposing ends of streams.

These features of Log(F) make it a nicely-limited sublanguage in which to write high-powered programs for stream processing and other performance-critical tasks. Special-purpose compilers can be developed for this sublanguage to produce highly-optimized code. Log(F) compilers can be much more sophisticated than the compiler described above. Among other things, they can ascertain the determinacy of Log(F) rules and prevent multiple reductions of common subexpressions.

In section 8.3 we grappled with the problem that it is not so obvious how to perform stream processing in Prolog. Specifically, it is not obvious how to implement control strategies like coroutining.

Log(F) offers a solution to this problem, since lazy evaluation gives us a method to implement coroutining. Recall that coroutining basically requires programs to suspend their execution temporarily while the executions of other programs are resumed. The result of lazy evaluation can be, for example, a term

```
[ partial_result | computation_to_resume_later ]
```

whose tail is a 'suspension', representing an unfinished computation. Designing transducers to yield this kind of result is precisely what we need to implement coroutining.

We pointed out earlier that it does not seem possible to implement merge join or merge sort directly in Prolog, because they are coroutining procedures by their very nature. In Log(F), on the other hand, it is easy to implement these procedures:

```
merge_sorted([ ],[ ]) => [ ].
merge_sorted([ ],[X|Y]) => [X|Y].
merge_sorted([U|V],[ ]) => [U|V].
merge_sorted([U|V],[X|Y]) => if(
                              U=<X,
                              [U|merge_sorted(V,[X|Y])],
                              [X|merge_sorted([U|V],Y)]
                            ).
```

We will illustrate with further examples in the next section that Log(F) provides enough to implement (even recursively-defined) networks of coroutined transducers, and thus demand-driven stream processing.

8.5   Stream Processing in Prolog

The Tangram Stream Processor is an extensible stream processing system that uses Log(F) to implement stream processing in Prolog. This section develops techniques for stream processing in Log(F) through a sequence of examples.

8.5.1   Implementing Transducers in Log(F)

Let us first review how the four basic kinds of single-input, single-output transducers can be implemented in Log(F). It is remarkable how much simpler they are than their Prolog counterparts.

Enumerators   Enumerators in Log(F) are typically compact:

```
enumerate => enumerate(initial_state).
```

```
enumerate(S) => [next_value(S)|enumerate(next_state(S))].
enumerate(_) => [ ].
```

The enumerator of integers is easy to develop, and the infinite stream version is even simpler:

```
% intfrom(M,N)  =>  the list of integers [M,...,M+N].
intfrom(M,N) => if(N=<0, [ ], [M|intfrom(M+1,N-1)] ).
```

```
% intfrom(M)  =>  the list of integers [M,...].
intfrom(M) => [M|intfrom(M+1)].
```

Maps   The generic map transducers for the function f can look as follows in Log(F):

```
f_mapstream([X|Xs]) => [f(X)|f_mapstream(Xs)].
f_mapstream([ ]) => [ ].
```

The Prolog examples given earlier can be adapted to Log(F) as follows:

```
% squares(L) => the result of squaring each member of L.
squares([X|Xs]) => [X*X|squares(Xs)].
squares([ ]) => [ ].
```

```
% project(I,L) => the list of I-th arguments of terms in L.
```

```
project(I,[X|Xs]) => [arg(I,X) | project(I,Xs)].
project(_,[ ]) => [ ].
```

It is also easy to develop the higher-order version of mapstream which takes a function as an argument:

```
mapstream(F,[ ]) => [ ].
mapstream(F,[X|L]) => [apply(F,X)|mapstream(F,L)].
```

Filters   Filters in Log(F) are like maps, but involve an if-then-else construct.

```
filter([X|Xs]) =>
      if( inadmissible(X), filter(Xs), [X|filter(Xs)]).
filter([ ]) => [ ].
```

A good example of a filter is provided by the generic selection transducer.

```
% select(S,T,C)  =>  the stream of terms in S
%                     matching T and satisfying C.
select([X|Xs],T,C) =>
        if(success(\+(X=T,C)),select(Xs,T,C),[X|select(Xs,T,C)]).
select([ ],_,_) => [ ].
```

Accumulators   Thanks to the functional notation again, accumulators are also easy to develop in Log(F):

```
accumulate(List) => accumulate(List,initial_state).

accumulate([X|Xs],S) => accumulate(Xs,next_state(X,S)).
accumulate([ ],S) => final_state_value(S).
```

A simple example is the sum transducer.

```
% sum(Stream,Sum)  =>  Sum is the result of
%                      summing the elements in Stream
sum(Stream) => sum(Stream,0).

sum([X|Xs],OldSum) => sum(Xs,X+OldSum).
sum([ ],Sum) => Sum.
```

The General Single-Input, Single-Output Transducer   The four kinds of transducers above are all special cases of a general single-input, single-output transducer. An advantage of using Log(F) is that the functional nature of the transducer – a sequential mapping between input stream items and output stream subsequences – is evident. Consequently, we can generalize nicely upon the four kinds. A general transducer can be defined by an initial state and three functions:

A single-input, single-output stream transducer T is a 4-tuple

```
(initial_state, output, next_state, final_output),
```

where:

initial_state is the state of the transducer when it is invoked;

output maps the current state and current stream input(s) to new stream output(s). Stream inputs can be ignored. A stream output can be [ ], specifying that the output stream is not to be changed;

next_state maps the current state and current stream input(s) to the next state;

final_output specifies the final output(s) to be written on streams when no input is left.

The general transducer can now be written as follows:

```
transduce(Stream) => transduce(Stream, initial_state).

transduce([ ],State) => final_output(State).
transduce([Input|Stream],State) =>
        append(
                output(Input,State),
                transduce(Stream,next_state(Input,State))
             ).
```

Note that although the third rule uses *append* for the sake of generality, in many cases it is possible to use only a cons instead.

8.5.2   Basic Statistical Time Series Analysis

Many basic time series analysis procedures can be formalized now as stream transducers. A standard deviation transducer that accumulates counts, sums, and sums of squares simultaneously can be written in Log(F) as follows:

```
stddev(Stream) =>
        sqrt(variance(count_sum_sumsq(Stream,0,0,0))).

variance([N,S,Q]) => if( N =< 1, 0, (Q-(S*S/N))/(N-1) ).

count_sum_sumsq([ ],N,S,Q) => [N,S,Q].
count_sum_sumsq([X|Xs],N,S,Q) =>
        count_sum_sumsq(Xs,N+1,S+X,Q+X*X).
```

This program assumes the existence of an eager square root function.

A transducer for moving averages is also straightforward to develop:

```
moving_avg(M,[ ]) => 0.
moving_avg(M,[H|T]) =>
        [ sum(first(M,[H|T]))/M | moving_avg(M,T)].

first(N,[ ]) => [ ].
first(N,[H|T]) => if( N=<0, [ ], [H|first(N-1,T)]).
```

Simple linear regression gives a good final example. Given two streams of values, $\mathbf{X}$ and $\mathbf{Y}$, we can find the simple linear regression coefficients b_0 and b_1 that minimize the mean square error of the approximation $\mathbf{Y} = b_0 + b_1\mathbf{X}$. Since the mean square error is $\sum_{i=1}^{n}(Y_i - (b_0 + b_1 X_i))^2/n$, where n is the number of elements in each of the streams, the coefficients minimizing this are

$$b_1 = \frac{(\sum_{i=1}^{n} X_i Y_i) - (\sum_{i=1}^{n} X_i)(\sum_{i=1}^{n} Y_i)/n}{(\sum_{i=1}^{n} X_i^2) - (\sum_{i=1}^{n} X_i)^2/n}$$

$$b_0 = (\sum_{i=1}^{n} Y_i)/n - b_1(\sum_{i=1}^{n} X_i)/n$$

and these can be computed in essentially the same way we computed standard deviations.

Log(F) permits us to expand upon conventional statistical time series analysis as we wish. With the power of Prolog at our disposal, we can build 'rule-based' analysis tools. Rather than blindly performing a simple linear regression, for example, we can write a transducer that decides first how *best* to fit $\mathbf{X}$ against $\mathbf{Y}$. An example of this kind of system is described by Gale in [Gal86].

8.5.3   Aggregate Computations

Aggregate operators can be of several kinds. Aggregate reductions, which apply an associative operator to a stream, are easy to define:

```
count(S) => count(S,0).
count([ ],N) => N.
count([_|S],N) => count(S,N+1).

sum(S) => sum(S,0).
sum([ ],T) => T.
sum([X|S],T) => sum(S,X+T).

avg([ ]) => 0.
avg([X|S]) => sum([X|S]) / count([X|S]).
```

Aggregate operators may also act as stream transducers, placing partial aggregates in the output stream as each input item is tallied.

8.5.4   Computing Medians and Quantiles

A useful way to capture the distribution of the values in a stream is to compute certain *quantiles* of the stream. The q-th quantile, $0 \leq q \leq 1$, of a stream S = $[X_1, X_2, ..., X_n]$ is the value X_j such that $\lfloor qn \rfloor$ members of S are less than or equal to X_j. For example, the 0.50-th quantile of a stream will be its *median*. Also, reaching the 0.98 quantile (i.e., the 98-th percentile, or top 2 percent) on examinations seems to be the only goal for some people.

Quantiles are sometimes called *order statistics*. They are important, since in many cases they give us more basic information than other measures, such as averages or standard deviations. Quantiles characterize the shape of the distribution of values we have, without requiring assumptions about its shape or basic nature.

Unfortunately, quantiles can be expensive to compute. To see this, consider the following approach for computing all M-th quantiles (so when M=2 we get the median and the largest value, when M=4 we get all quartiles, etc.), where *sort* and *length* are eager primitives defined elsewhere:

```
quantiles(S,M) => everyNth( sort(S), length(S)/M ).

everyNth(S,N) => if( N=<1, S, everyNth(S,[ ],1,N,N) ).

everyNth([X|Xs],_,I,Limit,N) =>
```

```
if( I>=Limit,
        [X|everyNth(Xs,[ ],I+1,Limit+N,N)],
        everyNth(Xs,[X],I+1,Limit,N)
).
everyNth([ ],Last,_,_,_) => Last.
```

This approach is expensive. The sorting will generally take time $O(n \log n)$, where n is the length of the stream S, and in addition we need to know the length of the stream before we compute any actual quantiles. Better algorithms for computing quantiles have been developed [BFP+72], and the time bound above can be reduced to $O(n)$, but at the cost of requiring all n members of the stream to be accessible in memory for comparisons. When the input stream is large, this approach will not be reasonable.

Fortunately, efficient approaches are now known for *estimating* quantiles. We present a surprising and simple technique developed by Pearl [Pea81], who noticed that quantiles of a random sequence are estimated by the values of specific minimax (or maximin) trees of the sequence. Specifically, if d_1 and d_2 are positive integers and q is the root of the polynomial $(1 - x - (1 - x^{d_2})^{d_1})$, then it turns out that the value of a maximin tree whose min nodes have branching factor d_1, whose max nodes have branching factor d_2, and whose leaves are the members of a random stream S, is an estimate of the q-th quantile of S.

To implement Pearl's approach we can first develop some stream operators that produce minimax values of a stream, assuming that *minimum/2* and *maximum/2* are eager primitives defined in Prolog:

```
min([X|Xs],N) => min(Xs,1,N,X).
min([ ],N) => [ ].

min([X|Xs],I,N,B) =>
        if( I<N, min(Xs,I+1,N,minimum(B,X)), [B|min([X|Xs],N)] ).
min([ ],I,N,B) => [B].

max([X|Xs],N) => max(Xs,1,N,X).
max([ ],N) => [ ].

max([X|Xs],I,N,B) =>
        if( I<N, max(Xs,I+1,N,maximum(B,X)), [B|max([X|Xs],N)] ).
max([ ],I,N,B) => [B].
```

```
maximin(S,D1,D2) => min( max(S,D2), D1 ).
```

```
minimax(S,D1,D2) => max( min(S,D1), D2 ).
```

With these, an estimate of medians is easily obtained. When $d_1 = 5$ and $d_2 = 3$ we have $q = 0.511$, which is fairly close to 0.50. Thus we can produce a median estimate from a maximin tree obtained by recursively taking maximins with this d_1, d_2:

```
medianEstimates(S) => maximin(S,5,3).
```

```
median([X|Xs]) => if( Xs==[ ], X, median(medianEstimates([X|Xs])) ).
median([ ]) => [ ].
```

The maximum tree if built bottom–up, with each level of the tree implemented by either a min or max transducer. On the stream [3, 14, 8, 1, 15, 11, 2, 7, 10, 6, 9, 4, 13, 12, 5] median will produce the value 9. This estimate is simple and cheap. Pearl points out that better estimates can be obtained by using $d_1 = 11$, $d_2 = 4$ (which gives $q = 0.495575$) or $d_1 = 44$, $d_2 = 6$ (which gives $q = 0.500034$).

A more general stream transducer to find the q-th quantile could be implemented with a similar transducer that first begins operation with some kind of search for the right parameters d_1, d_2 to obtain q. The transducer below does just this; the eager Prolog predicate *quantileParameters/2* performs a search through its available table of parameters looking for the best match to a request for a quantile value. Once the best d_1, d_2 values have been found, a simple maximin recursion can be used again.

```
quantile(S,Quantile) =>
      approxQuantile(S,quantileParameters(Quantile)).
```

```
approxQuantile([X|Xs],[D1|D2]) =>
      if(
         Xs==[ ],
         X,
         approxQuantile(quantileEstimates([X|Xs],[D1|D2]),[D1|D2])
         ).
approxQuantile([ ],_) => [ ].
```

```
quantileEstimates(S,[D1|D2]) => maximin(S,D1,D2).
```

This transducer needs the following eager quantile parameter selection code:

```
quantileParameters(Quantile,[D1|D2]) :-
        quantileTable(Table),
        bestMatch(Table,Quantile,1.0,2,2,D1,D2).


bestMatch([ ],_,_,D1,D2,D1,D2).
bestMatch([q(D1,D2,Q0)|T],Q,BestDiff,BestD1,BestD2,OutD1,OutD2) :-
        absDiff(Q0,Q,Diff),
        (Diff >= BestDiff ->
                bestMatch(T,Q,BestDiff,BestD1,BestD2,OutD1,OutD2)
        ;
                bestMatch(T,Q,    Diff,    D1,     D2,OutD1,OutD2)
        ).


absDiff(A,B,X) :- D is (A-B), ((D > 0) -> (X is D) ; (X is -D)).


% The table q(D1,D2,Q) below, for positive integers D1 & D2,
% gives values of Q -- the unique positive root of the polynomial
%       1 - x - ((1 - x ^ D2) ^ D1)
quantileTable([
q( 2,2, 0.618),   q( 2,3, 0.848),   q( 2,4, 0.920),   q( 2,5, 0.951),
q( 3,2, 0.389),   q( 3,3, 0.683),   q( 3,4, 0.805),   q( 3,5, 0.866),
q( 4,2, 0.282),   q( 4,3, 0.579),   q( 4,4, 0.725),   q( 4,5, 0.803),
q( 5,2, 0.220),   q( 5,3, 0.511),   q( 5,4, 0.666),   q( 5,5, 0.755),
q( 6,2, 0.180),   q( 6,3, 0.461),   q( 6,4, 0.622),   q( 6,5, 0.717),
q( 7,2, 0.153),   q( 7,3, 0.422),   q( 7,4, 0.587),   q( 7,5, 0.687),
q( 8,2, 0.133),   q( 8,3, 0.392),   q( 8,4, 0.558),   q( 8,5, 0.661),
q( 9,2, 0.117),   q( 9,3, 0.367),   q( 9,4, 0.534),   q( 9,5, 0.640),
q(10,2, 0.105),   q(10,3, 0.347),   q(10,4, 0.513),   q(10,5, 0.621),
q(11,2, 0.095),   q(11,3, 0.329),   q(11,4, 0.496),   q(11,5, 0.605)
]).
```

Of course, this program could be extended to find roots of the polynomial to any desired precision.

8.5.5 Pattern Matching against Streams

So far we have illustrated how Log(F) makes a fine language for expressing transductions of streams. In this section we show how, when extended slightly, it also makes a fine language for pattern analysis against streams.

It is not difficult to write transducers that detect patterns. For example, the transducer

```
bump(S) => t1(S).
t1([up|S]) => t2(S).
t2([up|S]) => t2(S).
t2(S) => t3(S).
t3([down|S]) => t4(S).
t4([down|S]) => t4(S).
t4(S) => S.
```

successfully recognizes all streams containing sequences of one or more copies of up followed by one or more copies of down. In short, the bump transducer recognizes the *regular expression*

```
( [up]+ , [down]+ )
```

where '+' is the postfix pattern operator defining the Kleene plus, and ',' defines pattern concatenation.

An interesting feature of our approach is that we can write transducers to implement *parsers* by specifiying patterns with *grammars*. For example, we can specify regular expressions and, more generally, path expressions, with grammar rules something like the following:

```
(X+) => X.
(X+) => (X,(X+)).
(X*) => [ ].
(X*) => (X,(X*)).
(X;Y) => X.
(X;Y) => Y.
([ ],X) => X.
([X|Y],Z) => [X|(Y,Z)].
```

These rules behave just like the context free grammar rules they resemble.

Pattern matching can be enforced with a *match* transducer, which takes its first argument a *pattern* describing the starting symbol(s) of some grammar used for the match, and as its second argument a Log(F) term that produces a stream. This transducer is defined as follows:

```
match([ ],S) => S.
match([X|L],[X|S]) => match(L,S).
```

With this definition, for example, the following definition for bump is equivalent to the one given earlier:

```
bump_pattern => ( [up]+ , [down]+ ).

bump(S) => match( bump_pattern, S ).
```

These grammars have many promising uses. For further examples in stream pattern analysis, see [CP89].

8.6   Connecting Prolog with Databases

We mentioned earlier the widely-held belief that Prolog has an impedance mismatch with database management systems (DBMS). In this section, we show how stream processing can remove this mismatch.

8.6.1   A Common Model for Prolog and DBMS

In Prolog systems, an 'inference engine' naturally works on single clauses at a time, with a particular control strategy (depth-first-search with backtracking). In DBMS, by contrast, an entire query is processed at once, by a query evaluator that selects among a variety of sophisticated algorithms. Since both systems go about work differently, it is difficult to connect the two systems in an efficient or easy-to-use way.

The key to the mismatch is that Prolog and DBMS follow different models of data processing:

1. Where the Prolog system can be said to be 'search oriented', seeking a single proof, the DBMS is viewed as 'set oriented', computing all proofs at once.

2. A DBMS provides a limited model of computation that it guarantees to handle well, while Prolog strives to provide a general model of computation or inference with neither real limitations nor blanket guarantees of performance.

In the past, attempts in coupling Prolog and DBMS have adopted one model of data processing or the other [BJ86, Nus89]. Tuple-at-a-time solutions (particularly Prolog-DBMS interfaces) [NH89, SW86, Zan86] follow the Prolog model. Query-at-a-time solutions that store the results of the query in the Prolog system workspace [CW86, GLS88, JCV84] follow the DBMS model. It is well known that tuple-at-a-time solutions can be inefficient, and query-at-a-time solutions can overwhelm the

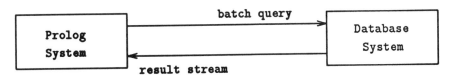

Figure 8.5: Coupling Prolog with a DBMS via Streams

Prolog system with data. A variety of combinations of these strategies have therefore been proposed [CGW87, ICFT89]. The EDUCE system, for example, provides complete tuple-at-a-time and query-at-a-time capabilities [Boc86a, Boc86b].

We can reduce or eliminate the mismatch if we can find a common model that will fit both systems. There is such a model: *stream processing*. We have shown that we can introduce stream processing into Prolog in a clean and natural way, and combining stream processing with DBMS models is not difficult, since databases naturally produce streams of results to queries [Par89]. Below we will sketch how a stream-based connection can be implemented.

8.6.2 Coupling Prolog and DBMS with Streams

The Tangram project at UCLA has integrated Prolog and relational DBMS. Although the integration can be used for 'tight coupling' of Prolog and DBMS, it can also be used for 'loose coupling'. By a *loose coupling* we mean a combination in which each system keeps its own identity, and both communicate through a well-defined interface. We see loose coupling not only as necessary because of economic, political, and other forces, but also as *a desirable division of labor* in many situations. One system does bulk data processing well, while the other performs arbitrary analyses on the results.

The stream processing approach for coupling a DBMS with Prolog is basically to have the DBMS yield a result stream in response to a query, and have Prolog applications analyze the result by stream processing, as shown in Figure 8.5.

Roughly, execution under the approach is as follows:

1. A DML (Data Manipulation Language) request can be sent from the Prolog system to the DBMS. Naturally, many extensions suggest themselves here, such as piggybacking of requests, translation from nice syntax to DML, semantic query optimization, and so forth. These requests can (and in our impression, should) be made with full knowledge of what is available in the DBMS, such as indices or other access paths.

2. The DBMS produces the result of the DML request.

3. The Prolog system consumes the result tuples incrementally (i.e., lazily), as
   it needs them. Important extensions here include eagerly fetching more than
   1 tuple at a time, performing unification or other pattern matching at the
   interface level, selectively retrieving only the needed fields from tuples, etc.

The diagram above shows the Prolog system and DBMS coupled directly, but
in fact an interface between the two can improve performance. Such an interface
can implement buffering and flow control, and sorting of results when this is not
available in the DML, since stream processing often requires sorted streams.

This general approach avoids many problems in traditional couplings between
Prolog and DBMS. Couplings that offer *only* access method tuple-at-a-time retrieval
from Prolog sacrifice the bulk query processing power of the DBMS, and make very
heavy use of the Prolog/DBMS interface. High-level-query-at-a-time couplings that
assert the entire query result in the Prolog database are slow since *assert* is slow,
and potentially dangerous since they can overflow Prolog data areas. A stream
processing approach permits us to take advantage of the best performance aspects
of both systems, tune the granularity of data blocks transferred from the DBMS
to Prolog, and give the Prolog system access to the data without requiring it to be
stored in the Prolog database.

8.6.3 Implementation of Prolog-DBMS Coupling

To couple Prolog with a DBMS for high-level queries, we can use something like
the code below:

```
reduce( sql_query(Query), Stream ) :-
       start_query(Query,Cursor),
       reduce(query_stream(Cursor),Stream).
reduce( query_stream(Cursor), Stream ) :-
       next_query_result(Cursor,Term),
       query_stream(Term,Cursor,Stream).

query_stream(end_of_file,Cursor,[ ]) :-
       end_query(Cursor), !.
query_stream(Term,Cursor,[Term|query_stream(Cursor)]).
```

This code requires several additional predicates: *start_query/2* sends a full SQL
query to the DBMS, *next_query_result/2* retrieves result tuples from the DBMS,
and *end_query/2* terminates processing of the query.

Consider the following scenario. In a relational DBMS we have both a relation of stocks, giving stock names and stock symbols and other relevant data, and a relation of daily high/low/close prices for stocks over the past few years. With the *moving_avg* transducer defined above, and a *print_stream* transducer for displaying data, we can quickly implement the query

show the 5-day moving averages for AT&T stock in 1989

by evaluating the following:

```
print_stream(
    moving_avg( 5,
        sql_query(
                    'select  quote.close
                    from     stock, quote
                    where    stock.name = "AT&T"
                    and      stock.symbol = quote.symbol
                    and      quote.date >= 89/01/01
                    and      quote.date =< 89/12/31'
        )
    )
)
```

The *sql_query* expression yields a stream, just like any other expression. This stream is then averaged and displayed.

The point here is not the syntax, since we can certainly translate from whatever-you-please to this representation. The point is that *the DBMS and the Prolog system both work on the same model of data.*

Some high points of this example:

1. We have done a brute force join query solely with the DBMS. This join might have been more expensive in Prolog.

2. We have performed some intelligent digestion of the result with a straightforward, easy-to-write transducer. (This would have been impossible in ordinary SQL.) The transducer takes definite advantage of the fact that the data is ordered.

3. Even display primitives can fit the stream processing paradigm.

One of the beautiful things about coupling via stream processing is that it permits us to use a low-level access method interface to obtain a stream from the DBMS as well as a high-level query interface. Access methods provide the sequential retrieval we need to implement streams. For example, we can define a tuple-at-a-time connection to the relations *stock* and *quote* with the following code:

```
reduce( stock, Stream ) :-
        open_relation(stock/3,Cursor),
        reduce(tuple_stream(Cursor),Stream).

reduce( quote, Stream ) :-
        open_relation(quote/5,Cursor),
        reduce(tuple_stream(Cursor),Stream).

reduce( tuple_stream(Cursor), Stream ) :-
        retrieve(Cursor,Tuple),
        tuple_stream(Tuple,Cursor,Stream).

tuple_stream(end_of_file,Cursor,[ ]) :-
        close_relation(Cursor), !.
tuple_stream(Term,Cursor,[Term|tuple_stream(Cursor)]).
```

Here the predicate *open_relation/2* sets up a cursor on a relation from which we can retrieve tuples by using *retrieve/2*. With these definitions we can implement the same query handled above with something like the following code:

```
print_stream(
   moving_avg( 5,
      project( 9,
         join(
            select( stock, stock(_,"AT&T",_,_), true),
            select( quote, quote(_,_,_,_,Date),
               ('89/01/01' @=< Date,Date @=<'89/12/31') )
         )
      )
   )
)
```

The point to see here is that we can allocate processing responsibility as we please to Prolog and the DBMS. Stream processing allows us to couple either via a high-level query-at-a-time interface, or a low-level tuple-at-a-time interface.

There is one final remark to make here. Just as we have used streams to get data from databases, we can use streams for getting results from files, or any other source of data. The following code implements streams from files:

```
reduce( file_terms(Filename), Stream ) :-
       open(Filename,read,Descriptor),
       reduce(file_stream(Descriptor),Stream).

reduce( file_stream(Descriptor), Stream ) :-
       read(Descriptor,Term),
       file_stream(Term,Descriptor,Stream).

file_stream(end_of_file,Descriptor,[ ]) :-
       close(Descriptor), !.
file_stream(T,Descriptor,[T|file_stream(Descriptor)]).
```

With similar code we could retrieve data across a network, or from some other specialized source. In other words, stream processing gives a simple technique for implementing *transparency* among data sources. Transparency will always be important in data analysis.

8.7   Background

Stream processing has traditionally been used in languages such as APL and Lisp. It is a powerful paradigm that can be viewed in different ways, and the variety of presentations in the literature is striking. Streams have been viewed as lists, functions, special cases of infinite objects, and sequences of values operated on by special stream functions. Similarly stream processing has been defined as a kind of coroutining, a kind of dataflow processing, a kind of 'normal-order reduction', and a kind of lazy evaluation. While these viewpoints are all closely related, they have different emphases that can lead to different implementations.

Landin introduced stream processing in the early 1960's. In [Lan65] he defined the term 'stream', and presented lambda calculus implementations of many basic stream transducers. At that time coroutines had just been introduced by Conway [Con63], and Landin also pointed out the connection between stream processing and coroutining in [Lan65].

Many programming languages have been influenced by the work of Landin, particularly by its presentation in the ISWIM family of languages [Lan66]. The programming language POP-2 [BCP71] implemented a version of streams called 'dynamic lists'. In [Bur75b, Bur75a] Burge presented a well-written tour of stream processing examples showing the potential of the paradigm, drawing directly on [Lan65]. The Lucid language [WA85], an elegant language that emphasizes processing of finite streams, borrows freely from ISWIM. In the mid-1970's the concept of lazy evaluation was popularized as an alternative evaluation scheme for functional languages, [FW76, HM76, Tur79] and stream processing also became established as an approach for developing networks of coroutines or parallel processes [KM77]. Aspects of this later work are summarized in [AS85, Hen80, PJ87]. Today lazy evaluation and stream processing are part of a modest number of functional and dataflow programming languages.

A rather different outlook on stream processing is offered by Goldberg and Paige [GP84], who take the point of view that 'stream processing is a technique that seeks to avoid intermediate storage and to minimize sequential search'. From this perspective, stream processing amounts basically to loop fusion, an optimization technique presented by Allen and Cocke for combining consecutive Fortran DO-loops into a single loop in [AC71]. Goldberg and Paige give a history of stream processing from this perspective, pointing out applications that have been proposed for it in file processing, data restructuring, and above all database query processing.

Stream processing in databases has been proposed a number of times in the past. Streams arise naturally in functional data models, first presented by Sibley and Kerschberg in [SK77] and subsequently developed in the SDM [McL78] and DAPLEX [Shi81] data models. DAPLEX has inspired features in many recent database systems, as functions provide both a mechanism for representing associations among objects, and a way to make databases extensible. However in DAPLEX, and in its successors, sets are the primitive data structure, not streams.

The earliest database system with stream processing concepts, to our knowledge, was the FQL system of Buneman et al [BF79, BNF81, BFN82]. FQL implemented lazy evaluation and stream processing in the manner proposed by Landin and Burge, with a syntax based on Backus' FP language[Bac78]. The FQL design reflected database performance considerations, through datatypes, the lack of environments, and direct implementation of a few higher-order operations. The GENESIS system of Batory very recently outlined in [BLW88] extends FQL and DAPLEX by placing all structures in a stream format, distinguishing sequences (structured streams) from streams, and viewing functions on streams as rewriting operators. Batory shows that the resulting system is extensible and easily handles non-first-normal-form data. Other recent database systems that have included stream concepts include FAD [BBKV87] and LDL [BNR$^+$87, TZ86].

Prolog systems supporting coroutining as a basic feature have been proposed

[CM79], but these systems are complex and are not generally available. Also, many stream processing extensions of Prolog have been proposed in the past few years. For example, many parallel logic programming systems have been developed essentially as stream processing systems. Typically, these systems fall into one of several camps:

1. They resemble PARLOG [CG85] and the other 'committed choice' parallel programming systems (Concurrent Prolog, GHC, etc.).

2. They introduce *'parallel and'* or *'parallel or'* operators into ordinary Prolog [LM86].

3. They are extended Prolog systems that introduce streams by adding functional programming constructs [BL86, DL86, Kah84, LP84, Nai85, SY84]. The thrust of this introduction is to make Prolog more like either Lisp or Smalltalk or both.

The approach we have described is like that of the third camp, but is more conservative in that no real change is made to Prolog.

We have seen how to implement stream data analysis in Prolog elegantly, even though an elegant implementation is not obvious at first. In fact, we have shown how many problems in using Prolog for stream processing can be overcome.

This raises a point: Prolog can be what you want. People may say Prolog 'cannot' do something, while in fact with a little ingenuity it is not only 'possible' to do what you want, it is natural. Prolog is a very powerful assembler for building larger systems.

Acknowledgement

The author is grateful to Scott Chase, Mike Coleman, Scott Kalter, Ted Kim, Cliff Leung, Dinh Le, Brian Livezey, Dick Muntz, Richard O'Keefe, Judea Pearl, Leon Sterling, and other members of the Tangram group at UCLA for comments and improvements they suggested on the manuscript.

Bibliography

[ABC+87] F. Allen, M. Burke, P. Charles, R. Cytron, and J. Ferrante. An Overview of the PTRAN Analysis System for Multiprocessing. In *Proceedings of the 1st International Conference on Supercomputing*, pages 194–211, 1987.

[AC71] F.E. Allen and J. Cocke. A Catalogue of Optimizing Transformations. In R. Rustin, editor, *Design and Optimization of Compilers*, pages 1–30. Prentice-Hall, 1971.

[AK83] J. F. Allen and J. A. Koomen. Planning using a Temporal World Model. In *Proceedings of the 8th IJCAI*, pages 741–747, 1983.

[All83] J. F. Allen. Recognising Intentions from Natural Language Utterances. In M. Brady and R. C. Berwick, editors, *Computational Models of Discourse*. MIT Press, 1983.

[App85] D. Appelt. *Planning English Sentences*. Cambridge University Press, 1985.

[AR89] H. Abramson and M. H. Rogers, editors. *Meta-Programming in Logic Programming*. MIT Press, 1989.

[AS85] H. Abelson and G. Sussman. *The Structure and Analysis of Computer Programs*. MIT Press, Boston, MA, 1985.

[AS88] W. C. Athas and C. L. Seitz. Multicomputers: Message-Passing Concurrent Computers. *IEEE Computer*, 21(8):9–25, August 1988.

[Ass88] Office of Technology Assessment. *Mapping Our Genes—Genome Projects: How Big, How Fast?* The Johns Hopkins University Press, Baltimore and London, 1988.

[ASU86] A. V. Aho, R. Sethi, and J. D. Ullman. *Compiler Principles, Techniques and Tools*. Addison-Wesley, Reading, Massachussets, 1986.

[Bac78] J. Backus. Can Programming be Liberated from the von Neumann Style? A Functional Style and its Algebra of Programs. *Comm. ACM*, 21(8):613–641, 1978.

[BBKV87] F. Bancilhon, T. Briggs, S. Khoshafian, and P. Valduriez. FAD, a Powerful and Simple Database Language. In *Proceedings of the 13th International Conference on Very Large Data Bases*, Brighton, England, 1987.

[BC84] R.A. Becker and J.M. Chambers. *S: An Interactive Environment for Data Analysis and Graphics*. Wadsworth, Inc., Belmont, CA, 1984.

[BCF+88] M. Burke, R. Cytron, J. Ferrante, W. Hsien, V. Sarkar, and D. Shields. Automatic Discovery of Parallelism: A Tool and an Experiment (Extended Abstract). *SIGPLAN Notices*, 23(9):77–84, September 1988.

[BCMD87] William R. Bush, Gino Cheng, Patrick C. McGeer, and Alvin M. Despain. Experience with Prolog as a Hardware Specification Language. In *Proceedings of the 1987 Symposium on Logic Programming*, pages 490–498. IEEE Computer Society Press, September 1987.

[BCP71] R.M. Burstall, J.S. Collins, and R.J. Popplestone. *Programming in POP-2*. Edinburgh University Press, 1971.

[BEJ88a] D. Bjørner, A. Ershov, and N. Jones, editors. *Partial Evaluation and Mixed Computation: Proceedings of the IFIP TC2 workshop on partial evaluation and mixed computation, Gammel Avernæs, Denmark, October 1987*. North-Holland, Amsterdam, 1988.

[BEJ88b]   D. Bjørner, A. Ershov, and N. Jones. Special issue on Partial and Mixed Computation. *New Generation Computing*, 6(2), 1988.

[BF79]   P. Buneman and R.E. Frankel. FQL – A Functional Query Language. In *Proc ACM SIGMOD International Conference on Management of Data*, pages 52–57, Boston, MA, June 1979.

[BFN82]   P. Buneman, R.E. Frankel, and Rishiyur Nikhil. An Implementation Technique for Database Query Languages. *ACM Trans. Database Systems*, 7(2):164–186, June 1982.

[BFP$^+$72] M. Blum, R.W. Floyd, V.R. Pratt, R.L. Rivest, and R.E. Tarjan. Time Bounds for Selection. *J. Comput. System Sci.*, 7:448–461, 1972.

[BJ86]   M. Brodie and M. Jarke. On Integrating Logic Programming and Databases. In L. Kerschberg, editor, *Expert Database Systems: Proceedings from the 1st International Conference*, pages 191–208. Benjamin/Cummings, 1986.

[BL86]   M. Bellia and G. Levi. The Reation between Logic and Functional Languages: A Survey. *J. Logic Programming*, 3(3):217–236, October 1986.

[BLW88]   D.S. Batory, T.Y. Leung, and T. Wise. Implementation Concepts For an Extensible Data Model and Data Language. *ACM Trans. Database Systems*, 13(3):231–262, September 1988.

[BNF81]   P. Buneman, R. Nikhil, and R. Frankel. A Practical Functional Programming System for Databases. In *Proceedings of the ACM Conference on Functional Languages and Computer Architecture*, pages 195–201, 1981.

[BNR$^+$87] C. Beeri, S. Naqvi, R. Ramakrishnan, O. Shmueli, and S. Tsur. Sets and Negation in a Logic Database Language (LDL1). In *Proceedings of the 6th ACM Symp. on Principles of Database Systems*, pages 21–37, San Diego, March 1987.

[Boc86a]   J. Bocca. EDUCE – A Marriage of Convenience: Prolog and a Relational DBMS. In *Proceedings of the 1986 Symposium on Logic Programming*, pages 36–45, Salt Lake City, UT, September 1986.

[Boc86b]   J. Bocca. On the Evaluation Strategy of EDUCE. In *Proceedings of the ACM SIGMOD International Conference on Management of Data*, pages 368–378, Washington, D.C., May 1986. Appeared as *ACM SIGMOD Record* 15:2, June 1986.

[Boy89]   Glenn. J. Boysko. A Complexity Analysis Tool for VLSI Systems. Master's thesis, Department of Computer Engineering and Science, Case Western Reserve University, Cleveland, Ohio, January 1989.

[Bur75a]   W.H. Burge. *Recursive Programming Techniques*. Addison-Wesley, Reading, MA, 1975.

[Bur75b]   W.H. Burge. Stream Processing Functions. *IBM J. Res. Develop.*, 19(1):12–25, 1975.

[CG85]   K. Clark and S. Gregory. Notes on the Implementation of PARLOG. *J. Logic Programming*, 2(1):17–42, 1985.

[CGW87]   S. Ceri, G. Gottlob, and G. Wiederhold. Interfacing Relational Databases and Prolog Efficiently. In L. Kerschberg, editor, *Expert Database Systems: Proceedings from the 1st International Conference*, pages 207–223. Benjamin/Cummings, 1987.

[CH87]   J. Cohen and T. Hickey. Parsing and Compiling Using Prolog. *ACM Transactions on Programming Languages and Systems*, 9(2):125–163, April 1987.

[CL86]   William F. Clocksin and Miriam E. Leeser. Automatic Determination of Signal Flow Through MOS Transistor Networks. *INTEGRATION, the VLSI journal*, pages 53–63, March 1986.

[Clo87]   William F. Clocksin. Logic Programming and Digital Circuit Analysis. *The Journal of Logic Programming*, 4:59(82), March 1987.

[CM79]   K.L. Clark and F.G. McCabe. Control facilities of IC-PROLOG. In D. Michie, editor, *Expert Systems in the Microelectronic Age*. Edinburgh University Press, 1979.

[CM87]   W. F. Clocksin and C. S. Mellish. *Programming in Prolog, (3rd Edition)*. Springer-Verlag, Berlin, Germany, 1987.

[Con63]   M.E. Conway. Design of a Separable Transition-Diagram Compiler. *Comm. ACM*, 6(7):396–408, July 1963.

[CP89]   L. Chau and D.S. Parker. Narrowing Grammars. In G. Levi, editor, *Proceedings of the 6th International Conference on Logic Programming*, pages 199–217. MIT Press, Lisbon, Portugal, June 1989.

[CW86]   C.L. Chang and A. Walker. PROSQL: A Prolog Interface with SQL/DS. In L. Kerschberg, editor, *Expert Database Systems: Proceedings from the 1st International Conference*, pages 233–246. Benjamin/Cummings, 1986.

[CW88]   M. Carlsson and J. Widen. SICStus Prolog User's Manual. Technical Report SICS R88007, Swedish Institute of Computer Science, P.O. Box 1263, S-16313 Kista, SWEDEN, February 1988.

[D+87]   P. J. Drongowski et al. *An Experimental Assistant to Support The Construction and Analysis of Control Graph - Datapath Designs*. Technical Report CES-87-03, Department of Computer Engineering and Science, Case Western Reserve University, Cleveland, Ohio, June 1987.

[Dar86]   N. Darvas. *How I Made 2,000,000 Dollars in the Stock Market*. Lyle Stuart, Inc., 120 Enterprise Ave., Secaucus, NJ 07094, 1986.

[DB88]   P. J. Drongowski and G. J. Boysko. *Agent: A Modelling and Analytical Tool for VLSI System architects*. Technical Report CES-89-09, Department of Computer Engineering and Science, Case Western Reserve University, Cleveland, Ohio, nov 1988.

[DBR+88] P. J. Drongowski, J. R. Bammi, R. Ramaswamy, S. R. Iyengar, and T. H. Wang. A Graphical Hardware Design Language. In *Proceedings of the ACM/IEEE 25th Design Automation Conference*, pages 108–115, June 1988.

[Des87]   Alvin M. Despain. A High Performance Hardware Architecture for Design Automation. Technical report, University of California, Berkeley and Xenologic, Inc., September 1987.

[DL86]   D. DeGroot and G. Lindstrom. *Logic Programming: Functions, Relations, and Equations*. Prentice-Hall, 1986.

[Dro83]   P. J. Drongowski. System speed, space and power estimation using a high level design notation. *Proceedings of the International Conference on Computer Design*, pages 468–471, October 1983.

[Dro85a] P. J. Drongowski. *A Graphical Engineering Aid for VLSI Systems.* Computer Science Series. UMI Research Press, Ann Arbor, Michigan, 1985.

[Dro85b] P. J. Drongowski. Representations in CAD: Model and Semantics. In *ACM Computer Science Conference*, pages 131–135, March 1985.

[Dro87] P. J. Drongowski. *An Organization Level Story Board for Agent – A VLSI designer's assistant.* Technical Report CES-87-08, Department of Computer Engineering and Science, Case Western Reserve University, Cleveland, Ohio, March 1987.

[Ers77] A. P. Ershov. On the Partial Computation Principle. *Information Processing Letters*, 6(2):38–41, April 1977.

[Est85] G. Estrin. SARA in the design room. In *ACM Computer Science Conference*, pages 1–12, New Orleans, March 1985.

[F+85a] G.A. Frank et al. An Architecture Design and Assessment System. *VLSI design*, August 1985.

[F+85b] G.A. Frank et al. An Architecture Design and Assessment System for Software/Hardware Codesign. In *Proceedings of the ACM/IEEE 22nd Design Automation Conference*, pages 417–424, Las Vegas, June 1985.

[FDP88] V. A. Norton F. Darema, D. A. George and G. F. Pfister. A Single-Program-Multiple-Data Computational Model for EPEX/FORTRAN. *Parallel Computing*, 7(1):11–24, April 1988.

[FF88] H. Fujita and K. Furukawa. A Self-Applicable Partial Evaluator and Its Use in Incremental Compilation. *New Generation Computing*, 6(2), 1988.

[Fis87] K.L. Fisher. *The Wall Street Waltz.* Contemporary Books, Inc., Chicago, 1987.

[FN71] R. E. Fikes and N. J. Nilsson. STRIPS: A New Approach to the Application of Theorem Proving to Problem Solving. *Artificial Intelligence*, 2, 1971.

[Ful76] W.A. Fuller. *Introduction to Statistical Time Series.* John Wiley & Sons, 1976.

[Fut71] Y. Futamura. Partial Evaluation of Computation Process - An Approach to a Compiler-Compiler. *Systems, Computers, Controls*, 25:45–50, 1971.

[FW76] D.P. Friedman and D.S. Wise. CONS Should Not Evaluate Its Arguments. In S. Michaelson and R. Milner, editors, *Automata, Languages and Programming.* Edinburgh University Press, Edinburgh, 1976.

[Gab88] E. Gabber. Parallel Programming Using the MMX Operating System and Its Processor. In *Proceedings of the 3rd Israeli Conference on Computer Systems and Software Engineering, Tel-Aviv, Israel*, pages 122–132, June 1988.

[Gab89] E. Gabber. VMMP: A Virtual Machine for the Development of Portable and Efficient Programs for Multiprocessors. In *International Conference on Parallel Processing, 1989, St. Charles, Illinois*, pages 11–14, August 1989.

[Gal86] W.A. Gale. REX Review. In W.A. Gale, editor, *Artificial Intelligence & Statistics.* Addison-Wesley, 1986.

[GBK72] E.L. Glaser, F. T. Bradshaw, and S. W. Katske. LOGOS – An Overview. In *IEEE CompCon '72*, September 1972.

[GFF89]   A. Garcia, D. J. Foster, and R. F. Freitas. The Advanced Computing Environ-
          ment Multiprocessor Workstation. Technical Report IBM Research Report RC 14491
          (#64901), IBM T.J. Watson Research Center, March 1989.

[GLS88]   S. Ghosh, C.C. Lin, and T. Sellis. Implementation of a Prolog-Ingres Interface. *SIG-
          MOD Record*, 17(2), June 1988.

[GM89]   G. Gazdar and C. Mellish. *Natural Language Processing in Prolog*. Addison-Wesley,
          1989.

[Gor85]   Mike Gordon. Why Higher-order Logic is a good formalism for Specifying and Verify-
          ing Hardware. Technical Report 77, University of Cambridge, Computer Laboratory,
          September 1985.

[GP84]   A. Goldberg and R. Paige. Stream Processing. In *Proceedings of the 1984 ACM
          Symposium on Lisp and Functional Programming*, pages 53–62, Austin, TX, August
          1984.

[GW83]   L. Gonick and M. Wheelis. *The Cartoon Guide to Genetics*. Barnes and Noble Books,
          New York, 1983.

[Hen80]   P. Henderson. *Functional Programming: Application and Implementation*. Pren-
          tice/Hall International, 1980.

[HM76]   P. Henderson and J.H. Morris, Jr. A Lazy Evaluator. In *Proceedings of the 3rd ACM
          Symposium on Principles of Programming Languages*, pages 95–103, 1976.

[Hof79]   D. R. Hofstadter. *Godel, Escher, Bach: an Eternal Golden Braid*. Basic Books, Inc.,
          New York, 1979.

[Hof85]   D. R. Hofstadter. *Metamagical Themas: Questing for the Essence of Mind and
          Pattern*. Basic Books, Inc., New York, 1985.

[HR72]   F. G. Heath and C. W. Rose. The Case for Integrated Hardware/Software Design
          With CAD Implications. In *IEEE CompCon '72*, September 1972.

[ICFT89] Y.E. Ioannidis, J. Chen, M.A. Friedman, and M.M. Tsangaris. BERMUDA – An
          Architectural Perspective on Interfacing Prolog to a Database Machine. In L. Ker-
          schberg, editor, *Expert Database Systems: Proceedings from the 2nd International
          Conference*, pages 229–256. Benjamin/Cummings, 1989.

[JCV84]   M. Jarke, J. Clifford, and Y. Vassiliou. An Optimizing Prolog Front-End to a Rela-
          tional Query System. In *Proceedings of the 1984 ACM SIGMOD International Con-
          ference on Management of Data*, pages 296–306, Boston, MA, June 1984. Appeared
          as *ACM SIGMOD Record* 14:2, 1984.

[Joh75]   S. C. Johnson. YACC - Yet Another Compiler-Compiler. Technical report, Bell
          Laboratory, Computer Science Technical Report, 1975.

[Jor87]   H. F. Jordan. The Force. In Leah H. Jamieson, Dennis B. Gannon, and Robert J.
          Douglas, editors, *The Characteristics of Parallel Algorithms*, pages 395–436. MIT
          Press, 1987.

[JSS85]   N. D. Jones, P. Sestoft, and H. Sondergaard. An Experiment in Partial Evalua-
          tion: The Generation of a Compiler Generator. *Lecture Notes in Computer Science*,
          202:124–140, 1985.

[Kah84]   K. Kahn. A Primitive for the Control of Logic Programs. In *Proceedings of the Symposium on Logic Programming*, pages 242–251, Atlantic City, 1984. IEEE Computer Society.

[KB88]   A. H. Karp and R. G. Babb II. A Comparison of 12 Parallel Fortran Dialects. *IEEE Software*, 5(5):52–67, September 1988.

[Kle52]   S. C. Kleene. *Introduction to Mathematics*. Van Nostrand, 1952.

[KM69]   R. M. Karp and R. E. Miller. Parallel Program Schemata. *Journal of Computers and System Science*, 3:147–195, 1969.

[KM77]   G. Kahn and D. McQueen. Coroutines and Networks of Parallel Processes. In *IFIP 77*, Amsterdam, 1977. North-Holland.

[Kom81]   H. J. Komorowski. *A Specification of an Abstract Prolog Machine and its Application to Partial Evaluation*. PhD thesis, Linköping Studies in Science and Technology, 1981.

[Lak89]   A. Lakhotia. A Code in Support of 'A Workbench for Developing Logic Programs by Stepwise Enhancement'. Technical Report 89-163b, Center for Automation and Intelligent Systems Research, 1989.

[Lan65]   P.J. Landin. A Correspondence Between Algol 60 and Church's Lambda-Notation, Parts I and II. *Communications of the ACM*, 8(2 and 3):89–101, 158–165, 1965.

[Lan66]   P.J. Landin. The Next 700 Programming Languages. *Comm. ACM*, 9(3):157–166, 1966.

[LM86]   P-Y.P. Li and A.J. Martin. The Sync Model: A Parallel Execution Method for Logic Programming. In *Proceedings of the Symposium on Logic Programming*, pages 223–234, Salt Lake City, 1986. IEEE Computer Society.

[LP84]   G. Lindstrom and P. Panangaden. Stream-Based Execution of Logic Programs. In *Proceedings of the Symposium on Logic Programming*, pages 168–176, Atlantic City, 1984. IEEE Computer Society.

[LS75]   M. E. Lesk and Schmidt. LEX - A Lexical Analyzer Generator. Technical report, Bell Laboratory, Computer Science Technical Report, 1975.

[LS87]   J. W. Lloyd and J. C. Shepherdson. Partial Evaluation in Logic Programming. Technical Report CS-87-09, Computer Science Department, University of Bristol, December 1987.

[LV88]   G. Louis and M. Vauclair. Algebraic Meta-Level Programming in Prolog. In *Proceedings of the International Conference on 5th Generation Computer Systems*, pages 555–564, 1988.

[MC80]   Carver Mead and Lynn Conway. *Introduction to VLSI Systems*. Addison-Wesley, 1980.

[McC86]   Michael C. McCord. Design of a Prolog-Based Machine Translation System. In *Proceedings of the 3rd International Conference on Logic Programming*. Springer-Verlag, July 1986.

[McL78]   D. McLeod. A Semantic Data Base Model and its Associated Structured User Interface. Technical report, Dept. EE&CS, MIT, Cambridge, MA, 1978.

[ME89]   C. S. Mellish and R. Evans. Natural Language Generation from Plans. *Computational Linguistics*, to–appear, 1989.

[Mel88]   C. S. Mellish. Natural Language Generation from Plans. In M. Zock and G. Sabah, editors, *Advances in Natural Language Generation, Volume 1*. Pinter Publishers, 1988.

[MPC88]   M.C. McFarland, A.C. Parker, and R. Composano. Tutorial on High–level Synthesis of Digital Systems. In *Proceedings of the ACM/IEEE 25th Design Automation Conference*, pages 330–336, June 1988.

[Nai85]   L. Naish. All Solutions Predicates in Prolog. In *Proceedings of the Symposium on Logic Programming*, pages 73–77, Boston, 1985. IEEE Computer Society.

[Nar87]   S. Narain. LOG(F): A New Scheme for Integrating Rewrite Rules, Logic Programming and Lazy Evaluation. Technical Report CSD-870027, UCLA Computer Science Dept., Los Angeles, CA 90024-1596, 1987.

[Nar88]   S. Narain. LOG(F): An Optimal Combination of Logic Programming, Rewrite Rules and Lazy Evaluation. Technical report, UCLA Computer Science Dept., Los Angeles, CA 90024-1596, 1988.

[Nar89]   S. Narain. Optimization by Nondeterministic, Lazy Rewriting. In N. Dershowitz, editor, *Proceedings of the 3rd International Conference on Rewriting Techniques and Applications*. Springer-Verlag, Chapel Hill, NC, 1989.

[Nar90]   S. Narain. Lazy Evaluation in Logic Programming. In *Proceedings of the IEEE International Conference on Computer Languages*, New Orleans, 1990.

[Neu88]   G. Neumann. *Metaprogrammeirung Und Prolog*. Addison-Wesley, 1988.

[NH89]   B. Napheys and D. Herkimer. A Look at Loosely-Coupled Prolog/Database Systems. In L. Kerschberg, editor, *Expert Database Systems: Proceedings from the 2nd International Conference*, pages 257–272. Benjamin/Cummings, 1989.

[NS73]   William M. Newman and Robert F. Sproull. *Principles of Interactive Computer Graphics*. McGraw Hill, 1973.

[Nus89]   M. Nussbaum. Combining Top-Down and Bottom-Up Computation in Knowledge Based Systems. In L. Kerschberg, editor, *Expert Database Systems: Proceedings from the 2nd International Conference*, pages 273–310. Benjamin/Cummings, 1989.

[O'K85]   R. A. O'Keefe. On the Treatment of Cuts in Prolog Source-Level Tools. In *Proceedings of the Symposium on Logic Programming, Boston*, pages 68–72, 1985.

[Owe89]   S. Owen. Issues in the Partial Evaluation of Meta-Interpreters. In *Meta-Programming in Logic Programming*, pages 319–340. MIT Press, 1989.

[Pag89]   T. Page. An Object Oriented Logic Programming Environment for Prolog. Technical Report CSD-890055(Ph.D. Thesis), UCLA Computer Science Department, Los Angeles, CA 90024-1596, September 1989.

[Par84]   Alice C. Parker. Automated Synthesis of Digital Systems. In *IEEE Design and Test of Computers*, pages 75–81. IEEE, November 1984.

[Par89]   D.S. Parker. Stream Processing: An Effective Way to Integrate AI and DBMS. Technical Report CSD-890005, UCLA Computer Science Dept., Los Angeles, CA 90024-1596, January 1989.

[Pea81]   J. Pearl. A Space-Efficient On-Line Method of Computing Quantile Estimates. *J. Algorithms*, 2(2):164–177, 1981.

[Per84]   F. Pereira. *C-Prolog User's Manual*. SRI International, Menlo Park, 1984.

[Pet81]   J. L. Peterson. *Petri Net Theory and the Modeling of Systems*. Prentice Hall, Englewood Cliffs, N.J., 1981.

[PJ87]   S.L. Peyton-Jones. *The Implementation of Functional Programming Languages*. Prentice/Hall International, Englewood Cliffs, NJ, 1987.

[PKP86]   C. D. Polychronopoulos, D. J. Kuck, and D. A. Padua. Execution of Parallel Loops on Parallel Processor Systems. In *Proceedings of the 1986 International Conference on Parallel Processing*, pages 519–527. IEEE Computer Society Press, August 1986.

[PMC89]   D.S. Parker, R.R. Muntz, and L. Chau. The Tangram Stream Query Processing System. In *Proceedings of the 5th International Conference on Data Engineering*, pages 556–563, Los Angeles, CA, February 1989.

[PPM88]   D.S. Parker, T. Page, and R.R. Muntz. Improving Clause Access in Prolog. Technical Report CSD-880024, UCLA Computer Science Dept., Los Angeles, CA 90024-1596, March 1988.

[PS87]   F. Pereira and S. Shieber. Prolog and Natural-Language Analysis. Technical Report Lecture Notes #10, Center for the Study of Language and Information, 1987.

[RBK72]   C.W. Rose, F.T. Bradshaw, and S.W. Katske. The LOGOS Representation System. In *IEEE CompCon '72*, September 1972.

[Rei87]   Peter B. Reintjes. AUNT: A Universal Netlist Translator. In *Proceedings of the 1987 Symposium on Logic Programming*. IEEE Computer Society Press, September 1987.

[Rei88]   Peter B. Reintjes. A VLSI Design Environment in Prolog. In *Logic Programming: Proceedings of the 5th International Conference and Symposium*, pages 70–81. MIT Press, August 1988.

[Ros72]   C.W. Rose. LOGOS and the software engineer. In *Fall Joint Computer Conference*, pages 312–314. IFIPS, 1972.

[RRD85]   C. D. Rogers, J. B. Rosenberg, and S. W. Daniel. MCNC's Vertically Integrated Symbolic Design System. In *Proceedings of the 22nd ACM/IEEE Design Automation Conference*. IEEE Computer Society Press, June 1985.

[Rub87]   Steven M. Rubin. *Computer Aids for VLSI Design*. Addison-Wesley, 1987.

[SA77]   R. C. Schank and R. P. Abelson. *Scripts, Plans, Goals and Understanding*. Lawrence Erlbaum, 1977.

[Sac77]   E. D. Sacerdoti. *A Structure for Plans and Behaviour*. Elsevier-North Holland, 1977.

[SB89]   L. S. Sterling and R. D. Beer. Meta-Interpreters for Expert System Construction. *Journal of Logic Programming*, 6(1 & 2):163–178, March 1989.

[Shi81]   D.W. Shipman. The Functional Data Model and the Data Language DAPLEX. *ACM Trans. Database Systems*, 6(1):140–173, March 1981.

[Shi86]   S. M. Shieber. An Introduction to Unification-Based Approaches to Grammar. In *CSLI Lecture Notes No 4*. Chicago University Press, 1986.

[SK77]   E.H. Sibley and L. Kerschberg. Data Architecture and Data Model Considerations. In *Proceedings of the AFIPS National Computer Conference*, pages 85–96, June 1977.

[SS86]   L. S. Sterling and E. Y. Shapiro. *The Art of Prolog*. MIT Press, 1986.

[SS88]   P. Sestoft and H. Sondergaard. A Bibliography on Partial Evaluation. *SIGPLAN Notices*, 23(2):9–18, February 1988.

[SW86]   E. Sciore and D.S. Warren. Towards an Integrated Database-Prolog System. In L. Kerschberg, editor, *Expert Database Systems: Proceedings From the 1st International Workshop*, pages 293–305. Benjamin/Cummings, Menlo Park, CA, 1986.

[SY84]   P.A. Subrahmanyam and J-H. You. Conceptual Basis and Evaluation Strategies for Integrating Functional and Logic Programming. In *Proceedings of the Symposium on Logic Programming*, pages 144–153, Atlantic City, 1984. IEEE Computer Society.

[SY89]   L. S. Sterling and L. Ü Yalçinalp. Explaining Prolog-Based Expert Systems Using a Layered Meta-Interpreter. In *Proceedings of 11th IJCAI*, pages 66–71, 1989.

[SZ88]   P. Sestoft and A. Zamulin. Annotated Bibliography on Partial Evaluation and Mixed Computation. In D. Bjorner, A. Ershov, and N. Jones, editors, *Partial Evaluation and Mixed Computation: Proceedings of the IFIP TC2 workshop on Partial Evaluation and Mixed Computation, Gammel Avernæs, Denmark, October 1987*. North-Holland, Amsterdam, 1988.

[Tat85]   A. Tate. A Review of Knowledge-Based Planning Techniques. In M. Merry, editor, *Expert Systems 85*. Cambridge University Press, 1985.

[TF86]   A. Takeuchi and K. Furukawa. Partial Evaluation of Prolog programs and its Application to Meta Programming. In *Information Processing 86*, pages 415–420. North-Holland, 1986.

[TGF88]   S. Thakkar, P. Gifford, and G. Fielland. The Balance Multiprocessor System. *IEEE Micro*, 8(1):57–69, February 1988.

[Tic88]   E. Tick. *Memory Performance of Prolog Architectures*. Kluwer Academic Publishers, Norwell, MA, 1988.

[Tsa87]   E. P. K Tsang. TLP - A Temporal Planner. In J. Hallam and C. Mellish, editors, *Advances in Artificial Intelligence*. John Wiley, 1987.

[Tur79]   D.A. Turner. A New Implementation Technique for Applicative Languages. *Software - Practice and Experience*, 9:31–49, 1979.

[TZ86]   S. Tsur and C. Zaniolo. LDL: A Logic-Based Data Language. In *Proceedings of the 12th International Conference on Very Large Data Bases*, pages 33–41, Kyoto, Japan, 1986.

[VD88]   R. Venken and B. Dameon. A Partial Evaluation System for Prolog: some Practical Considerations. *New Generation Computing*, 6(2), 1988.

[Ven84]   R. Venken. A Prolog Meta-Interpreter for Partial Evaluation and its Application to Source-to-Source Transformation and Query-Optimisation. In *ECAI*, pages 91–100, 1984.

[vH89]   F. van Harmelen. Personal Communication. E-mail, March 1989.

[WA85]   W.W. Wadge and E.A. Ashcroft. *Lucid, the Dataflow Programming Language*. Academic Press, Orlando, FL, 1985.

[War80]   D.H.D Warren. Logic Programming and Compiler Writing. *Software Practice and Experience*, 10(2), 1980.

[Wat79]   R. Waters. A Method for Analyzing Loop Programs. *IEEE Trans. Software Engineering*, 5(3):237–247, 1979.

[WE85]   Neil H. E. Weste and Kamran Eshraghian. *Principles of CMOS VLSI Design: A Systems Perspective*. Addison-Wesley, 1985.

[Wes81]   Neil H. E. Weste. MULGA - An Interactive System for the Design of Integrated Circuits. *Bell System Technical Journal, AT&T Bell Laboratories*, 60(6):823–857, July 1981.

[Wil82]   D. E. Wilkins. Using Knowledge to Control Tree Searching. *Artificial Intelligence*, 18, 1982.

[Wil83]   R. Wilensky. *Planning and Understanding*. Addison-Wesley, 1983.

[Wir74]   N. Wirth. *Pascal User Manual and Report*. Springer-Verlag, 1974.

[YS89]   L. Ü. Yalçinalp and L. S. Sterling. An Integrated Interpreter for Explaining Prolog's Successes and Failures. In *Meta Programming in Logic Programming*, pages 191–203. MIT Press, 1989.

[Zan86]   C. Zaniolo. Prolog – A Database Query Language for All Seasons. In L. Kerschberg, editor, *Expert Database Systems: Proceedings From the 1st International Workshop*, pages 219–232. Benjamin/Cummings, 1986.

The MIT Press, with Peter Denning as general consulting editor, publishes computer science books in the following series:

ACM Doctoral Dissertation Award and Distinguished Dissertation Series

Artificial Intelligence
Patrick Winston, founding editor
J. Michael Brady, Daniel G. Bobrow, and Randall Davis, editors

Charles Babbage Institute Reprint Series for the History of Computing
Martin Campbell-Kelly, editor

Computer Systems
Herb Schwetman, editor

Explorations with Logo
E. Paul Goldenberg, editor

Foundations of Computing
Michael Garey and Albert Meyer, editors

History of Computing
I. Bernard Cohen and William Aspray, editors

Information Systems
Michael Lesk, editor

Logic Programming
Ehud Shapiro, editor; Koichi Furukawa, Jean-Louis Lassez, Fernando Pereira, and David H. D. Warren, associate editors

The MIT Press Electrical Engineering and Computer Science Series

Research Monographs in Parallel and Distributed Processing
Christopher Jesshope and David Klappholz, editors

Scientific and Engineering Computation
Janusz Kowalik, editor

Technical Communication
Ed Barrett, editor